CIVIC PRIDE

Salisbury, The Guildhall. (Salisbury City Council)

Civic Pride

The Public Buildings of Wiltshire Towns

TOWN HALLS
MARKET HALLS
LAW COURTS
MUSEUMS & ART GALLERIES
LIBRARIES & READING ROOMS
COUNCIL BUILDINGS
POLICE STATIONS
POST OFFICES
SWIMMING BATHS

James Holden

HOBNOB PRESS
for the
WILTSHIRE BUILDINGS RECORD

First published in the United Kingdom in 2024
on behalf of the Wiltshire Buildings Record
by The Hobnob Press, 8 Lock Warehouse, Severn Road, Gloucester GL1 2GA.
www.hobnobpress.co.uk

© James Holden 2024, text and photography

All rights reserved. No part of this publication may be reproduced, stored in a retrieval system, or transmitted, in any form or by any means, electronic, mechanical, photocopying, recording or otherwise, without the prior permission of the publisher and copyright holder.

British Library Cataloguing in Publication Data
A catalogue record for this book is available from the British Library.

ISBN 978-1-914407-74-1

Typeset in 10/12 pt Adobe Garamond Pro.
Typesetting and origination by John Chandler

The Wiltshire Buildings Record is a voluntary society and educational charity, with members in historic Wiltshire and beyond. The archive of the Record, gathered together since 1979 from fieldwork and from a variety of sources, covers over 18,500 sites representing buildings of all dates and types. The collection is housed at the Wiltshire & Swindon History Centre, Cocklebury Road, Chippenham, Wiltshire SN15 3QN, telephone 01249 705508, www.wiltshirebuildingsrecord.org.uk. It is open to the public on Tuesdays, 9 a.m. to 5 p.m. or by arrangement.

Also available from Wiltshire Buildings Record:
Wiltshire Farmhouses and Cottages 1500-1850	£6
Medieval Houses of Wiltshire	£6
Wiltshire Town Houses 1500-1900	£6
Wiltshire Farm Buildings 1500-1900	£5
Architects and Building Craftsmen with Work in Wiltshire (Part 1)	£5
Architects and Craftsmen with Work in Wiltshire (Part 2)	£5
Wiltshire Village Reading Rooms (Ivor Slocombe)	£8
Wiltshire Gate Lodges (James Holden)	£8

All plus £1.50 per copy post and packing.

The Dovecotes and Pigeon Lofts of Wiltshire (J & P McCann)	reduced to £5
Wiltshire Almshouses and their Founders (Sally Thomson)	£10.50
Wiltshire Nonconformist Chapels and Meeting Houses (James Holden)	£20

All plus £2.50 per copy post and packing

You can help the Record by allowing us to copy photographs, drawings and any other information, structural or historical you may have about Wiltshire buildings. Please join the Record and help to record buildings in your locality or assist us by drawing our attention to threatened buildings which may be worth recording.

Contents

Acknowledgements vii

1	Introduction	1
2	Town Halls	4
3	Market Halls	47
4	Law Courts	68
5	Museums and Art Galleries	90
6	Libraries and Reading Rooms	108
7	Council Buildings	145
8	Police Stations	177
9	Post Offices	206
10	Swimming Baths	228

Notes 243
Note on Sources 275
Index of Buildings 277
Index of Architects 281

All photographs are by the author except where otherwise indicated

Front cover: The Town Hall, Marlborough. Cover design by Jenny Holden. Back cover: The Station Road Post Office, Warminster (Warminster Historical Society).

The Baths, Westbury.

Acknowledgements

In writing this book I have called extensively on the local knowledge of many people, particularly the members of the local history societies which thrive in most Wiltshire towns and also the staff and volunteers of the county's museums. Those whose help I particularly want to record are: Gil and Ray Alder (Chippenham), Melissa Barnett (Chippenham Museum), Nick Baxter (Marlborough), Sue Boddington (Calne), Jean Booth (Mere), Beth O'Brien (Chippenham Town Hall), David Buxton (Devizes), Julian Carosi (Corsham), Clive Carter (Swindon), David Chandler (Marlborough), Roger Clark (Bradford on Avon), Alan Clarke (Salisbury and South Wiltshire Museum), Owen Collier (Wootton Bassett), Yvonne Crossley (Wilton), Kevin Dickens (Marlborough, Merchant's House Museum) Barbara Fisher (Amesbury, Antrobus House), Graham Fry (Salisbury City Council), Jim Fuller (Amesbury), Peter Goodhugh (Amesbury), Steve Hobbs (Westbury), Lucy Lewis (Purton for Wootton Bassett), Peter Maslen (Melksham), Darryl Moody (Swindon Libraries), Eric Peddle (Warminster), Rosemary Pemberton (Salisbury), Nikki Ritson (Trowbridge Museum), Jane Schon (Wiltshire Museum), Roger Smith (Wootton Bassett), Tom Smith (Swindon), Mike Stone (Chippenham), Christine Suter (Highworth), Charles Vernon (Malmesbury), Pat Whalley (Corsham) and Karen Young (Wiltshire Museum, Devizes).

Many of the museums and historical societies listed here have made photographs available for use in this book, for which I am most grateful: these are acknowledged in the photograph captions.

As before, I would like also to thank Pam Slocombe and Dorothy Treasure of the Wiltshire Buildings Record for their continuing support; Julian Orbach for information, for his invaluable index to Wiltshire architects and for kindly giving me access to his notes for the new edition of the Wiltshire Buildings of England; John Chandler for information and for his work as Hobnob Press in producing this book to such a high standard; and the ever-helpful staff of the Wiltshire and Swindon History Centre.

Tracing the various public buildings through time can be an elusive business. The people named above have contributed greatly to my attempts to resolve these and many other points but any errors and omissions which remain are my responsibility.

James Holden

Trowbridge, County Hall, the 2013 linking block.

1
Introduction

A FINE BUILDING in the countryside – a church say, or a manor house or a grand old barn – soon catches our attention. But in the town, distracted by traffic, by crowding pedestrians and by the lure of shop windows, we struggle to notice our built surroundings. Yet there are many fine buildings to be found here if we can raise our eyes from these obstacles. The most interesting of these, and often the finest as well, are the public buildings, and the purpose of this book is to describe Wiltshire's many examples and to tell their stories.

A public building is one which helps make the town function as a town. The need for such buildings in earlier times was minimal: an outdoor space for markets, some sort of assembly room for meetings and social events and perhaps a lock-up. But all that changed in the 19th century when growing population, a move from the countryside to the towns precipitated by the industrial revolution, and a gradually awakening concern for welfare transformed the picture.

Towns became more complicated places, and public initiative was needed to help run them better for the benefit of their inhabitants. Initiatives gradually built up through the century: the introduction of the county police in 1839 was followed by the first public museums in mid-century, accompanied soon by swimming baths and then by the local government reorganisations towards the century's end which were linked with such a large increase in council responsibilities. Post office services grew substantially towards 1900, requiring larger and more specialist premises, and finally the first stirrings of a comprehensive public library service were felt at the start of the 20th century, aided by the Carnegie trust.

The idea of 'civic pride' is elusive but it certainly played a part in these changes. Nationally the Great Exhibition of 1851 provides the most prominent example of how the nation's self-confidence had grown on the back of industrial success, but the same spirit acted locally also: why else would town halls, for example, be so assertively dominant in their design? No doubt pride of place existed long before this but it was the 19th century which saw it demonstrated so clearly in concrete form. What ordinary people thought on the subject is largely unrecorded but the leading townspeople, though also capable of remaining outstandingly parsimonious, were those who promoted so much of the century's new public building. Amongst these were to be found a few influential men whose impact was particularly great: people like Joseph Neeld in Chippenham and William Laverton in Westbury shaped their towns. Self-interest no doubt played a part – good public services helped the town to thrive which also helped the individual's business and his wider ambitions – but whatever the motives, the impact on the town's built environment was considerable.

So the 19th century produced many more public buildings. Inevitably some of these were dull but a large number were not: civic pride, increased confidence and a desire to enhance the urban environment worked together to produce numerous buildings of distinction and many more with strong character. And it is not just the obvious ones like town halls which please the eye, for 19th century police stations, as one example, can offer a harmony of design a world apart from their crudely functional modern counterparts.

The 20th century brought some continuation of this same trend but recession between the wars and for periods postwar curtailed investment and, though there are good examples, they are not plentiful. A different economic climate ruled at the millennium and after, with the result that most of the services provided by public buildings have been cut back and many buildings converted or destroyed. One interesting trend of recent years, though, is a new approach to combining services in one place, such as the Melksham community campus which opened in 2022 and offers a library, swimming pool and parish council offices in the same building. In doing so, it replicates in different form that mix of services which was so characteristic of 19th century town halls.

A high proportion of 19th and 20th century public buildings, and a few from earlier, still survive and are described here. In earlier times many civic functions were not seen to require specialist buildings, obviously in the case of post offices but equally so for council offices and also libraries, police stations and even on occasion law courts. This led to the extensive adaptation of other town buildings, some of which are themselves of considerable interest: these also are described here. Of the approximately 300 buildings still standing and described in this book, just under half were purpose-built and the remainder were adapted to their new use.

In the text which follows I attempt to define briefly the history of each service – law courts, market halls and so on – in each town, associating that with the buildings occupied for that purpose. The description includes buildings both purpose-built and adapted, standing and demolished, but with a level of detail proportional to the interest of each. To highlight them, the various extant buildings are titled in bold italics on first mention; those no longer here are given just in bold. Buildings of particular interest are asterisked as an indication, of course subjective on my part, as to those which are most worth seeking out.

A word is needed on definitions. Firstly, the text covers all of the old county of Wiltshire so includes what was formerly Thamesdown Borough and is now Swindon Borough. Secondly, on what constitutes a public building, I have included those which have a 'civic' function but not those, like cinemas, which are run on a purely commercial basis. Thirdly, although numerous villages have post offices, police stations and sometimes libraries, I have kept just to the towns in this book in order to prevent its becoming too sprawling. There are 19 in total and, with apologies to them, I have omitted Ludgershall and Tidworth, both of which expanded into towns through the arrival of the military in relatively recent times and consequently lack most of the buildings which characterise those of earlier foundation.

The nine main chapters of the book each cover one of the building types. Each starts with a general introduction and this is followed by a description town by town in alphabetical order. The text is completed by an index of the extant buildings described and a further index, with some biographical details, of the architects whose work has been identified here.

The photographs, except where otherwise noted, are mine. I have included, with acknowledgement, a considerable number of historical photographs: the low quality of some of these is evident but I have added them where I think they contribute significantly towards telling the story of the building in question. I hope the many such stories in this book will give interest and pleasure.

2
Town Halls

Introduction

WILTSHIRE HAS 19 town halls still standing. All are interesting, several are of exceptional architectural value and nearly all have prominent positions which give them strong presence as town centre buildings. Most are of the 19th century but they range in date from Wootton Bassett, whose hall of c1700 was old-fashioned even for then, to Cricklade with a 1933 building which itself looks backwards in style, if only to the turn of the century.

We now think of the 'town hall', almost in the abstract, as the place where local government is exercised. But when most town halls were built local government consisted only of occasional meetings of committees with the few paid officers working from their own premises, so no such specific space was required.

In addition, most earlier town halls were not built specifically as such but rather as market halls with rooms above. 12 of Wiltshire's 19 were built before the mid-19th

The Town Hall, Wootton Bassett.

The 1933 Town Hall, Cricklade.

century and of these, eight were constructed with open space beneath for the use of markets, the rooms above supported on either arches or columns. This pattern, so common then, is illustrated by Veneering in 'Our Mutual Friend' who, wanting to buy a parliamentary seat, proceeds 'to a feeble little town hall on crutches, with some onions and bootlaces under it, which the legal gentleman says are a Market; and from the front window of that edifice Veneering speaks to the listening earth.'[1]

A covered market hall helped strengthen the town's markets against competition from elsewhere, and adding rooms on the first floor, for which the precedents go back many centuries,[2] gave the opportunity to provide more facilities, above all a large assembly room. The developers of these buildings, often private companies set up for the purpose and often with major contributions from the local gentry, were motivated both by the desire to help the town to thrive and, perhaps more in hope than expectation, by the wish to make a profit from their investment.

Almost without exception town halls included such a large room, usually double height and parallel to the street across the front of the building; this acted as an assembly room for meetings, concerts, balls and the like. Law courts were often incorporated from the start, with the necessary cells, and sometimes police offices and fire stations. The various local government boards might use the rooms for meetings but this did not make these municipal buildings.

If this was the usual pattern there are of course exceptions, notably Salisbury, whose Guildhall was known as the Council House until the early 20th century and was the culminating building following the long competition between city and bishops. Similarly, later town halls were built as explicitly municipal, for example Trowbridge, late on the scene in 1889 with council chamber, committee rooms and offices from the start alongside the law court.

Town hall design naturally followed the fashions of the times, generally Classical up to the mid-19th century and a mix of Tudor and Northern Renaissance thereafter but with a substantial amount of symmetry apparent even in some later buildings. The influence of the Gothic Revival is apparent in a few but little in Wiltshire is overtly Gothic, in contrast to some other parts of the country.

Those of the Classical period were generally restrained in design but in the later 19th century town halls became much more demonstrative, with first-floor balconies for declaring election results and otherwise haranguing the populace, very large windows, often mullioned and transomed, and clock towers of impressive height. The tower at Calne was a late addition to the plans and those at Swindon (new town hall) and Trowbridge were increased in height from the architect's plans, all to meet the hubristic aspirations of the local politicians. Interiors also were heavily decorated

Calne Town Hall, the 1st floor assembly room, typically well lit and Queen Victoria still watchful

in the later period, with stained glass, carvings, coats of arms and pictures all demonstrative of civic pride and perhaps also of a wish in some way to 'improve' the taste of people who entered the building. Such exuberance was not always the case, though, and the final version of Marlborough's much-altered town hall, designed in the 1880s, reverted to a late 17th century style.

Nearly all were designed by architects, mostly those with a local rather than a national practice. Competitions between architects, typically with between 20 and 30 invited to submit designs and costings, were common nationally[3] although only two are recorded in Wiltshire, at Calne in 1883 and at Swindon in 1887. Devizes Corn Exchange (see Chapter 3) was also the subject of a competition.

The importance of town halls was reducing by the early 20th century. Local markets were declining and nearly all those town halls with markets beneath filled in the arches and used the space for different purposes, from housing a fire engine at Malmesbury to shops at Westbury. Local government was becoming more comprehensive in its scope and required more room for its offices, so councils often moved to purpose-built premises elsewhere; and where police accommodation had

Swindon, the New Town Hall, new Library to the right.

been incorporated a similar move took place. Law courts were amongst the last to remain in the town halls and local authorities made considerable efforts to retain them – particularly the quarter sessions - because of the local trade and prestige they brought: successive re-buildings at Marlborough were for just this purpose.

The decline led to the typical problem of what to do with large old buildings which have outlived their original purpose but the response, in Wiltshire at least, has often been positive. Some are now put to other uses, like the Baptist church at Wilton and the museum at Wootton Bassett, and some have been taken over by the town councils as successor authorities following local government reorganisations, like Corsham and Devizes. A small number – Warminster and Westbury quietly fading and Old Town Swindon in lamentable decline – have not found a new use.

It will be apparent from the descriptions above that there is a considerable overlap between town halls and market halls. The buildings themselves and their history are described in this chapter but Chapter 3 gives the wider background to the operation of markets in each town and describes other buildings which were built specifically and only as market halls.

The Buildings

Amesbury

In the middle ages Amesbury had a market hall which was also called a guildhall, a town hall or court house.[4] The town was sometimes called a borough, but it never had an institution for self-government.[5] The market hall was taken down in 1809.[6]

Bradford on Avon

The *Town Hall**, at the junction of Church Street and Market Street, dominates the centre of Bradford. Perhaps it was always too grand for a town of such modest size but it is nevertheless one of the finest in the county.

The previous market house had been at the east end of the Shambles and contained a room on the first floor, above the colonnaded market, which had been used for meetings of the manorial court. The building was referred to as the town hall

Bradford Town Hall as proposed, from the Civil Engineer & Architect's Journal, *Volume 17, 1854. (Google Books).*

but by the late 18th century it was dilapidated and it collapsed in 1820 and was soon demolished.[7] The various local government bodies had since the late 18th century been meeting usually in the *Swan Hotel** at the foot of Market Street but there was a wish to bring these bodies, and the market, together in new premises. This led to the formation of a company specifically to build and lease back a new town hall and market.

Bradford Town Hall as built, different in some details from the original design

The architect was Thomas Fuller of Bath and the new building, his major work in England before emigrating to Canada to design the Ottawa parliament building, was completed in 1855. In Jacobean style and made of weathered ashlar, it makes full use of its corner position, with the major wing along Church Street containing the council offices and that up Market Street containing mainly the police quarters. Joining them, on the angle and almost a separate building, is the substantial entrance tower, broad-shouldered below, square above and culminating in an octagonal bell tower with an ogee cap. The dominant feature on Church Street is the substantial oriel at first floor level fronting the main council chamber. The Market Street side, of three storeys with large chimney blocks, is less assertive but retains scroll inscriptions for 'Police' and 'Superintendent' above the two doors.

The Church Street wing contained on the first floor the main hall, large and well illuminated with oriels to front and side, and a committee room, with offices

Bradford Town Hall Council Chamber, now the Roman Catholic church of St Thomas More.

below. The Market Street wing contained the police offices and living accommodation below, the reading room and library for the Literary Institution on the middle floor above (see Chapter 6), and police sleeping apartments in the attic floor. Police cells were behind this block and lean-to sheds for the market were placed in the substantial rear yard, accessed off Market Street. The yard was also home to the fire brigade.

The town hall was used from the outset by the various local government bodies, the police and the petty sessions, but by the turn of the century the costs and space restrictions of this single base for so many services were beginning to tell. The fire brigade moved out in 1903 and the market was closed by 1911 but the police, though long dissatisfied with their accommodation, were unable to move until 1936. In 1911 the Urban District Council weighed up the relative costs of staying put or moving to *Westbury House* – described in Chapter 7 – and decided on the latter option.

Bradford Town Hall in the early 20th century. (WBR)

The town hall was then put up for sale but failed to sell for a number of years and had various tenuous uses before eventually being sold to the Midland Bank. The petty sessions (see Chapter 4) remained there until the end of 1954 when they had to move out, the hall having been sold to the Clifton Diocese for conversion into the Catholic Church of St Thomas More. They use the main hall as their church, the walls stripped of plaster perhaps for aesthetic reasons or because of some problem with damp. The ground floor police offices were converted into two shops in 1993/4, the architect Esmond Murray of Bath.

Calne

There was a guildhall in Calne from as early as the 13th century and from at least 1581 until 1829 the burgesses met in what is now Church House at the north end of the churchyard, though this building has since been much altered.[9] The market

Calne Old Town Hall. (Wiltshire Museum, Devizes)

house, by the junction of Market Hill with High Street, had a corn store on the first floor before the early 1820s after which this floor was converted into the town's first **Town Hall**.[10] The north end was rebuilt, a Classical portico added with a semi-circular iron fence protecting it, and the first floor windows replaced by sashes. In mid-century the ground floor was converted into a corn exchange, with the arches infilled and glazed.[11]

The town hall, the sides of six bays, was evidently large enough for the needs of the borough council for some years[12] but by later in the century its weaknesses were apparent: it was described as unsightly and inconvenient, the staircase up to the first floor dangerous and the council chamber inferior.[13] The council considered improving it but in the end decided to look elsewhere: it was demolished in 1882 and the following year the Marquess of Lansdowne, who owned the site, gave it to the corporation on the condition that it should remain as public open space.[14] It is not clear why the old town hall was demolished before its replacement was built but the council had to return to Church House for its meetings in the meantime.[15]

Calne New Town Hall, architect's drawings of elevations. (WSA)

Calne New Town Hall.

A larger site was needed for the new *Town Hall** and was obtained by demolishing the former town mill towards the south end of the town centre and building on its site. A limited competition was held to choose an architect and the choice was C Bryan Oliver of Bath, who produced a building of considerable presence, Tudor-Gothic in rock-faced stone, opened in 1886.[16] The total cost was £9400, paid for largely by subscribers, Alderman Harris of the bacon family and the Marquess of Lansdowne prominent amongst them, and the new town hall contained not only the council chamber, assembly rooms and magistrates' room but also the corn exchange, a police station with 2 cells, a volunteer drill hall and an armoury.[17]

The building's impact is increased now that it is no longer dominated by the vast Harris bacon factory which used to stand opposite. The front facing north up the street, and thus most prominently in view, has a large gable at the left, mullioned and transomed windows, and a four-stage tower which was a late addition to the plan.[18] To the right of these are the former police quarters, with a carriageway arch through and two smaller gables. The buttressed east wall contains the main entrance, a row of large nine-light windows at first floor level illuminating the council chamber, and a crenelated roofline which, clearly inappropriate, nevertheless seems to enhance the building. Inside, the council chamber and mayor's parlour retain their wood panelling.

Calne New Town Hall, the mayor's parlour.

Chippenham

Chippenham's first town hall was the building known, again now as it was in the 16th century, as the *Yelde Hall**.[19] It was built between 1446 and 1458, replacing an earlier building on the site, and originally stood alone in the market place, though in the

Chippenham, the Yelde Hall.

following centuries more buildings were constructed nearby and several of these were attached directly to the hall. It was used by hundred and manorial courts as well as for church entertainments and as a council chamber for the burgesses. The council moved to the new Town Hall in 1841 after which the Yelde Hall functioned as an armoury for the Chippenham Rifle Corps; part was also used as a police lock-up. From c1870 the south-east end was used as a fire-engine house; the fire service was given the full use of the building from 1911 when the armoury moved out, and they themselves moved out in 1945 to their new base in Dallas Road. The use of the building as a museum had been discussed as early as 1909 but it finally opened as such in 1963. In 1999, the Yelde Hall having become too small, the museum moved to its present location (see Chapter 5) and the hall was used as a tourist information centre for a time before in 2012 again becoming a part of the museum, used for temporary exhibitions.

The hall is now grade 1 listed. Its exterior has large-panelled half-timbering on a stone plinth under a stone slate roof, much of this only visible again after the attached buildings were removed in

Chippenham, the Yelde Hall before demolition of attached buildings. Note bell turret used for the fire service. (WBR).

left: Chippenham Yelde Hall, the council chamber. Small for such a function but larger meetings were held in the main hall downstairs (below). Note hat pegs above the window and slots for rifle butts in the bench seat, from its time as an armoury. right: Chippenham Yelde Hall, lock-up below the council chamber, showing two of the vertical timbers with which it was originally fully lined

the years up to 1963. The porch at the north-west end is a 16th century addition occupying two of the end three bays on the north-east side. Both are gabled, one with the town's arms in the head with the date 1776 when extensive repairs were carried out, and the door is below. Large doors, with a circular window above, were inserted into the south-east end for the use of the fire service; these were removed and replaced by a single window in the 1963 renovation but when the hall reopened as display space in 2012 the present more modest doors were inserted. Amongst other alterations through the years was the addition of two bell turrets for the use of the fire service.

Inside is a fine hall, the stone plinth and timbering also exposed here beneath an open ceiling of tie beam, collar trusses and wind-bracing. To the rear and at a slightly lower level is the lock-up, this with solid stone walls and still retaining two of the substantial vertical timbers with which it was originally fully lined; the larger side window and the safe are later additions. Above this, up a stairway in the porch, is the council chamber, a small room for this purpose but larger meetings were held downstairs. 16th century panelling, with a bench and long table original to the room, give a good feel for its original appearance and the window seat has slots cut into it to hold rifle butts, an alteration dating from its period as an armoury.

The present *Town Hall**, towards the lower end of the High Street, appears modest for a town of Chippenham's size, but the explanation lies in the fact that it was not built as such. The building was the gift of the town's MP, Joseph Neeld of Grittleton, and was constructed with ground floor open arches for market purposes as part of the development of the adjacent market, described in Chapter 3.[20] Designed by James Thomson, an architect much used by Neeld at Grittleton, it opened in 1833 as the New Hall.[21] The first floor was intended originally as a school but in the end the location was considered unsuitable for this purpose and instead it was used for the meetings, concerts and the like which had previously been held in the Yelde Hall.[22] In 1841 the corporation moved here for its meetings as well and the New Hall became in effect the town hall.[23]

Chippenham New Town Hall

The building is in fine ashlar with three broad open arches at the ground floor, now glazed; above are three triplet round-arched sash windows. Plain pilasters divide these, the central pair carried up either side of the central bay, which is stepped forward, to a parapet which carries Neeld's arms. These were added with an inscription in 1851 after he had paid for an extension to the market facilities to cope with the expanding cheese market.[24] The building to the right, of the same date, was not then associated with the hall.

The 1850 extension added a large double-roofed shed to the rear for the cheese market, open to the yard at the side and replacing various smaller previous buildings. Beyond this was built a small exchange room for financial business, in ashlar with a hipped roof and an apse-like extension to the far wall; the doorway, now hidden in a store-room, has 'Exchange' incised in the lintel and previously had a clock above.

Chippenham New Town Hall, the council chamber. Joseph Neeld in fake-Roman splendour above the fireplace

To the east of the cheese market a three-storey 'cheese warehouse' had already been built in 1841, in rubblestone but again hipped-roofed.[25] This arrangement of buildings lasted until 1911 when, with the cheese market long in decline, alterations to the market were coupled with the building of a new public hall to replace the cheese market shed and provide a larger entertainment space for the town. Designed by the Chippenham architect Thomas Fogg, it was paid for by Sir Audley Neeld and became known as the Neeld Hall.[26] The final change came in 1996 when the 'Neeld Lounge', a lean-to extension to the side of the Neeld Hall, was demolished and a new entrance, bar and cafe for the hall were built at the rear.[27] These, in neat ashlar, were placed alongside the former exchange.

The vaulting of the ground floor in the town hall is both heavy and low, giving more the appearance of a basement than of a market trading space. The stairway to the council chamber makes some attempt at grandeur, split to the half-landing where it joins into one, but the approach is through the vaults and not even in a straight line from the main entrance, perhaps more evidence of the originally planned role as a school. The chamber itself, though, is grand enough with a high ceiling, three pairs of entrance doors with plaques above, the town arms in the central one, and busts of Joseph Neeld and his brother John (who followed him as MP for the town) at either end of the room above ornate fireplaces.

Chippenham, the Neeld Hall.

The Neeld Hall has round and segmental-arched windows to the market yard side where the Neeld Lounge previously stood, a roof supported by iron girders and a stage at the town hall end. But for its substantial size it would have much of the feel of a village hall of the period, although the stage and associated equipment were designed to be of a quality to attract major theatre companies.[28]

In 1911 the New Hall finally became known officially as the Town Hall after the council agreed to lease it from Neeld, although it had been known unofficially as that from at least the 1870s,[29] and in 1947 the council bought both halls. They were then renovated, though in the 1960s and 1970s there were repeated attempts to demolish the Neeld Hall as part of redevelopment. In 1974, with local government reorganization, management of the halls passed to North Wiltshire District Council but in 1996 that responsibility was taken by the town council, which later gained the ownership of both halls and continues to run them.³⁰

Corsham

A building of probably mid-17th century date served as market hall, court building and probably as an early **Town Hall**. Of two storeys and an attic, it had two gable dormers and a ground floor arcaded shambles. The interior space on the ground floor was untypically enclosed; there was a blind house alongside and on the first floor were rooms marked on an 18th century sketch plan as court rooms.³¹

This may have been on the site of the present town hall but there is equally some evidence that it was instead located close to the church in Church Square, then much more a focus for town activity than it is now.³² It was certainly gone by the 1780s and may have been demolished as part of the 1760s 'Capability' Brown scheme for alterations to Corsham Court and its grounds.³³

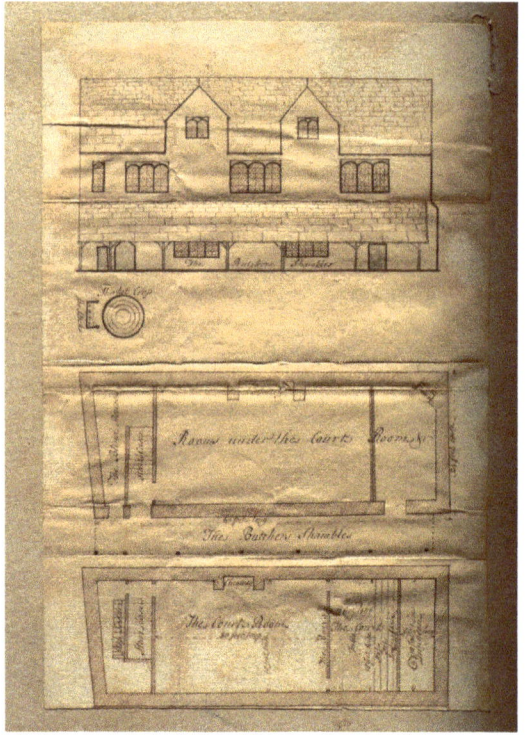

Corsham, the 17th century Town Hall. (Courtesy of James Methuen-Campbell).

A new market house was built in 1784, paid for by Paul Methuen of Corsham Court. This was single-storey, in ashlar with five arches to the street, the middle three brought forward and pedimented with the Methuen arms in the tympanum.³⁴ The arches at each end were infilled, that to the south serving as a lockup.³⁵ This was an attempt by Methuen to promote a market in the town but it was not successful and there was a call as early as 1815 to have it all infilled and converted to a Sunday school. The conversion did not happen but by late in the century the market was moribund.³⁶

At some date, probably in the 1870s, Thomas Poynder of Hartham Park came up with the idea of converting the market house into a town hall and commissioned WH Bromley of Corsham to produce a design.³⁷ Poynder died not long afterwards but the planning was taken forward by the Methuens and the new **Town Hall***, funded by them and by public subscription, opened in 1883.³⁸ The conversion left the ground floor substantially the same but added a first floor above, relocating the original pediment with the Methuen arms above that.

The resulting building is harmonious. Four of the ground floor arches are converted to round-arched windows and betray little of their past; the central one is

Corsham Town Hall.

Corsham Town Hall, the assembly room. One mechanism drives both internal and external clocks.

contained within a substantial doorcase above which sits a balcony, altered in 1897 by Harold Brakspear with a plaque and inscription for Victoria's diamond jubilee.[39] At the first floor the five round-arched windows front a large main hall, said to seat 400,[40] which is approached by a surprisingly grand double staircase. The hall, well lit by its multiple windows, is of simple design with exposed roof timbers and a clock on the front wall driven by the same mechanism used for the external clock. On the ground floor, where the town council offices now are, there were originally the rooms for the Mechanics' Institute, described in Chapter 6.

The town hall served as a VAD hospital during the first world war[41] but otherwise has been occupied continuously by the local council.

Cricklade

A market house, erected probably in the 1660s, stood in the High Street north of Calcutt Street. It had the typical pattern of an open space below with ten pillars supporting an enclosed room above, which seems to have been used as a town hall.[42] It was demolished in 1814.[43]

A new *Town Hall* was built by J W Lansdown, a local businessman, with the intention that it should serve both as the town hall and as his own business premises.[44] On High Street, south of Calcutt Street, it opened in 1862 and is entirely unpretentious in coursed rubblestone, an archway leading through to the rear no doubt for Lansdown's business use. On the first floor three large 20-light sash windows illuminate the council chamber which stretches across the whole front of the building.

In 1933 it was sold to serve as Ockwell's glove factory and most of the existing rear extensions probably date from this period.[45] Ockwell's ceased trading in 1993,

Cricklade, the 1862 Town Hall

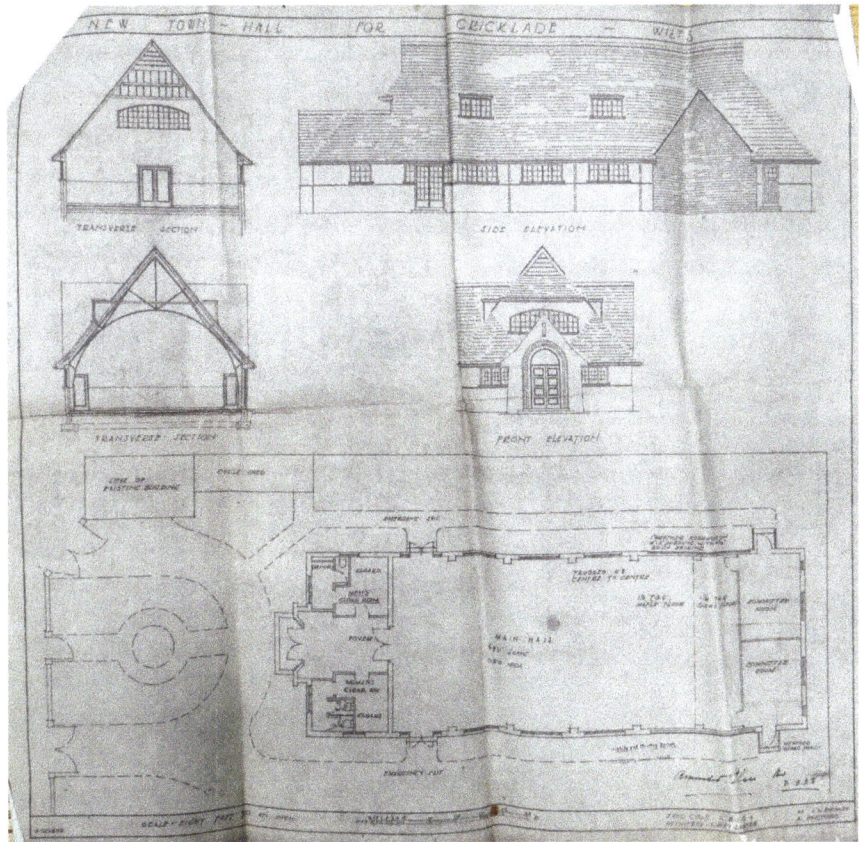

Cricklade, architect's plan and elevations of the 1933 Town Hall (photograph of town hall in chapter introduction). (WSA).

North Wiltshire District Council bought the building in 1995 and, after conversion, the library opened in the former council chamber in 2002.[46] In 2023 the building also contained the offices of the town council and a doctor's surgery.

It seems that the council had committed to selling the old town hall before they had new premises but they then moved with considerable speed, holding a public meeting in January 1933, starting work in February and opening the *New Town Hall* in July.[47] It stands on land given to the town in 1919 for a public building to serve as a war memorial hall, further south down High Street and alongside a temporary recreation hall. The new town hall contained two committee rooms and a recreation room in addition to the main hall and a stage. Its design, by Eric Cole of Cirencester, seems to have been made first in 1932, so anticipating future events.[48] The building is in white-painted brick with a single row of windows weighed down by the vast slope of the roof in a style reminiscent of Voysey. A barn-like porch at the front contributes to the top-heavy feeling. There were plans for wings to be added, which never materialized,[49] but the recreation hall was removed at some point and replaced in 1958 by an annexe in plain stone blockwork.[50]

Devizes

Devizes has many fine buildings in its central area but the *New Hall** and the *Town Hall** stand out even in this company, both dominating the view south from the Market Place down into St John's Street.

The history leading up to the construction of these was complex, and the various previous buildings were used more for markets than for municipal government. The New Hall, in particular, was intended as a public hall but in practice barely used for that purpose. The histories are entwined and so are recounted here rather than in Chapter 3.

An 'old' town hall is recorded in 1451 and by the 16th century a guildhall and council house stood adjacent to each other and were used for various municipal and law court functions; their location is not recorded.[51] Where the town hall now stands there was a yarn hall at the beginning of the 17th century. This was rebuilt in 1615-16 as a market house for wool and yarn; it was repaired at various dates in the 17th century, in 1689 the cheese market and fairs were moved into it and a council chamber was added c1733. It was known for most of its life as the Wool Hall but also after c1750 as the Old Hall, to differentiate it from the New Hall then recently built.

The **Wool Hall** in its final form was of two storeys and five bays under a hipped roof, the ground floor open between columns for market trading and with sash windows to the first floor. Corinthian columns either side of the central entrance rose through both storeys to a pediment with above that a clock turret surmounted by a bell cupola.[52]

In 1750 it was decided to pull the guildhall down and to erect a public hall on a site on the south side of Wine Street. This *New Hall* was nearly finished by 1752 but, unexpectedly, was thereafter used mainly as a market house, including some market activities previously carried out at the Wool Hall; it also served as a militia depot. It

left: Devizes, the Old Wool Hall. Image from Dore's map of the town. (Wiltshire Museum, Devizes).
right: Devizes, the New Hall. Image from Dore's map of the town. (Wiltshire Museum, Devizes).

above: Devizes, the New Hall when in use as a wine merchant's with the Town Hall in the distance. (WSA). below: the same view now.

fulfilled a municipal function only briefly during the rebuilding of the old Wool Hall (see below) and in 1809 was leased out, being sold in 1825. It was subsequently bought in 1836 by William Cunnington to house his wines and spirits business, and the town's literary and scientific institution used the first floor for a period from 1848.[53] It has remained in commercial use.

The New Hall's ashlar front facing north towards the Market Place is exceptionally fine. The ground floor is arched and rusticated, the arches originally open,

Devizes, the Town Hall.

and above that five Ionic columns separate tall 24-light sash windows below a broad pediment decorated with cherubs and scrolls. A clock was added by Cunnington's son

Devizes Town Hall, the assembly room

in 1871.⁵⁴ The side to St John's Street is similar but more modest, the columns replaced by pilasters. It is now grade 2* listed.

Returning to the Wool Hall, it was condemned by James Wyatt in 1803 as beyond repair and was subsequently rebuilt between 1806 and 1808 as the new *Town Hall*, to the designs of Thomas Baldwin of Bath.⁵⁵ The front was pulled down and replaced by a new sessions court on the ground floor and an assembly room above. Walls to the rear were retained but the interior was altered to provide, amongst others, a first floor council chamber. Below this was an enclosed open space into which the cheese market was moved from the New Hall.

The chief architec-tural delight of the Town Hall, appropriately enough as it is the most conspicuous, is the splendid north front. Three of its five bays are taken up with a generous bow and the ground floor is rusticated with windows in arched recesses. The first floor has engaged Ionic columns between tall 12-light sash windows, the central three pedimented. The hall's rear is curved following the outline of the preceding building, with a surviving basement lock-up and, above at the centre, the three sash windows of the council chamber. The sides are plain, with many windows blind, but contain two doors each, to different parts of the building. The interior is modest but dignified, the assembly room with recessed arches at each end, a musicians' gallery on the back wall and a ceiling with the feeling of Adam. The town hall also is now grade 2* listed.

Highworth

There appears to be no evidence that Highworth has ever had a town hall.

Malmesbury

After the Dissolution of the monasteries the town's corporation bought *St Paul's church* and in 1542 were using the east end as a town hall, although it was said to be in ruinous condition at that time.⁵⁶ Meetings of various bodies were held there until at least 1709, it was used as a poorhouse in the late 18th century, later served as a timber warehouse and was finally demolished, all but the tower, in 1852.⁵⁷

The corporation also owned *No 9 Oxford Street**. It was known as the Guildhall and may have been used for meetings in the 18th century though that use had ceased by 1794.⁵⁸ The building is 15th century, altered later and at some point divided into a pair of cottages, this reversed on restoration in 1990.⁵⁹ The exterior, of painted rubble with ashlar dressings, betrays its age, though the front to Oxford Street has inserted 19th century shop windows either side of a central door with a six-light sash above, all under a half-hipped gable. The chief feature of the side return is another gable half-way along housing a substantial chimney stack topped with brick. The interior, a single hall at right angles to Oxford Street with exposed roof timbers revealed in the 1990 restoration, was a restaurant in 2023. The roof is 15th century, with four arch-braced collar trusses and wind bracing: a delight, it is grade 2* listed.

The borough is also said to have used the *Old Courthouse*, described in Chapter 4, for meetings at one time.⁶⁰ This may refer primarily to the more administrative elements of the work of the borough sessions.

The *Town Hall** at the north end of Cross Hayes was built as a market house but soon became known as the town hall.[61] It was promoted by the Malmesbury Market House Company in an effort to strengthen the town's market and was funded by subscription,. Designed by Francis Niblett, it opened in 1848.[62] By the end of the century it was being rented out to auctioneers and it was subsequently bought by the council in 1920. In 1926 the council also bought part of the former malthouse joined to it to the west, rebuilt the front of that and opened it as a town hall extension the following year. In 1970 the remaining offices facing Market Lane, and the former Methodist Chapel[63] to the north, were bought and added to the premises, with infill construction to join the various blocks of building together. In 2006, with the transfer of the town hall from the district council to the town council, there was a major refurbishment and another small extension to the north. The Athelstan museum is now housed in the 1848 building and the town council in the remainder.

The design and layout of the building is as complex as might be expected from the description above. The town hall proper is in Tudor style, in stone block and incorporating some fabric from a 17th century building

Malmesbury, the Town Hall

Malmesbury Town Hall, the connected building, re-fronted in 1927, paying homage to the design of the original.

previously on the site.⁶⁴ The buttressed front has three four-centred arches below, originally open for market activities but since infilled. The fire brigade moved in soon after the council bought the building and the opening to the left was for long used as an entrance and exit for the town's fire engine – fire engines were narrower then - and so lacks the replacement mullioned and transomed stonework fitted into its counterpart to the right. Above are three tall mullioned and transomed windows, the central one a canted oriel under a narrow gable. To the west is the 1927 extension, the front altered from the previous industrial-looking façade to mimic the front of the town hall, albeit with coarser stonework.

Most rooms inside are much altered, though the council chamber in the former malthouse shows the roof timbers of the original building. The assembly room, in the usual position at first floor front of the 1848 town hall, is a fine interior, with the arch-braced roof timbers exposed and a small stage and proscenium arch at one end.

Malmesbury Town Hall assembly room, the stage perhaps original

Marlborough

Marlborough town hall is in an enviable position, dominating the fine High Street from its position at the east end. It has been there in different forms since the early 17th century and there was a building on this site previously to that. The town hall has perhaps the most unified set of rooms and offices in the county, making its interior as interesting as the exterior.

The town had a guildhall from at least 1270, perhaps located on the north side of High Street at its east end, and that building or its successor was still standing in 1583.⁶⁵ A 'high cross', probably actually a timber building on piers set in a stone base and used as a market house, was standing on the present site of the town hall by the early 17th century. Both this and the guildhall were replaced in c1630 by the first **Town Hall**, which continued to have market activities in the space beneath. This was destroyed in the major fire which damaged so much of the town in 1653 but was replaced in 1654-5 by the second **Town Hall**, probably of similar style. Images of this show much of it to be conventional enough, with a ground floor open on piers for markets and a first floor with what look like mullioned and transomed windows. Above that, however, different images all show it with a tall, convex-curving roofline with two tiers of dormers, the whole drawn up into two points almost like spires, each capped by a weathervane. The fact that at least three different images show this suggests that it is not artistic licence, but if correct it was truly bizarre.⁶⁶

Marlborough, the 1655 Town Hall with its amazing double-peaked roof. (WBR)

The third **Town Hall** was a rebuild by John Hammond in 1792-3, the outline of this one still discernable in the present building. The ground floor was again open on stone piers, possibly the previous ones re-used, but the section to the rear was enclosed and contained the lock-up. At first floor level the main hall had three windows facing the High Street, the central one broader under a semi-circular recessed head. The side elevation was of seven bays and the roof, returned to a more rational hipped configuration, was capped by a cupola.[67]

The poor quality of the quarter sessions accommodation here became a matter of increasing concern. The borough was anxious not to lose the sessions and the associated income for the town so further alterations were made in 1867 to resolve the problem. The architect was Samuel Overton and the works included removing the dividing wall between the previous sessions court and the assembly room and refacing the west front.[68] This front, dour in its rebuilding, had a round-arched entrance up steps at the centre – the sloping site made steps necessary in every version of the town hall – with round-arched blind windows either side.

Marlborough, the 1867 Town Hall. (WBR).

Marlborough Town Hall, Ponting's rebuilding of 1902.

The first floor echoed this with a triplet window at the centre and one either side, and the central section was brought forward beneath a parapet.[69]

The judicial authorities were still dissatisfied with the 1867 alterations and this resulted in the final rebuilding, in 1901-2, to designs by C.E. Ponting which he had actually drawn up in the 1880s.[70] This fourth *Town Hall** is in late 17th century style. The west front, brought forward from that of its predecessor, is dominated by a large stone canted oriel with a balcony, and there is a second balcony above beneath the town's arms in stone. The oriel is supported on brackets which are in turn held by paired columns either side of the central door, the whole a remarkably satisfying composition. Either side of the door are round-arched windows, now glazed but originally open to the stairs.[71]

There are echoes of the 1793 hall still in the side elevations, with four bays of mullioned and transomed windows to the front with round-windowed dormers above,

Marlborough Town Hall assembly room, perhaps the finest in the county.

and two bays to the back. The whole is in brick below and render above, the quoins in brick but other dressings in ashlar. The cupola remains and the new roof is double-angled in a faint echo of its 1655 predecessor.

Ponting made use of many of the original piers, and the importance now given to the court room is demonstrated by its being separate and directly behind the main doors on the ground floor, the bench panelled and the cells at basement level accessed by steps leading to trap doors in the floor. Other rooms are also panelled, the first-floor council chamber at the rear lined with photographs of past mayors in typical fashion, but the highlight is the assembly room on the first floor. This is oak-panelled to above head height and its two-tier curved ceiling is lit by round dormers in generous semi-circular arches, the whole producing a remarkable effect. The west end has double doors onto the balcony and there is a stage with proscenium arch at the east end.

Melksham

Like so many others, the *Town Hall** at Melksham was built as a market hall. By the mid-1840s the markets here were struggling and there was a particular concern about competition from the thriving markets at Chippenham which were benefitting from the investment of Joseph Neeld.[72] On the positive side, the new railway line serving the town was due to open shortly and that would provide the opportunity to serve a wider area from Melksham market.

Melksham Town Hall.

The result was a public meeting in December 1846 which resolved to build a new cheese market, with £3000 to be subscribed in £20 shares. The subscription was raised without difficulty, the contract to design and build was awarded to Daniel and Charles Jones of Bradford on Avon, construction started in March 1847 and the new hall opened in September of that year.

The building facing the Market Place is handsome in good ashlar, the modest front of three bays and the sides of four. The ground floor had open arches, later infilled, and the first floor has paired arched windows between giant pilasters below a plain frieze and a central pediment, above which is a small bellcote. The sides are plain at first floor level and the rear was originally a simpler version of the front but now has a modest central extension, added in the late 1990s, in matching ashlar.[73]

As built, the ground floor was to be used as a market for poultry and eggs. Above were the main assembly hall and two smaller rooms, one of which was intended as a reading room though it seems it may not have been used as such.[74] The assembly room is in the usual position behind the front first-floor windows and is of modest size and plain.

The cheese market itself was not in the hall but in a quadrangle of buildings behind, which contained the trading floors and store-rooms.[75] It was accessed by arched

TH44   Melksham Town Hall with Police Station alongside, showing the consistency of design. 1978 drawing by John Worsfold (WSA).

gateways on either side of the hall; one of these remains but the other was removed in 1950 to the detriment of the overall appearance.[76] The former police station, adjoining the right hand arch and built at the same time, is described in Chapter 8.

It seems that the hall very soon became known as the town hall and was used for the usual range of activities.[77] The market company appears to have been wound up in 1898, at which date the town hall and accompanying buildings, including the police station, were sold to Charles Awdry and, after his death, were put up for auction in 1914. They were then bought by the urban district council and were later taken over by the town council, which continues to use the town hall.[78] In the meantime the rear building of the cheese market had been replaced by a new drill hall in 1907, with an iron-framed roof of 118ft by 50ft.[79] It had been used for flower shows and other events as well but after the Second World War it ceased functioning as a drill hall and reopened as an *Assembly Hall*, a use which continues to the present day.[80] The building, the main structure of which is hidden, was re-roofed and otherwise refurbished in 1979/80.[81]

Mere

Mere's medieval **Market House** or **Guildhall** was in the Market Place where the clock tower now stands. It appears from a surviving print to have been of modest size, buttressed at the corners with open arches to the ground floor, two to the front and one to the sides. On the first floor there was a three-light window to the front with a hoodmould, and a clock above.[82] The ground floor was used for markets and the upper, called the Cross Loft, had various uses including by the manorial court of the

Duchy of Cornwall and for a period as a school.[83] The market weakened during the early 19th century and the market house was demolished in 1863. The successor clock tower was erected in 1868.[84]

Mere, the Old Market Hall. (Wiltshire Museum, Devizes).

The *Victoria Hall*, nearby on the south side of the Market Place, was built by the Conservative Association in 1899 to commemorate Queen Victoria's diamond jubilee and was intended from the start to be not only a Conservative club but also a town hall for the use of all.[85] It seems not to have retained that function for long because by the 1920s it was in use as a cinema; in the 1940s it was converted into a car showroom and in 2023 it housed the town's Co-operative store.[86] The building, gable facing the road, is of coursed rough stone under a tiled roof with roof ventilators. There is now a full-width shop-front and above that are a plaque for the diamond jubilee and a pair of sash windows with ashlar dressings and exposed relieving arches.

Salisbury

Salisbury's *Guildhall** has a history which makes it stand out from every other town hall in the county. Most have their roots in market houses, their function widened or replaced as they were turned into civic buildings during the 19th century, but in

Salisbury, the Guildhall as built in 1795. (Salisbury Museum).

Salisbury the roots lie elsewhere, in the long battle to wrest control of the city from the bishops.[87]

Salisbury belonged to the bishops from its foundation and the seat of government from which the bishops executed justice and controlled the markets was the **Bishops' Guildhall**, located in the marketplace on the site of the present Guildhall. First mentioned in 1314, it also housed the city gaol beneath. Rectangular, of six bays separated by buttressing pilasters, it had mullioned and transomed windows to the

Salisbury, the Bishop's Guildhall during demolition in the 1780s (Salisbury Museum).

main first floor meeting space. The entrance end had arched windows with Gothic tracery and there was a bell turret above the roof.

Through the 14th and 15th centuries leading citizens, angered by their lack of power, pushed back against the bishops and in 1415 built their own **Council House** in the cheese market at the west end of the marketplace. This was replaced in 1584 by a new **Council House** directly in front of the Bishops' Guildhall. The new Council House was of modest floor plan but tall, timber-framed above an open arcaded ground floor. The first floor had oriel windows; above that the attic floor, jettied out, had gabled windows, and at the centre was a

Salisbury, the 1584 Council House as built. (Salisbury Museum).

Salisbury Guildhall. (Salisbury City Council).

tower with a belvedere on top. At a later date the ground floor was infilled, in the pattern later to be repeated in many other town halls, and the footprint was extended in the 17th century by the addition of side colonnades.

By the later 18th century both the Council House and the Bishops' Guildhall were in poor repair, the latter by now having lost much of its function to the corporation. A major fire in the Council House in 1780, though the damage was repaired, only added to the urgency of planning a replacement. The Earl of Radnor offered to pay for a new building provided it was to his design and in the centre of the marketplace. The city objected because they did not want to lose market space and eventually, in 1787, a compromise was reached with both the Earl and the new bishop. In this, the Bishops' Guildhall and the Council House would both be demolished and the new Guildhall would be built on the site of the former. The city took over the running of the markets and the gaol, using the county gaol at Fisherton Anger, and the bishop was able to use the new Guildhall without charge for his law courts. The Earl of Radnor, for his part, would acquire a permanent testament to his family's generosity, still recorded in a plaque on the front of the building.

Salisbury Guildhall, the dedicatory plaque.

The architect for the new Guildhall was Sir Robert Taylor, replaced by his pupil William Pilkington on his death in 1788. When it opened in 1795 it had one main storey and consisted of tall blocks either side of a lower central section recessed behind a colonnaded portico. The block to the east contained one large room, initially the council chamber, and that to the west housed a courtroom and behind that what was designated as a guildhall but could also be used as a courtroom; the central block contained service rooms.

Salisbury Guildhall, the banqueting hall.

In 1825, fearful of losing the county assize to Devizes following a complaint from the assize judge, the city hired Thomas Hopper to make improvements; the work was completed in 1830. He rebuilt the northern portico to project forward from the building, creating space for a grand jury room above and giving the front, with its new portico, the appearance it retains.

In 1889 a separate portico which had given direct access to the courtrooms from the west side of the building was demolished and replaced with more cells. In 1896/7, following renewed fears that the city might lose the assizes, this time to Trowbridge, alterations were made to create several rooms, particularly the courtroom now called the Oak Court.[88] There have been various more minor alterations since, including a refurbishment in 1991-3, but the exterior appearance was set at that time. It is now grade 2* listed.

The Guildhall is built of a creamy-yellow brick, now much discoloured, with stone dressings rusticated and heavily vermiculated. To the front, tall round-arched windows – Taylor had specified Venetian but Pilkington changed this - have brick surrounds within the rusticated arch, and between them stands Hopper's new portico with six Roman-Doric columns, probably those from the original portico. This sits beneath the three smaller round-arched windows of his new jury room and above is the plaque to the Earl of Radnor, relocated from the parapet of the original portico. To the east a canted bay fronts what is, inside the building, a semicircular space, and to the west the 1889 extension, matching the materials and design of Hopper's work, provides generous tall windows for what was built as a two-storey cell block. The rear is more plain.

Inside, the entrance hall is lit from above and has the chimneypiece of c1580 from the old Council House; the staircase is probably also part of Hopper's alterations. The large room, originally called the council room but known as the banqueting hall from the mid-19th century, is distinguished by the generous semicircular bay on its east wall and the ceiling plasterwork of 1794. The original crown court, top-lit, has a gallery to the rear and one side, supported on columns, and retains a canopy above what was the judge's chair. The Oak Court, added with the inserted floor in 1896/7 and furnished on the diagonal so as to maximise space, has the judge's dais, the dock, curved bench seating and a public gallery all, as the name implies, in oak. Its three windows on the rear of the building are above the lower ground floor entrance there.

The building was known as the Council House from its opening but in 1927 the city moved its offices to St Edmund's College, Bourne Hill – see Chapter 7 – and that building became the new Council House. The former Council House was thereafter known as the Guildhall.

Swindon

Swindon before the railway was one of the smallest towns in the county, 16th largest in 1841 with a population then of 2459.[89] The arrival of the Great Western Railway in the 1840s precipitated a rapid growth in overall population such that in 1861 it was third largest at 6856 and by 1881, at 19904, it was by some margin the largest. This pattern of growth helps to explain why there were no early moves to establish a town hall: the place was too small to justify it

The Old Town Hall

As so often, the *Old Town Hall** started off as a market hall. Swindon already had a covered market of sorts in the earlier 19th century[90] but it was evidently considered inadequate because the Swindon Market Company was formed in 1852 with the intention of improving market accommodation.[91] It employed Sampson Sage to design a new building for the same site on the south side of the Market Square and this opened in 1853.[92] However, the open arches on the ground floor, which had been intended to house a produce market, were almost immediately filled in and used as a wine store, the wine company taking over the whole of the ground floor in 1873.[93] The large room on the first floor was used for various purposes, including as a court room until 1873,[94] and the whole building was soon known as the Town Hall.

Market provision was still inadequate, not helped by the failure of the 1853 building to function as intended, and to help remedy this the Swindon Central Market Company was founded in 1863. It built the new *Corn Exchange* in 1866, to designs by W J Willcox of Wilson and Willcox of Bath.[95] This was set at right angles to the Town Hall, the two buildings forming an L shape, and had a triangular extension to the east, perhaps for a butter market.[96] The link at the corner of the L was provided by an 80ft tall Italianate tower. The two market companies combined in 1874 to bring both buildings under single ownership.

TOWN HALLS

Swindon, the Old Town Hall as built: what a handsome building this once was. (Local Studies (Swindon Library & Information Service))

The Old Town Hall, although one might not think so to look at it in its present condition, was a fine building. It is of two storeys and five bays in Grecian style with giant pilasters, the central three bays brought slightly forward under a pediment with a clock in the tympanum and a bellcote above; the ground floor with its filled-in arches is rusticated.[97] The Corn Exchange was mostly in coursed rubblestone, the triangular section to the east arcaded in round arches with ashlar dressings; the windows elsewhere, including those in a wall between the triangular section and the main rectangular block, were dressed in brick. The tower, in four stages, has Venetian windows in the top stage and a balustraded belvedere above.

The Corn Exchange closed at the start of the 20th century in the face of a decline in corn production in the district and the building then saw use from 1910 as a skating rink, a cinema and from 1949 a Locarno ballroom.[98] The Town Hall was used, amongst other

Swindon, the Old Town Hall and Corn Market, framed by the bell of the Bell Hotel and already in decline in the 1960s. (Local Studies (Swindon Library & Information Service))

Swindon, the Old Town Hall and Corn Market, forlorn in 2023

things, as a masonic lodge in 1920.[99] Both buildings closed in 1984[100] and there then followed a long saga of failed attempts to redevelop them. In the meantime both lost their roofs and windows, the damage made worse by arson attacks in 2003 and 2004. In 2023, boarded up, they presented a desolate sight, matched in the town only by the equally desolate Mechanics' Institute described in Chapter 6.

The New Town Hall

It must have been clear from mid-century that the Old and New Towns would eventually merge, such was the rapid expansion of the latter, but in 1864 new public health boards were created for both and two separate district councils were created in 1894.[101] By this date the towns had physically merged so the decision to maintain separate councils is, with hindsight, difficult to understand. The two councils were famously uncooperative with each other but the problem was solved in 1900 when they were at last combined into one borough.[102]

The New Swindon Local Board built their **New Town Hall*** in 1891 in Regent Circus, a location mid-way between the Old and New Towns chosen with an eye to the likely future incorporation of the town.[103] The site had been bought in 1886 and there was then a competition with 20 entries to find a suitable architect, Brightwen Binyon of Ipswich being chosen, perhaps because he had already designed several buildings in the town and his cost estimates were lower than those of many of his competitors.[104] At this late date there was no attempt to combine functions with a market hall or similar: the building provided just public offices.[105] It became the offices of the new corporation from 1900.[106]

The New Town Hall, in Northern Renaissance style, makes a considerable impact. It is of two storeys plus attic, in brick with stone dressings and string courses, the windows mullioned and transomed. The front has nine bays, the two at each end under gables, with entrance doors located in

Swindon, the New Town Hall in the early 20th century. (Local Studies (Swindon Library & Information Service))

the third bay from each end, that at the north in an elaborate surround with heavy brackets carrying a balcony above. This same bay rises into a substantial clock tower with ogee roof and cupola, the tower made taller than the architect had specified at

Swindon, the New Town Hall, New Library visible to left hand side.

the demand of the Board. The result was some unbalancing of the design but also the creation of a tower taller than that of the Old Town Hall, which may have been the intention.[107]

The side wings, that to the south plainer than the northern one, now butt up against the new library. Inside, the entrance hall and many of the rooms are of modest size but there is a well-lit first floor landing with three round-arched windows overlooking the rear courtyard and there is also a four-bay theatre with a panelled barrel vault and a balcony.

The Town Hall eventually became too small for the council and much of the administration moved elsewhere in 1938. The building, still well maintained in 2023, was then occupied by a dance studio.

Trowbridge

Perhaps the central question about the town hall at Trowbridge, opened in 1889, is why it was so late on the scene. There might be some explanation in the facts that the town was not incorporated so had no over-arching local government body and that it already had public halls such as the Court Hall - described in Chapter 4 - and Hill's Hall. It also already had a market house, opened in 1861, so there was no incentive for the type of mixed-use building found elsewhere. But Trowbridge, throughout the 19th century, was one of the two or three most populous towns in the county, with civic aspirations to match, so the question remains.

Whatever the explanation, no building appeared until Roger Brown, a rich local manufacturer, announced his intention to give a town hall in commemoration

Trowbridge: The Local Board site plan for the Town Hall. Note lack of a road link at that date from Silver Street to Castle Street. (WSA)

of Queen Victoria's golden jubilee provided a suitable town centre site could be found.[108] The site chosen was immediately adjacent to the Market Hall where a substantial two-storey house with an 18th century façade, The Limes, previously for some time a post office, was acquired and demolished to make way for the new building.[109] The *Town Hall**, designed by Alfred Goodridge of Bath, was opened in June 1889.[110]

It is nearly square in plan and built of local stone in Northern Renaissance style. The front is asymmetrical but well balanced with a larger shaped gable to the left and a smaller to the right, separated by a doorway with the obligatory balcony above. This in turn sits beneath a 101ft tall clock tower with conical top, the height increased from the architect's plans in what – see also Swindon – may be a typical display of municipal pride.[111] The ground floor fenestration is modest but on the principal floor a very large, round-arched, mullioned and transomed window fronts the assembly room and a smaller one, similar but flat-headed and an oriel, provides the illumination to the committee room. The larger window was also originally an oriel but, after cracking and being repaired in 1896, it became dangerous again in 1974 and was then brought back flat to the wall.[112] As a footnote to the construction, the floors were of reinforced concrete,[113] perhaps one of the first times such a material had been used other than in an industrial building.

The rear is less assertive but follows the same pattern with asymmetrical gables and large windows illuminating the principal rooms: it could well be the front of some affluent burgher's late 19th century house in any North European city. Inside, the main rooms on the ground floor are the courtroom and board room, both facing the rear, with cells beneath in the basement. A large entrance hall leads to a grand staircase, all much wood-panelled with a large stained glass window at the half-landing, and this gives at the first floor onto the three doors leading to the assembly room. Here was the major disappointment for anyone viewing the building up to 2023, for what was originally a single space 90ft by 40ft with a 40ft high mock-hammerbeam ceiling[114] had been subdivided into individual rooms and its whole impact lost: a major refurbishment programme starting in that year was due to reinstate the room to its former condition. The council chamber is the other principal room on this floor and its stained glass windows, like many others elsewhere in the building, contain a proud mixture of symbols, inscriptions and coats of arms.

Trowbridge Town Hall. (Trowbridge Museum).

The town hall was managed from the start by the local board,[115] later the district council, and was also used for meetings of the county council before the erection of County Hall (see Chapter 7).[116] It was also used for the usual variety of functions beyond its core purpose. By the late 1950s a link had been made at first floor level with the market hall next door so that rooms there could be used as additional offices.[117]

The local government use was lost following reorganization in 1974 but after conversion work to create more courtrooms the town hall became for another 30 years a magistrates' court. Following that it was used for a period as a coroner's court for service personnel but when that ceased there seemed no obvious purpose for it until

Trowbridge Town Hall, the Great Hall before it was subdivided, in use for an exhibition. (Trowbridge Museum).

a trust was formed in 2010. The trust is restoring the building under a lease from Wiltshire Council and is exploiting its potential for local events of all kinds.[118] Work started in 2023 on a major refurbishment scheme.

Warminster

The town's first town hall seems to have been in place by the late 14th century, was repaired in 1563-4, and was believed to have stood on what later became the eastern corner of Weymouth Street and Market Place. It was later an inn and either it or a replacement was finally demolished in the 1830s, presumably to make way for the premises of the Literary and Scientific Society described in Chapter 6.[119]

A new hall, called the 'yelde hall' in 1516-17 and later more commonly the **Guildhall**, stood in the centre of the road outside where the Athenaeum was later built.[120] A 'little shed house' which was there in 1575 had been replaced a century later by a newly erected hall with a partly open space underneath for a market, and there may have been further alterations or repairs in 1711. It was used for the summer quarter sessions as well as for balls and assemblies. A print shows a building with no pretensions, the main block of three bays with two storeys and an attic, the ground floor open behind pillars in two of the bays. A lower single-

Warminster, the old Guildhall. (Warminster History Society).

bay section at the east end contained the main door.¹²¹

Its position in the middle of the highway was a serious obstacle and around 1830 a proposal to construct Weymouth Street as a new road to Sambourne gave the opportunity to replace it with a new building at the junction of that road with the Market Place.¹²² This is the **Town Hall***, paid for by the Marquess of Bath, designed by Edward Blore and opened in 1832 at the same time as the new road.¹²³ It is nearly square in plan, of modest size compared to later examples but nevertheless with considerable presence. The ashlar front has two-storey square bays either side of the door in tactful emulation of the design of Longleat, with pilasters and mullioned and transomed

Warminster Town Hall, a mid-19th century print (Wiltshire Museum, Devizes.

Warminster Town Hall in 2023, the front remarkably unchanged

windows as in the original. Above the round-arched doorway the Thynne arms stand proud of the wall, which is inset between the two first-floor bays, and above that are a clock and a bell turret, the latter set into the parapet. The side to Weymouth Street is mainly in rubblestone, with a subsidiary door and four-light windows, two of them blind, and the rear has sash windows. A parapet hides most of the hipped roof.

The architect was under no obligation to provide market space, available elsewhere (see Chapter 3). Emulating Longleat produced an attractive street frontage but would have made it difficult to site the main assembly room in the usual position lengthways at the first floor front, so instead it is across the rear. The courtroom was vertically beneath this, again stretching the full width of the building, with cells under. Additional cells were added in 1888 for prisoners held for the quarter sessions.[124]

The Town Hall operated successfully for many years and was given to the town by the fifth Marquess in 1903.[125] It came into the ownership of the new district council in 1974 but was sold off by them in 1979, though courts remained in the building until their move to Trowbridge in 1991.[126] The Warminster Preservation Trust, formed in 1987 to restore historic buildings in the town, attempted without success to buy the building in 2011 and has worked with subsequent owners on various unsuccessful attempts since to restore it and provide it with a viable future. The exterior does not betray this unhappy situation but in 2023 a resolution to the problem appeared to be as far away as ever.[127]

Westbury

A guildhall is mentioned in 1599, said to have been on the north-west corner of the junction of the Market Place and Fore Street, and this appears to be confirmed by a plan of 1762, although this would have placed the guildhall, with a public house

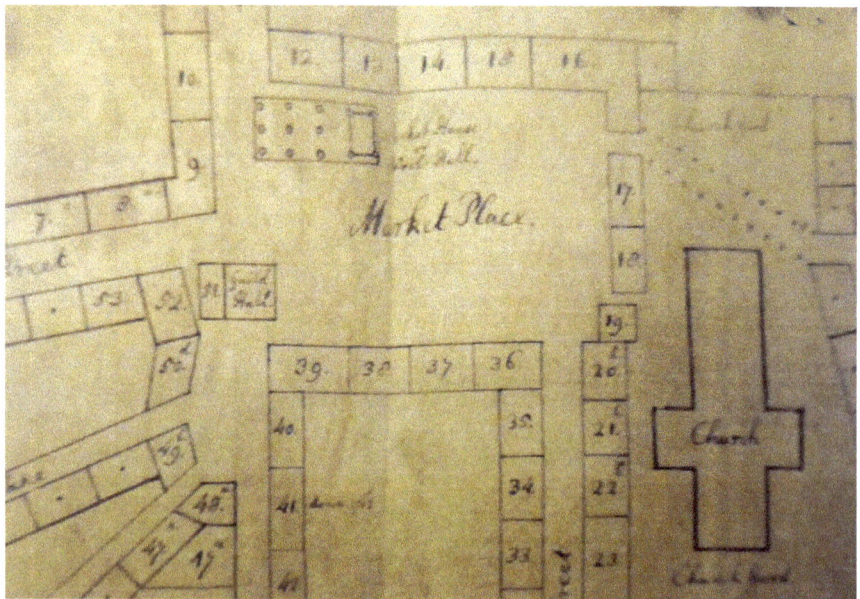

Westbury, burgage plan showing the predecessor Guildhall, Market House and Wool Hall. (WSA)

TOWN HALLS

Westbury Town Hall, the inscription to Lopes still just visible. (Further photograph with introduction to Chapter 3.)

attached to the rear, directly in front of the early 18th century Marlborough House which still stands.[128] It seems that there was also a previous **Market House and Wool Hall**, on the same site as its later replacement but aligned at right angles to it. The plan which shows this is not explicit but there may have been a covered market hall on columns to the north and the wool hall to the south.[129]

The present *Town Hall**, built as a Market Hall but soon expanding its functions in the typical way, was built in 1815. It was the gift of Sir Manasseh Massey Lopes, born in Jamaica of a family of Portuguese origins, who exploited the pre-Reform Act electoral system to buy several constituencies including that of Westbury with its two MPs.*[130]*

Though early in date, the Town Hall was of conventional appearance with an open space below for markets and rooms above for civic use behind a Classical ashlar façade, the stone of which was specified to come from a quarry at Monkton Farleigh.[131] Below are four rusticated piers, each separated by two Roman Doric columns, in front of what is now a series of glass shop fronts. Above, each of the three bays has an arched recess, with sash windows in the outer two, the centre one blind and containing a clock. The central bay is brought forward slightly in typical fashion and is topped with a pediment containing the arms of Lopes; the plain frieze has an inscription noting his gift.[132] The returns are similar in style, with two further columns each, and the rear is in plain brick between various outbuildings. It was designed by Richard Ingleman of Southwell.[133]

The result is neat, even if for some tastes the ground floor may be too low relative to the first and the central bay with its pediment too narrow. Law courts sat here from the outset and it seems to have been used for the usual range of town hall functions even though there was very limited space.[134] Underneath there was originally what was described as a 'prison', removed c1830, though two cells remained at the rear of the ground floor for the use of the court.[135] It may be that the first floor front was originally one long room in the typical pattern – certainly its use as any sort of assembly room would seem to have demanded that – though it is suggested that it may have been divisible into two by removable partitions from the outset.[136] Even so it was deemed to be too small for the newly formed Urban District Council and in 1899 this started to hold its meetings in the Laverton Institute, described in Chapter 7, which soon became viewed as the chief assembly place for the town.[137]

By the turn of the century, and presumably following the council's withdrawal, the first floor front was more permanently divided into two with the police court to the right and wide double doors to a public room to the left. To the rear were a judge's room and a witness room, the law courts function thereby taking up the whole of the usable space.[138] This use remained until the court was withdrawn in the late 1930s,[139] and the upper floor was also used for two periods as a public library (see Chapter 6). In the meantime, the magistrates complained in 1925 about the condition of the building and the council, it seems grudgingly, agreed to some repairs. A suggestion that the ground floor should be turned into offices and the whole building used again by the council may not have progressed although a plan was drawn up.[140]

The library moved out in 1970 and the Town Hall was sold in 1972 and then converted for commercial use by the insertion of shop units into the open ground floor.[141] It was used for a period as solicitors' offices, was sold again in 2013 and since then appears to have languished.[142]

Wilton

The medieval Guildhall stood on the site of the present Town Hall and was a two-storey building with a row of shops underneath, a penthouse attached on the Market Place side and an outside stairway to the north.[143] The gaol was situated immediately behind it.[144]

The present *Town Hall** was built in 1738 on the Guildhall site.[145] It is in brick under a hipped tiled roof with ashlar dressings, six bays wide with the door placed asymmetrically in the fourth bay from the left: there was previously a second door in the second bay.[146] The first floor windows are 16-pane sashes in ashlar surrounds, the ground floor segmental-arched in brick. The south side is of three bays, one first floor and both ground floor windows blind, the latter probably infilled at a later date. The north side has an unrelated mid-19th century building attached to it, at one stage used as a fire station.[147] To the rear of the town hall small extensions incorporate what are said to be remnants of the old gaol, although an 1857 drainage map shows a lock-up in the building to the north where later the fire station was placed.[148]

At an early date, perhaps when first built, the Town Hall had a clock with a single face mounted on a turret at the centre of the roof. This presumably modest structure was replaced in 1889, to mark Victoria's golden jubilee, by the present disproportionate effort, the turret tile-hung and the clock above altered to have four faces.[149]

Wilton Town Hall.

The town council left the Town Hall in 1948/9 and moved to Kingsbury Square (see Chapter 7), after which the hall remained used for public functions until the opening of the new community centre in 1978.[150] By 1980 the district council was attempting to have it turned into housing but the external changes they thought necessary to achieve this were too great.[151] The application failed and the Town Hall was instead taken over in 1981 by the Baptist church. They use as their main worship space the assembly room which runs to the full depth and much of the length of the first floor.

Royal Wootton Bassett

The *Town Hall** in Wootton Bassett is unlike any other in the county, a world away from Victorian civic grandeur or Georgian elegance. It was traditionally said to have been given to the town in 1700 by Lawrence Hyde, Earl of Rochester,[152] and was of simple, almost anachronistic design even for that relatively early date.

It had a largely open ground floor on 15 stone Tuscan columns, with a small lock-up at one end. The first floor was timber-framed and rendered, with a single room inside and an attic over. It thus provided the same mix of facilities on a small scale as its later equivalents elsewhere. By the late 19th century, however, it was in a poor state, much of the render falling off, and Sir Henry Meux of the brewery family,

Wootton Bassett Town Hall before restoration. (Royal Wootton Bassett Town Hall Museum).

Wootton Bassett Town Hall, restored. (Royal Wootton Bassett Town Hall Museum)

who had bought the manor, paid for its restoration.[153] The original half-timbering was exposed and renewed, the sash windows were replaced by casements, the lock-up was removed and new stairs were provided.[154] The first floor room, previously with a panelled ceiling and dormers in the chamber above, was opened up to the roof and a previous fireplace and chimney removed.[155] Outside, the Meux arms were added in panels at each end together with the 1889 date of planned completion for the restoration, though in the event it did not reopen until 1890.[156]

Sir Henry died in 1900 and Lady Meux, having first tried to sell the Town Hall to the town, gave it to them in 1906. It was run from 1909 by a charity which itself combined with the Town Trust in 1912 to form the Town Hall and Trust Charity.[157] The building has since served as town hall, school, library and town meeting place, and since the start as a museum. The museum was taken over by the town's historical society in 1971.[158]

3
Market Halls

Introduction

WILTSHIRE TOWNS HAD street markets from early medieval times, often clustered around a single market cross – Malmesbury is a good example – but more spread-out in more important places like Devizes and Salisbury, with markets for different commodities in various parts of the central area.[159] They were centred on the trade in foodstuffs, both for the day to day requirements of the populace and as a main means for farmers to sell their produce, particularly corn, livestock and wool, with little differentiation between wholesale and retail marketing. The butchers' shambles, where animals were slaughtered and meat sold, were for obvious reasons often separated from other traders' stalls, and livestock of course required a different type of provision.

Markets like this continued for centuries. People could buy from the gradually increasing number of shops, from pedlars and from occasional fairs, but markets remained central to the local economy. The great majority of sellers used temporary stalls put up for the occasion, covered or not depending on the produce on sale. However, other more permanent buildings sometimes joined them and a common feature of market squares, exemplified by Chippenham and Salisbury, is the gradual reduction in their area as other buildings encroached.

Chippenham, the Butter Cross

The markets remained no doubt often squalid, usually inefficient and sometimes subject to exploitative tolls by the market owner. But they worked after their fashion. So why did many towns, late on in their history, build market halls and take much of the activity under cover?

The reasons are complex and probably no single one fully explains any particular case. First might have been an altruistic wish to improve conditions for the traders and their customers, linked in some cases with a desire to take a grip on the often unruly conduct and illegal and fraudulent practices of those involved.[160] So for example the Trowbridge market house – the name generally used at that time – was erected in 1862 to meet just such concerns.

A second reason stems from the increased economic activity and improving transport links which from the late 18th century onwards led to more competition between adjacent market towns and, for some, risked a decline in market prosperity. A typical response to this threat might be to reduce or remove entirely the market tolls and thus make the market more attractive, itself a recognition that it had a wider social function and was not just a means of making money for the owner. But an alternative might be to build a market hall and so counter the threat of competition by making the whole process of buying and selling more comfortable. Two early examples here are Corsham and Westbury but several others were also motivated by the fear of competition.

Westbury Town Hall in the 1950s before the infilling of the former market space; photograph taken from the church tower. (Westbury Heritage Society)

If altruism, greater control and response to competition were the main motivations, another factor often played a part, namely the wish of one prominent individual to make his mark upon the town by funding a prominent public building. William Stancomb at Trowbridge and Sir Manasseh Massey Lopes at Westbury might come into this category, and the efforts of Joseph Neeld in Chippenham surpassed even theirs. Although the underlying motives of these men might be questioned there was at least an element of altruism present, in contrast to the motives of the lords of the manor who had owned most markets throughout earlier times and generally saw

Trowbridge, the Market House in 2023.

them simply as a means to extract money from the traders. It was only when local authorities began to acquire markets, aided by legislation in 1858, that exploitation was replaced more generally by investment for the community.

Some perishable goods particularly benefitted from being sold under cover. Corn was a specific case: generally when sold outdoors small 'sample' bags were shown to the potential purchaser but the preferred system was that of the 'pitched' market where a whole sack would be pitched out onto the ground, giving a better appreciation of the quality of the grain. There was clearly substantial risk of the grain spoiling when this was done outdoors, hence the priority given to building corn exchanges and the status they brought with them. The Devizes corn exchange is perhaps the county's finest example.

The ground floor open space of market houses was used for the most perishable goods and also for market administration – weighing, payment and collection of tolls. However, as has been seen in Chapter 2, many were soon transformed into town halls. The near-universal pattern was for the ground floor arched entrances to be infilled and the space then used for other purposes. Only in a small number of places, for example the corn exchange and market house in Devizes and the corn exchange in Marlborough, was the local economy strong enough to justify a completely separate building. A different type, unique in Wiltshire, was the market hall provided at the rear of the Mechanics' Institute in Swindon in 1855, built because the New Town at that date was thought not yet to have acquired enough shops for the increasing local population.

The modern market hall, of which examples include that at Castle Walk in Trowbridge, is a full-time part of the local shopping 'offer', open six or seven days a week and selling a wide range of products, certainly not just food. 19th century market halls, by contrast, were much focussed on food until late in the century and functioned only on certain days, sometimes one and seldom more than two or three days a week. This meant that they were empty for much of the time and so available to be used for other activities, from meetings, dinners and indoor sports to military drill. Market days were a major opportunity for social contact and the addition of these other activities underlined the role of the market hall as one of the town's most important public buildings.

There were periods of greater and lesser prosperity based on economic conditions, the state of farming and competition from elsewhere, but most market halls remained in generally good health into the 20th century. However, a number of factors began to undermine them, including increased competition from shops:

Swindon, the octagonal market house behind the Mechanics' Institute, awaiting demolition c1892. (Local Studies (Swindon Library & Information Service))

these were seen to offer a more attractive environment, particularly stores like the Co-operative and, much later, the new supermarkets. Farmers were also finding that sales of their produce direct to wholesalers offered greater profits, and at the same time there were more imported foodstuffs. The buildings themselves became increasingly run-down and, particularly after the Second World War, increasingly unfashionable when the emphasis was so strongly on modernity.

All this led to changes of use or to demolition and in 2024 the only market hall in the county still in use for nearly its original purpose was that in Devizes. Conversely, street markets, which were never entirely displaced by market halls, have in recent years thrived again, albeit serving a somewhat different purpose.

The history of markets is a large one, about which much has been written both generally and locally. In this chapter the focus is kept on the market halls themselves, with only enough background information on a town's markets to provide the context.

The Buildings

Amesbury

There may have been a market in Amesbury since the 13th century but it is thought never to have been important.[161] The market house operating in 1635 stood at the west end of the market place, approximately where the former Lloyds bank stands on the corner of Church Street and Salisbury Street. The market house was repaired in 1759, perhaps in late response to the great fire of 1751, and at that stage still retained a shambles. However, it was demolished in 1809, by which date the remaining market was probably no more than nominal. A directory of 1855 refers to Amesbury as 'formerly a market town'.[162]

Bradford on Avon

There was a market in Bradford in 1086 and continuously thereafter, descending with the manor until it was sold to the town commissioners in 1882 with the expectation that this change would make the markets and fairs more 'convenient and orderly.'[163] The market, however, though still active in 1903, had ceased by 1911.[164]

A **market house**, its date of construction not recorded, once stood at the east end of the Shambles.[165] It comprised a basement at street level, a colonnaded ground floor facing north and occupied by butchers' stalls, and a first floor at one time used as the court room for the manor. By the late 18th century the first floor room was in such poor repair that it was abandoned and meetings of the court leet were held instead in the Swan Hotel at the foot of Market Street.[166] By 1820 the whole building was dilapidated and not long afterwards it fell down. The market house, also known as the town hall, was attached to a late medieval building with a 15th century doorway, still standing, which was the *Tolsey*, the building where market tolls were collected.[167]

No further off-street provision was made for markets until the new town hall, described in Chapter 2, was opened in 1855, and even then there was no market hall as such. Instead the yard behind the new building, accessed from Market Street[168] and also through a small arch from Church Street, was used for markets. It was intended to have market buildings against the three enclosed sides, with a covered shed to the east and north and a hay loft over a further shed to the west.[169] In fact it appears that only the shed to the east was built, and later that to the north.[170] The northern one was presumably removed on closure of the market and the other was demolished after 1922.[171]

Calne

There was a market in Calne from at least the first half of the 13th century, believed to have been held on the triangle of land where later the first **market hall**, then **town hall**, was built.[172] This building, described in Chapter 2, was of the late 17th century or early 18th century. It had an open arcaded ground floor, except for a blind house at one corner, and a market bell above. In the days before its conversion to a town hall the first floor was used as a corn store, with a windlass to haul sacks up, and there was a covered shambles for the sale of meat on the west side. The declining market for corn in the 1820s presented the opportunity to convert the first floor into a town hall and, in mid-century, the shambles was demolished and the ground floor was enclosed with windows and converted into a corn exchange.

The river running across the Strand, outside what was the town mill and was later replaced by the new town hall, was fully culverted in the 1840s and it seems the market moved to this space soon after that date.[173] The new Town Hall contained a corn exchange, presumably a direct replacement for that in the old town hall.[174]

Chippenham

Chippenham's first markets, from 1205 or earlier, were located in what is still called the Market Place, at the south-eastern end of High Street.[175] By the 14th or 15th century the open space contained not only the Yelde Hall, described in Chapter 2, but also a shambles and shops. In c1570 the *Butter Cross* was built here, on the south side of

Chippenham, the New Hall, later Town Hall, in use as a market hall. (Chippenham Town Council)

the Shambles towards the east end; this was a roofed-in open market space, the roof supported by six Doric columns.[176]

From the late 18th century the market was in decline, and by the early 19th century there appears to have been some doubt as to whether the town actually needed a market at all,[177] a question which was answered by Joseph Neeld's initiative in erecting the *New Hall*, described in Chapter 2. The ground floor of this building was intended as a market for cheese, butter, bacon and poultry, and it was so successful that in 1835 Neeld agreed to expand into the yard behind, building a number of sheds there for more traders.¹⁷⁸ In 1837 he added a wool market in further sheds, but it was the cheese market which had most success and in 1841 Neeld replaced a previous building with a 'cheese warehouse' on three floors. Growth continued, necessitating the construction in 1850 of a new cheese shed behind the town hall, 156ft long with a grand entrance alongside 5 High Street in what is now Borough Parade; this and the cheese warehouse are also described in Chapter 2. At this time the Chippenham cheese market was said to be the greatest in the west of England.

Chippenham, dealers in the 1850 Cheese Hall, later replaced by the Neeld Hall. (Chippenham Town Council).

The stalls and shambles in the Market Place were still used for a small outdoor market in 1888, even though Neeld's new cheese hall had taken away much of the trade, but by that date the Butter Cross was already out of use.¹⁷⁹ It was sold to the owner of the manor house at Castle Combe for use as a garden gazebo and remained there until, 100 years later, the Chippenham Civic Society bought it and had it re-erected in the Market Place in 1995, close to its original site.

The main cheese market had itself entered a steep decline - in 1911 it was said that cheesemaking had almost entirely gone from the district - and the largest shed was then replaced by the **Neeld Hall**, also described in Chapter 2.¹⁸⁰ At the same time the cattle market in the Market Place, which had become increasingly unacceptable in that location, was moved here in lieu of the now much reduced market trading in other commodities, the space being considerably enlarged to accommodate the cattle pens and a new access opened from River Street. But this site too became congested and eventually, after a long delay, a new livestock market was opened in Cocklebury Lane, partially in 1951 and fully in 1954.¹⁸¹ This allowed the previous market to be closed and the site redeveloped. The Cocklebury Lane market closed finally in 2005 and was replaced in part by the Wiltshire and Swindon History Centre.

There had been market trading elsewhere in the town: a livestock and poultry market took place at The Wharf, now the bus station, and there was a general market on the site of what is now the Emery Street car park.¹⁸² The latter was moved to Bath Road when the Emery Gate shopping centre was built in the 1980s, the long row of gabled open sheds providing shelter for the traders, their pale-brick rear walls facing the street. This too declined and eventually ceased and the site is now just a car park.

Corsham

There was a market cross in Corsham from an early date¹⁸³ and a **Market Hall**, described in Chapter 2, was in place by the mid-17th century; this had butchers' shambles under a front arcade and an enclosed room on the ground floor which may have been the market hall itself. However, the market was evidently in decline when Paul Methuen of Corsham Court paid for the erection of the **Market House** in 1784. This, also described in Chapter 2, may have had some success initially but in 1815 the announcement of a new weekly market for 'grain and other commodities' suggests that it might already have been struggling.[184] By 1843 the poor results at a Corsham fair were put down to competition from other monthly markets[185] and it seems that the town's markets may have ceased to function at all soon after that, for a meeting in 1872 to consider the establishment of a market in the town brought out only seemingly distant memories of the previous one.[186] The proposal, which seems not to have progressed, was for a fortnightly market to be held on-street, implying that the space in the Market House was already committed to other activities.

Cricklade

Cricklade had a market from before 1275.[187] The market may have struggled at various periods since but there was a market cross in the High Street from the 14th century and a **Market House** was constructed c1663. This was apparently in the middle of High Street between the junctions with Calcutt Street and Mutton Lane (now Gas Lane) and was open on the ground floor with an enclosed room above supported on 10 stone pillars. A new weekly Saturday market was granted in 1663, perhaps coincident with the erection of the market house, but by the early 19th century the market was in decline. The market house was demolished in 1814 and in 1830 the market was said to be almost moribund.

A new monthly cattle and corn market was established in 1837 and was more successful, though the previous Saturday market was described in 1855 as 'almost nominal'.[188] The monthly market was held in the High Street, though for what may have been a short period around 1944 it was held in the station yard. The last market was held in 1953.

Devizes

Devizes market was first mentioned in 1228 and expanded over following centuries into a group of markets for different commodities in various locations through the town centre:[189] so profuse were they that for many years they must have dominated completely the central area. Most were accommodated on-street, those for produce having stalls of varying degrees of permanence, but others used at varying times what became four of the town's most notable buildings. Of these, the *New Hall* and *Town Hall*, previously the Yarn Hall then Wool Hall, are described in Chapter 2. The Market House and Corn Exchange are described here.

New shambles were built in Short Street in 1568, to the rear of the site of the later market house.[190] They were rebuilt in 1600 but by 1738 shambles were back in the market place and stayed there until a donation from a local MP was used to build another permanent building, again in Short Street. A further donation in 1791 allowed this to be either completed or rebuilt and by now it was in its present location, forming the rear half of what is now the market house, though it was at that stage not roofed over. In the same year a further donation allowed the construction of another market house to the west of the butcher's shambles, for produce other than meat, corn, cheese and livestock. This was finished by 1803 and in 1838 the butcher's shambles was roofed over and the two buildings became in effect one *Market House*, the changes said to have been designed by one Pollard of Frome.[191]

The 1838 roofing of the shambles must have involved substantial rebuilding since the two halves of the Market House are now nearly identical, separated only by steps up from the front to the rear through a tall archway with the town's arms and the date 1838 above. The roofs have a continuous clerestory above the central aisle, the ceilings to either side supported on rows of columns. The lean-to construction is of brick and the front to the market place has a three-bay Classical façade, the ground floor rusticated with three round-arched entrances, the central one brought forward and pedimented. Above are three blank panels separated by pairs of pilasters below a clock turret.

Devizes, the Market Hall.

A corn hall existed in 1560 and in 1615 a 'measuring house' for corn was erected in the market place; a map of 1759 indicates it in a central position there.[192] It seems to have been demolished between 1787 and 1791 and thereafter corn was bought and sold against railings in the open.[193] Protest against this unsatisfactory state of affairs resulted in a petition in 1837 for the provision of a covered market but, though the town council made an approach to the Treasury for borrowing approval and produced a plan of a potential building, evidently no progress was made.[194] The 1837 proposal was for a site unidentified but not in the Market Square; however, when the matter was raised again in 1855 all the three potential sites were there. Two of them were close to the shambles and the third and chosen site was in the Bear Inn yard.[195] The Assembly

Devizes Market Hall, the two buildings joined in 1838.

Rooms of the Bear Inn stood here and had first to be removed and rebuilt at the rear of the Inn, at right angles to their original orientation. The new building, to designs by William Hill of Leeds, was opened in 1857, providing a large full-height room for a pitched, rather than sample, **Corn Exchange***.[196]

The building was soon used for a variety of other civic purposes also, including dinners, dances and meetings, and remained a functioning corn exchange up until the 1960s.[197] By the 1980s, however, it was a run-down, draughty hall with a plastic false ceiling hiding the roof. A major refurbishment in 1995 included the insertion of an intermediate floor, with function rooms on the ground and first floors and also in the basement.

The front, in Bath stone, has four semi-engaged Corinthian columns between rusticated angle piers, between which are three doorways in round-arched surrounds and, at each end, round-arched windows at a higher level. Above is an entablature and stone balustrade with a central plaque giving name and date, and above that, on a conspicuously tall base, is a statue of Ceres, the goddess of the harvest. The first three bays of the north side follow the same pattern, the columns replaced by pilasters, making this part of the building appear almost separate from that further

Devizes, the Corn Exchange.

Devizes, rear of the Corn Exchange with at right the Assembly Rooms rebuilt at the rear of The Bear.

back with strikingly harmonious effect. This design is repeated at the end of this side and in a single bay at the centre, with four windows either side, creating a symmetrical north façade. The rear and what can be seen of the south elevation is plain and in rubblestone. Inside, a low clerestory provides extra illumination but the effect of the arched roof trusses is obstructed by the inserted floor.

Highworth

The first known charter for a market at Highworth was in 1206.[198] The market place, at that time much larger than now and encompassing the whole space between High Street and Sheep Street, was the site of what became a prosperous market, though it had a downturn in the early 17th century. Ownership of the market had passed through various hands and in 1686, by which time it seems to have regained its prosperity, it was sold to Thomas Freke of Hannington for £800. He had a **Market House** built in the market square for the 'farmers and traders to stand out of the rain and for the safe storage of their corn and other goods'. A sketch in a 1775 map indicates that it was similar in appearance to that still standing at Wootton Bassett.[199]

The Market House was taken down in the early 19th century to facilitate the movement of traffic through the town[200] and it was replaced by a **Toll House**, located in the northwest corner of the market place where there now stands a brick building of 1903, in 2023 a charity shop.[201] The toll house is thought to have burned down, the date uncertain, but the market was in decline from the mid-19th century and, despite attempts to revive it, was closed by the 1930s.

Malmesbury

Malmesbury had a market from before 1225 but it seems it was always overshadowed by those of surrounding towns, notably Chippenham, Tetbury and Cirencester.[202]

Different markets were held at different points in the town, with the focus on Abbey Row where the market cross was built in the 15th century. The Saturday market had ceased by 1890; amongst other markets, a general market operated in Cross Hayes until the mid-20th century. There was still a monthly cattle market in 1931 but this was moved from Cross Hayes to the Railway Hotel meadow in 1950.[203]

The *Market House*, opened in 1848 and described in Chapter 2, was intended to help revitalize the town's market. The arches opened onto an area for pitching corn and selling cheese, and behind this there were intended to be butter and poultry markets.[204] However, although it was established by the Malmesbury Market House Company, it is not clear to what extent, and for how long, it was used for market purposes: it is likely the arches were infilled at about the time the building was taken over by the council in 1920.[205]

Marlborough

Early markets on the site of what became the *Town Hall* are described in Chapter 2. A Wednesday market place, also with a **Market House** and perhaps also in High Street, was mentioned in 1625.[206] There was a butchers' shambles, also in High Street, from the later 16th century or earlier and this was demolished in 1812.[207]

For many years the corn market was a sample market, conducted by rails outside the Castle and Ball Inn.[208] In 1862 the Marquess of Ailesbury paid for a new Riding School to be built for the Royal Wiltshire Yeomanry south of the High Street.[209] At that time the corn market was in decline but the expected arrival of the new branch railway line to the town gave some hope that efforts to revitalise it might

Marlborough, the former Corn Exchange, passageway to rear Riding School through left hand arch. (Courtesy of Nick Baxter).

prove fruitful, particularly if they could replace the sample market with a covered, pitched market.[210] The Marquess of Ailesbury agreed that the riding school could be shared for this purpose and a section 40ft square was partitioned off from that building, which was 90ft by 40ft overall. The new *Corn Market* opened in June 1864.[211]

There were various conflicts with the Yeomanry as to priority for the use of the building – the partition mentioned may not have lasted long – and by the 1880s the market was in any event almost dead.[212] A movement to resuscitate the exchange in 1883 appears not to have had a long-lasting effect and by 1900 it had ceased functioning.[213] The building was converted c1914 into a cinema, which closed in 1970,[214] and in 2024 it was a Waitrose supermarket.

The Corn Market is of modest size, of ashlar with an arcaded front. Of the four arches, that at the east end leads through to the rear yard, still called Riding School Yard but now smaller in extent as the supermarket has a much larger footprint than had the original riding school. The first floor has four sash windows above the arches, and a parapet masks the roof.

Melksham

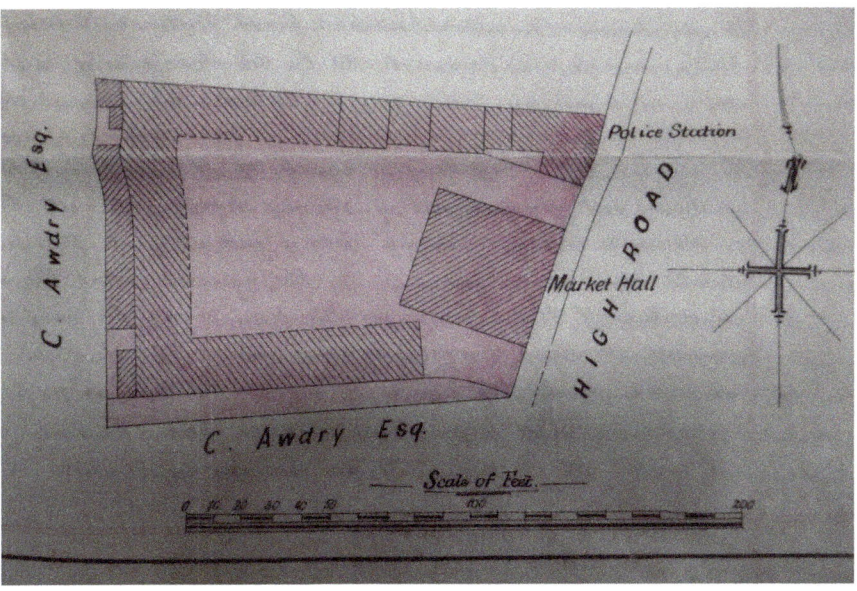

Melksham, original ground plan showing the extent of other market buildings to the rear of the Market Hall, later Town Hall. (WSA)

A Friday market was granted to Melksham in 1219 and various markets and fairs were held up until 1939.[215] The 1847 Cheese Hall, soon to become known as the *Town Hall*, is described in Chapter 2 and there is believed to have been no other market building in the town.

Mere

Mere had a market place in 1297 and perhaps considerably earlier.[216] Various markets lasted well into the 19th century, centred on the market place and the **Market House** described in Chapter 2. This was demolished in 1863 and replaced in 1868 by the clock tower still standing.[217] It seems that the remaining markets may then soon have died out.[218]

Salisbury

Rights to a market in the new Salisbury were first granted in 1227, though markets had been held for some time before that.[219] The various markets for different products remained mainly in the market place and the complicated story of their development, and the competition between the bishops and the citizenry for control of them, is detailed in the Victoria County History.

By the early 19th century there were growing concerns that the prosperity of the markets was under threat, partly because of congestion in the central area and partly because the ad hoc mix of temporary stalls, exposed to the weather, was proving increasingly unattractive. In response to this the corn market was moved shortly after 1823 from its existing position to a space in front of the Council House, the ground newly paved and a temporary awning supplied to cover it. In 1851 the newly established monthly cheese market was held in a temporary building put up each market day.

Salisbury, the Market House, now Library and Art Gallery.

Despite these moves, there appeared to be a danger that some of the markets might collapse unless better accommodation was provided.[220] A scheme in 1854 for a market house near the council house soon gave way to a proposal for a building on the present site, with the twin advantages that it did not encroach on the market place and could be served by a short railway branch line joining the main line close to the

MARKET HALLS

Salisbury, the Market House as built, railway siding to left. (Salisbury Museum)

London and South Western Railway (LSWR) station.[221] A private company, the Salisbury Railway and Market House Company, was formed to raise funds and secure the necessary parliamentary approval and the **Market House***, designed by John Strapp, engineer to the LSWR, opened in 1859. The LSWR ran the service to the Market House although the lines were laid to both broad and standard gauge so that they could be used also by the Great Western Railway.

The new Market House was successful and within a few years the pressure on space was such that it had to be restricted to use only for cheese and wool, together with a corn market. It suffered various vicissitudes over the years, including a claim against the architect in 1863 for two roof girders which had given way, but remained generally buoyant until the first world war when it was largely given over to the use of the army. Continued profitability, however, masked its decline: the cheese market had ceased to function by 1903 and the rail connection had been removed by 1923.[222] Around 1940 it was used mainly as a wool exchange, though the empty space was increasingly used for meetings, sports and other purposes. After the Second World War its only remaining market use was for a weekly sale of corn by sample. The company finally went into liquidation in 1966 and the building was sold to the city council before being turned into the new library, opened in 1975.

Salisbury, the Market House in use for the sale of wool. (Salisbury Museum)

The library retains the three-bay arcaded front of the original, striking with its three rusticated arches, the middle one larger and brought forward beneath a pediment with a clock in the tympanum. The side arches have ornate cast iron gates by Hill and Smith of Brierley Hill. The Market House itself was of iron and glass with low galleries either side. A single line of railway came across the millstream – the bridge still there and now used by pedestrians – and entered behind the left-hand arch.

The conversion into a library, by G Walters of Salisbury City Council,[223] demolished all but the front arcade. The alignment of the railway was kept as a pedestrian thoroughfare and the rest of the ground floor, and the whole width on higher floors, was rebuilt as the library and replacement Young art gallery (see Chapter 6), on three floors. The rear of the new building has rectangular lead-clad oriels over the millstream, mercifully not widely visible.

Swindon

There was a market in Swindon before 1274.[224] The first evidence of a permanent building is from the late 17th century when Thomas Goddard converted the former church-house into a Market House; it is not clear whether this was the small market house in the centre of the market square which was pulled down in 1793.[225]

Chapter 2 describes how the 1853 *Market Hall* in the market square never met its intended purpose and soon became known as the Town Hall. The *Corn Exchange*, built alongside in 1866 and also described in Chapter 2, at least functioned in the way intended until the turn of the century.

In the New Town, meanwhile, the builders of the *Mechanics' Institute* in 1855 added a *Market House* to the south end of the building to make up for the lack of other local shops at this early stage in development, as described in Chapter 6. The hall was octagonal, with low walls to the perimeter, and the roof was supported on metal

Swindon, the Commercial Road market in its original form. (Local Studies (Swindon Library & Information Service))

Swindon, the market after roofing in 1903. (Local Studies (Swindon Library & Information Service))

columns. In 1892 this was demolished to make way for an extension to the Mechanics' Institute, but it had already been replaced in 1891 by a new market on Commercial Road at its junction with what was then called Market Street, designed by H J Hamp, the borough surveyor.[226]

Swindon, the 'tipsy tent' Market, closed and beginning to be vandalised in 2023

The new **Market Hall** was triangular, essentially a low wall surrounding an open space in which were erected numerous stalls with canvas covers, with more permanent buildings to the south and north-west sides.[227] In 1903 it was roofed over to create a substantial building containing in 1920 17 shops and 80 stalls.[228] The sides were of brick in large panels below lines of gables, the entrance with ornate iron gates, the metal trussed roof supported on iron columns with long ventilated clerestoreys above.[229]

It was demolished in 1977, the site used for a car park for a time until the market hall was replaced on the same site in 1995 by the new *Market Hall*, designed by Harrison Patience.[230] This, conceived as a 'tipsy tent', has a roof of white fabric braced by external supports as if for a large marquee but with five unequal points at various angles. The walls below are mostly of glass blocks. It has not had a long life, closing in 2017, and despite planning approval in 2020 for a replacement building it was still empty in 2023.[231]

There had been a cattle market in Swindon for many years but this was apparently in decline when a new cattle market was proposed in an effort to boost trade. It was conveniently sited off Marlborough Road and adjacent to the Swindon Town station; designed by W H Read, it opened in 1887. It was alongside an existing cattle sale yard there and was praised for the quality of the provision in the sale sheds and pens.[232] Seemingly no substantial office or similar building was erected.[233] It closed in the 1980s and the site is now largely occupied by housing in Dewell Mews.

Trowbridge

The town was awarded a Tuesday market in 1200 and had a Saturday market by 1311, as well as a defined market place, believed to have been initially in front of the main entrance to the castle, a position whose modern equivalent is at the top of Castle Street.[234] By 1467 there was a 'high cross' nearby, described c1540 as octagonal with a pillar in the middle so perhaps similar to that at Malmesbury. It was taken down c1784.

After that there was no market house of any kind. There was an attempt in 1828 to have an assembly hall built with a covered market beneath but this seems to have failed because of opposition from the then lord of the manor, and a similar attempt in 1851 to have a covered market incorporated into what was later built as the *Court Hall* (see Chapter 4) failed because no suitable site could be found.[235] Faced with growing concerns about the unpleasant conditions offered by the open markets, civic dignitaries approached William Stancomb, the then lord of the manor, who agreed to have a new *Market House** erected at his expense.[236]

The new building opened in 1862 and offered over 100 stalls for meat, vegetables and 'sweetmeats etc' in a market hall 71ft by 110ft.[237] There was a smaller room below for a potato market and, above the portico at the front of the building, five rooms for public use. The market hall had an iron roof by Stothert and Pitt of Bath, supported on tall iron columns, and a skylight running full length above the centre of the room.

The architect was C E Davis of Bath and he provided a façade which has been described as being in the style of the Tuscan Trecento.[238] It relies for its effect on a repeating pattern of five openings: a five-bay arcade has above it five arched windows linked by a band of stone foliage and, in the attic storey, five much smaller windows below a deeply-eaved roof. The arcade arches have biblical texts above, though the central one is dedicated to recording Stancomb's generosity, and a sculpted lamb and flag at the apex of the building is inset into an ornate oval surround.

Stancomb leased the market rights to the local board, eventually selling them in 1892. To the left, the Market House was later joined to the Town Hall of 1889 and, to the right, an archway led through to the substantial market yard with its large cattle

MARKET HALLS

Trowbridge, the Market House in use for a flower show, showing the prodigious height of the roof. (Trowbridge Museum)

market, also initially under Stancomb's control. A pitched corn market was set up in the Market House in 1892,[239] presumably coincident upon the takeover by the local board, and the market seems to have thrived until well into the 20th century.

The cattle market closed in 1964[240] and the Market House not long after. The cast-iron market hall was demolished, leaving only the frontage building, and the space was redeveloped into the Castle Walk shopping centre and car park, opened in 1974, designed by John Simmons Associates, and accessed via the former archway to the market yard.[241] The frontage building was converted into a public house but in 2023 that had been closed for several years. The shopping centre and car park were sold in 2023 amidst speculation about possible redevelopment.

Warminster

There was a market in Warminster from at least the first half of the 13th century.[242] Most notable was the corn market, which was a pitched market in the Market Square, and right up to the end of the 18th century this was thought to be one of the largest in the west of England. A reduction in trade in the early 19th century was put down to the lack of a canal serving the town but the arrival of the railway in 1851 helped to boost custom back to previous levels, as did the construction of the **Market House**, in 1855.

The Market House, built with the usual intention of strengthening the market, was paid for by the Marquess of Bath on a site on the south side of the market place and immediately west of the former Barclays Bank.[243] Designed by T H Wyatt, it had a frontage of five arches between rusticated pilasters with a sculpted coat of arms above, presumably those of Lord Bath.[244] Three of the arches gave access to the interior, which was a square with an open centre and covered arcades to the sides, the roofs held up by cast-iron supports.[245]

Trade declined towards the end of the century and was described as 'almost dead' in 1894.[246] Lord Bath sold the Market House with other town centre property in 1920[247] and it was later converted into a garage, retaining only parts of the original before eventual demolition and replacement by a supermarket in 1967. The supermarket was later converted into the two shops now on the site.[248]

The corn market was evidently not completely moribund when the Market House was sold, as replacement buildings were erected consecutively at the rear of the Three Horse Shoes hotel in 1921 and near the station as part of the cattle market in 1929.[249] Both have since been demolished.

Other produce was bought and sold from stalls and shambles in the market place, some using for shelter the arcades which several of the inns possessed in earlier times.[250] A secondary place for the markets had been around and under the former town hall (see Chapter 2), and the new town hall of 1832 was accompanied by a new set of shambles to its rear, accessed from Weymouth Street.[251] These were still there, derelict, in the early 1960s[252] but have since been replaced by a row of single-storey shops. Finally, cattle had been sold since at least the 18th century and in 1922 a cattle market was opened by the railway station adjacent to Fairfield Road.[253] It was struggling by the 1940s and closed in 1968.[254]

Westbury

Westbury had a weekly market from at least 1252.[255] In 1540 it was described as small, in 1751 it was called a 'good one for corn', but it may already have been under threat from competition from Warminster when in 1815 Sir Manasseh Massey Lopes presented the new *Market Hall* (described in Chapter 2), perhaps chiefly as a means of stimulating trade. If so it did not succeed, for in 1835 the business was said to have passed to Warminster and the Westbury market was described as purely nominal. By 1876 it was extinct.

A cattle market in the market place was started, or perhaps re-started, in 1889 but it seems to have struggled from the outset and may have lasted only a very few years.[256]

Wilton

Wilton probably had markets in Anglo-Saxon times and in the later medieval period fought hard, sometimes with violence, to safeguard its market against what it considered to be unfair competition from Salisbury.[257] It was a losing battle: by the 15th century the greater economic strength of the city had made the Wilton markets more or less moribund. Despite efforts to resuscitate them, by 1888 all the markets had closed. There appears to be no evidence of a market house having been provided at any time.

Royal Wootton Bassett

A weekly market was granted in 1219 and may have met from early on in the High Street near to where the town hall was later built.[258] This market might not have lasted long but it was replaced later, though at no time did the market manage to become established strongly enough to act as a centre for neighbouring areas. The failure is thought to be largely due to competition from Swindon which, a small town itself before the arrival of the railway, nevertheless overshadowed its neighbour.

In 1836 the market was revived on a monthly basis and appeared to have some success for a considerable time, but by c1938 business had declined so much that it was closed. There is no evidence of market accommodation, apart from shambles, being provided at any time although the space under the town hall was no doubt used for market purposes.

4
Law Courts

Introduction

THE SYSTEM OF courts in the medieval and early modern periods was complex and a fascinating subject for study, but not here: the courts almost certainly all met in existing buildings whose main purpose was otherwise, and they have left no lasting mark on the built environment. With only a few exceptions, the story of court buildings really begins in the 19th century.

By the middle of that century the court system in shire counties had been brought into a relatively cohesive hierarchical structure, although outposts of earlier courts still persisted in places, usually with roles which were more or less nominal. At the top of the hierarchy were the Assize Courts, of ancient foundation, which were presided over by external judges and formed part of the national machinery of government. The circuit brought the judges to the county twice a year to try the most serious cases, events attended by considerable pomp and ceremony. Wiltshire was in the Western Circuit and Salisbury was the usual assize town until Devizes joined it in 1835, after which the two alternated.

At the next tier down were the Quarter Sessions, also of ancient foundation and part of the system of county government. The quarter sessions tried less serious cases and, until the advent of county councils late in the century, also had a major role in local administration, one which was often exercised through separate committees. The historic pattern was for the sessions to be held in successive quarters at Salisbury, Devizes, Warminster and Marlborough. There was a brief period in the early 18th century when they met at Chippenham instead of Marlborough but other attempts to change sessions towns were rejected. By later in the 19th century the increasing administrative workload made the annual trek round four towns inefficient and there was a move in 1867 to have all four sessions held in Devizes. This too was rejected and the administration problems remained until the foundation of the county council removed that part of their work.

Two of the municipal boroughs – Marlborough and Salisbury – had their own borough quarter sessions.[259] Malmesbury had applied for the same in 1750 but failed to secure them and Swindon, much later in 1899, considered its own application, though if this was made it apparently failed.

While the assizes were presided over by judges, the quarter sessions were run by justices of the peace, invariably the landed gentry plus other local worthies attending in relatively large numbers, typically up to ten. The justices often worked on individual cases in smaller groups and this process evolved into the Petty Sessions, the lowest tier of court for criminal matters. Petty sessions may go back to the late 16th century in Calne and appeared to have become well established in the county by 1670. They evolved in a largely unstructured way until formalized into divisions by the Division of Counties Act of 1828. Most Wiltshire towns were at the centre of a petty sessional division and the magistrates usually met monthly or fortnightly to deal with the lowest level of criminal case, referring the more serious ones up to the quarter sessions. As with quarter sessions, some boroughs had separate borough petty sessions concurrent with the county ones. The formation of the county police force led to close working between the police and the petty sessions and for that reason the sessions were sometimes referred to as police courts, particularly where the court was located alongside or within the police station as was the case for a period in Swindon. In later years they were known more generally as magistrates' courts, a designation which was formalized by the Justices of the Peace Act in 1949.

The next in the set of 19th century courts were the County Courts. These were judge-led and dealt with civil cases involving debts or damages; they replaced earlier courts under an Act of 1846 and as a result nearly all Wiltshire's 12 such courts were formed in early 1847. County courts have survived later changes in court structure though not in the same locations.

The final type was the Coroner's Court. There were two coroners in 1835, both in the northern half of the county, but the number was increased to three in 1859 and the county divided more logically into north, middle and south.[260]

The set of institutions described above lasted until the post-war period. Assize courts and quarter sessions were replaced in 1972 by the new Crown Courts, which gave a continuing presence where previously the attendance had been intermittent. Petty sessions, now known as magistrates' courts, continued but a process of consolidation started with a 1991 order which abolished 15 of the existing divisions and replaced them with just four.[261] This process has continued and as of 2023 there were courts only in Salisbury and Swindon, with also a single coroner's court based in the former place.

After this preamble it has to be added that buildings erected specifically for use as courts are few and far between. Court sessions were generally not frequent enough to justify this and instead sittings were held in hotels, town halls and other places. Coroner's courts are an extreme example: they were generally held at short notice and so had to find space where available. They did meet in normal court buildings but also, for example, at Swindon railway station (1848), the Three Horse Shoes inn in Bradford on Avon (1866), the cemetery lodge in Devizes (1892), Salisbury infirmary (1893) and at the workhouse in Chippenham (1939).[262] Because there were generally no specific buildings for coroner's courts they are not discussed further in the text below, save for the remaining one in Salisbury.

Courts need basic furnishings: the bench, the dock, a witness stand, benches for the lawyers and some provision for the public as well as sometimes cells in which prisoners could be held. The quarter sessions towns and some others had permanent accommodation within their town halls so that these furnishings could remain in place, although at Marlborough and perhaps elsewhere there was still shuffling around to be done when the ground floor room was set out for a court session. For many of the petty sessions, particularly those held in hotels and the like, the effort in setting up must have been considerable and it is likely that the arrangements were often decidedly informal. Court sessions in town halls not equipped with a room set aside for the purpose were generally held in the first floor assembly room, though smaller courts sometimes used the council chamber.

There were only ever 11 purpose-built courtrooms in the county but the arrangements made in town halls and elsewhere to accommodate the assizes, the quarter and petty sessions and the county court are also of considerable interest.

The Buildings

Amesbury

Amesbury market house was sometimes referred to as a court house so may have been used for that purpose up until its demolition in 1809.[263] The manor courts were of declining importance from the 18th century and the last was held in 1854.[264] Amesbury was in the Salisbury and Amesbury petty sessions division and, from 1847, in the Salisbury county court district. Despite the joint designation for the petty sessions division there appears to be no evidence that sessions were ever held in the town.[265]

Bradford on Avon

By the third quarter of the 19th century petty sessions were being held twice monthly and the county court, founded in 1847,[266] was meeting in alternate months at Bradford and Trowbridge.[267] In the early 20th century the pattern was much the same though petty sessions were then held only monthly. By 1915 the county court was meeting monthly in Trowbridge but only quarterly in Bradford and it seems likely that sittings in Bradford ceased entirely soon after 1918.[268]

The old market hall (see Chapter 3) had been used as a court room for the manor court but was abandoned in the late 18th century as its condition deteriorated.[269] Meetings were held thereafter in the *Swan Hotel* at the foot of Market Street, and also in the former *Pippet Street* (Market Street) Methodist chapel, until the *Town Hall*, described in Chapter 2, opened in 1855.[270] Meetings of the petty sessions and the county court were held there thereafter but in 1909 the town hall company and the petty sessions magistrates fell out because the former wanted a renewed lease to be for seven years and the latter for only three. This led to a period of nearly a year in which the sessions were held in unsuitable premises – the swimming baths, the temperance hall and the old school on Masons' Lane – before the disagreement was resolved.[271] Petty sessions were then held at the town hall until the end of 1954, at which date they moved to *Westbury House* (described in Chapter 7) following the sale of the town hall to the Clifton Diocese for conversion into a Roman Catholic church.[272] The magistrates' court closed in the 1991 revisions.[273]

Calne

The town had manorial courts and views of frankpledge from an early date.[274] It is not recorded where most such courts met but that for the Eastman Street manor held its meetings in the later 18th century in the Catherine Wheel Inn, later the *Lansdowne*

Arms and now renamed the Lansdowne Strand Hotel. A court of requests for the recovery of debts was held from 1765 and was superseded by the county court (see below) in 1847.[275]

Petty sessions were well established by 1851: a new Calne county petty sessions division was formed in that year and sessions were held until the early 1990s.[276] There were also borough petty sessions from at least 1863 and perhaps earlier.[277] Both sets of sessions were held successively in the old then the new *Town Halls*, described in Chapter 2: county sessions were monthly until c1900 and fortnightly thereafter; borough petty sessions were fortnightly in the 1890s but may have been combined with the county sessions around 1900.[278]

The county court met in Calne from its inception in 1847, also at the Town Hall, and was still meeting there until the mid-1950s.[279] A proposal from the Lord Chancellor in late 1956 that the court should be discontinued because of the small amount of business done was accepted by the rural district council.[280] The magistrates' court closed in the 1991 revisions, having used the town hall until the end.[281]

Chippenham

The *Yelde Hall*, described in Chapter 2, was being used for hundred, manor and other courts from an early date.[282] A court of requests was set up in 1765 for the recovery of debts and there had been some form of borough court, although this was apparently gone by 1835. The town was also established as a petty sessional division under the 1828 Act. All these met at the Yelde Hall and later at the *New Hall*, later redesignated as the *Town Hall* and also described in Chapter 2. During the 1830s the

Chippenham the former County Court now registry office. The link to the Museum building at the front is modern.

petty sessions were sometimes held at the *Angel Inn*, immediately adjacent to what is now the museum.

Chippenham was the head of a county court district following the passing of the 1846 Act, with meetings held initially at an inn.[283] In 1854 the clerk to the court purchased land for the erection of the *County Court* building behind what is now the museum in the market place, a seemingly obscure location for an important building but perhaps explained by the fact that Jacob Phillips, the prime mover in its creation, owned the building in front.[284] It opened in November 1854[285] and is of plain ashlar, two storeys under a hipped roof with the court room of four bays on the first floor. The façade is almost entirely lacking in ornamentation and the court room itself is high-ceilinged with large windows but otherwise equally plain. Double doors give access from the rear of what is now the museum as well as from stairs leading to the courtyard entrance; a door in the same wall leads presumably to the judge's room and in the opposite wall a door opens to a subsidiary staircase, understood to have been used by defendants. The County Court was a separate building until a linking section was built in the later 20th century and access was probably gained previously through what was an open archway which now forms the entrance to the museum.

The petty sessions remained at the Town Hall until c1946 after which, the magistrates having complained of poor conditions there, they moved to the County Court and the building in front, now the museum. One court was in the County Court room and the other in what is now the museum's education room in the opposite wing.[286] The magistrates moved out in 1996: the County Court room became the register office in place of the previous office in what is now one of the museum's downstairs galleries, and the remainder became the museum.

Chippenham Magistrates Court, Pewsham Way, soon after closure, the royal arms above the entrance already removed. (Courtesy of John Scragg)

Both courts moved in 1996 to the new **Chippenham Magistrates' Courts** at the junction of Pewsham Way and Avenue la Fleche. These, by Wiltshire County Architects, were of substantial size with four main courts on the first floor and were rectangular with a front wing alongside a semi-circular entrance front with tall post-modern classical columns, all in stone blockwork.[287] This building, of considerable character, was to have only a short life. In 2013 the area covered by the court was expanded to cover much of that of the former Trowbridge County Court (see below) but it itself closed only four years later, in 2017, under government measures to reduce the cost of the courts service. It was demolished and replaced by a supermarket.

Corsham

Early court sittings were held in the 17th century *Town Hall*, described in Chapter 2, which had a court room on the first floor with a lock-up below. The town became part of the Chippenham petty sessional division and was served alternately with Chippenham from at least 1846 and quite possibly earlier.[288] The 1784 *Market House* had no room suitable for sessions and courts were held instead at the *Methuen Arms* at the south end of High Street, but by 1889 the sessions were being held three-weekly at the *Town Hall* (see Chapter 2), so presumably moved there soon after that was rebuilt from the market hall in 1883.[289] The petty sessions, now redesignated as a magistrates' court, were still being held at the town hall in 1969 but may have closed soon thereafter.[290]

The town was in the Chippenham county court district and there appears to be no evidence of county court meetings being held here.

Cricklade

There was a borough court and view of frankpledge from an early date; in the early 19th century the view was held annually in the old town hall prior to its demolition and from 1822 in the *White Hart Inn* in the High Street. By mid-century the court had only nominal duties.[291]

The town was in Swindon county court district but had petty sessions from at least 1839[292] and perhaps some years before that, as part of the joint Cricklade and Wootton Bassett petty sessional division. In earlier years the sessions were presumably held in hotels but from 1862 they met in the new *Town Hall* (see Chapter 2).[293] They stayed there, although in 1896 the magistrates complained about the accommodation.[294] In 1933 they transferred to the second new *Town Hall*,[295] also described in Chapter 2, and remained there until the magistrates' court closed in 1993.[296]

There appears to be no evidence of sittings of the Swindon county court being held in the town.

Devizes

The story of law courts in Devizes underlines the town's long claim to be second only to Salisbury in importance in the county. It argued repeatedly, and often successfully, for the different courts to visit or be located here and in the *Assize courts* has what was for long the most significant court building in Wiltshire.

Devizes had been established as a county quarter sessions town in 1383, a role it was to retain until 1972. There was an attempt in 1867 to make it the sole quarter sessions location for Wiltshire but the attempt was unsuccessful.[297]

By the middle of the 19th century the town had one of the two annual assizes for Wiltshire, one of the four annual county quarter sessions, borough quarter sessions,

Devizes, the Assize Courts when newly built. (Ackermann print courtesy of Wiltshire Museum, Devizes)

a county court, and petty sessions for both county and borough.[298] The assizes are discussed further below. The county quarter sessions appear to have been held at the **Town Hall**, described in Chapter 2, from probably well before this time but had transferred to the Assize Courts by 1852.[299] The borough quarter sessions, set up in 1836,[300] were held generally within a week of those for the county[301] and were likely held at the same place.

The county court was established in 1847[302] and met initially at the Town Hall but by 1889 was meeting at the Assize Courts and stayed there.[303] The county court office was at **33/34 St John's Street** and it was almost certainly here that the monthly meetings of the county petty sessions and the fortnightly meetings of the borough magistrates were held.[304] The building, now grade 2* listed, is 16th or 17th century, timber-framed, the first floor jettied but the whole stuccoed in the 18th century. The front is of three storeys and six bays, relatively shallow but with a much larger extension to the rear, perhaps the site of the court room. Concern was expressed in 1895 about the inadequacy of these premises and there was a proposal to move the petty sessions to the police station in Bath Road[305] but in the event both petty sessions were still meeting in St John's Street in 1931. However, by 1939 they too had migrated to the Assize Courts.[306]

The Assize Courts* are evidence of the strong local belief in the importance of the town. An Act of 1833 allowed the appointment of new assize towns and Devizes promptly petitioned the Privy Council to be one such, then started a subscription from the town and surrounding gentry to pay for a suitable premises.[307] Both were successful and T H Wyatt was commissioned to design the new assize courts. The first assize was held in the completed building in August 1835[308] and thereafter the summer assize for Wiltshire was held here until in 1857 the spring assize was substituted.[309] Meetings of most of the other courts were later also held here. From 1869 **Northgate House** opposite, described in Chapter 7, was used as the judges' lodgings.[310]

The front of this impressive building, now grade 2* listed, has a temple centre with a four-column portico of Ionic columns between lower three-bay wings, all in fine ashlar. Inside, a central entrance hall has a coffered ceiling with later skylights, and rooms to either side, that to the west the grand jury room and that to the east originally a records room.[311] Behind the side rooms but taller are the two courtrooms, their hidden sides in brick and with a space between them: lower ancillary rooms in this space were later demolished. The courtrooms carry round the entablature from the portico and are under hipped roofs. They are illuminated by high-level round-arched windows, were panelled in wood to half height and had galleries at the rear accessed by stairs from the hall. Cells were initially contained in the basement, with stairs direct to the docks in the courtrooms, but these were later moved to the ground floor.

Devizes, the Assize Courts in the 1960s; note shared use by the police. (Wiltshire Museum, Devizes).

Court No.2 at the Assize Courts, Devizes, far from splendid in later days. (Wiltshire Museum, Devizes)

The police had moved here in 1937 (see Chapter 8) but following the passage of the 1971 Act the last assizes were held in October 1971.[312] The building was still used as a lower level crown court and for magistrates' courts but its deteriorating condition meant that eventually the two courtrooms had to be abandoned and magistrates' courts were held in a small and inconvenient upstairs room. By 1984 the courts had moved to the Town Hall, almost equally inconvenient,[313] and the assize courts building finally closed c1986.[314] It was replaced by a temporary **Court Building** for the magistrates' courts, purchased secondhand from the library service and located at the south end of the car park behind Northgate House, but this too closed in 2009 and was later demolished.[315] The decision to close was taken in 2002 but implementation was delayed until the new combined courts complex in Wilton Road, Salisbury was opened in September 2009, after which Devizes had no courts.

Devizes, 33/34 St John's Street, used by various courts in the later 19th and early 20th centuries

The Assize Courts, now empty, deteriorated severely over a prolonged period while developers attempted to come up with viable plans for their conversion to residential or office accommodation. Eventually, in 2018, the Dubai-based owners were persuaded to sell the building to the newly formed Devizes Assize Court Trust and planning then started for its conversion into a new home for the Wiltshire Museum. At the time of writing initial support had been received from the National Lottery Heritage Fund and the target date for opening was set at 2030.

Highworth

By the middle of the 19th century Highworth came under Swindon for both county court and petty sessions.[316] There appears not to have been any court activity in the town from that time onwards.[317]

Malmesbury

Malmesbury had a borough court from at least 1600 but the manor court seems to have had a dominant role for a considerable time.[318] In 1750 the borough attempted, without success, to gain the right to hold separate quarter sessions but it had acquired petty sessions by 1821 if not earlier.[319] It was also the centre of a county court district by 1855 and probably from 1847.[320]

Early sittings of the petty sessions appear to have been held at the *White Lion Inn*[321] at what is now 8 Gloucester Street, a building with 15th century origins but much altered later and now grade 2* listed and converted to a private house. They may have moved from there to the *Town Hall*, described in Chapter 2, soon after its opening in 1848 and were certainly meeting there by 1851.[322] The county court met at the Town Hall from the start.[323]

Malmesbury, the Court House. (Athelstan Museum).

It seems that neither of these bodies used the *Court House**, much the oldest court building in the town and one of great interest, now grade 1 listed. It is on the site of the medieval Hospital of St John and is likely a conversion of one of the original buildings, carried out c1623 after the corporation bought the site in 1580. It was then used both as a courthouse and, from c1629, for a free school, but its court use seems to have been confined to the borough court, whose function by the 19th century had

Malmesbury, the Court House in use by the warden and freemen of the town. (Athelstan Museum)

become more or less nominal.[324] The old corporation held meetings here from around 1600 and continued to do so, albeit with few remaining responsibilities, after the 1886 alterations to the borough's status (see Chapter 7). It remains in use for meetings by the Warden and Freemen of Malmesbury.

The Court House is attached to the rear of 27 St John's Street and accessed via an archway alongside. It is of modest dimensions: of three bays, narrow and single-storey in rubblestone under a stone slate roof, probably originally extending further to the east. The interior has battered walls and early 18th century fittings including a raised bench at the west end separated from a pit originally intended for the 24 assistant burgesses; this in turn is separated from public benches at the east end. Fittings include the court chest with six locks, a high steward's chair the gift of Joseph Neeld of Grittleton in 1842, and royal arms dated 1693. The exterior may give little away but the interior is a remarkable survival.[325]

The surviving magistrates' court in the Town Hall continued to sit until closure under the 1991 revisions.[326] There are now no courts in the town.

Marlborough

The early status of the town is illustrated by the fact that in 1280 there was consideration of transferring the county court here from Wilton.[327] County quarter sessions were held here from 1383 or earlier and there was a king's court, the later town court or court of civil pleas, first mentioned in 1473. There was also a mayor's court and by the early 18th century there were borough quarter sessions, which ceased in 1835. A county court, created in 1847,[328] took over most of the duties of the king's court and borough sessions resumed in 1851.

With rare exceptions, it seems that all of these various courts used the **Guildhall**, and later the various versions of the *Town Hall*, (both described in Chapter 2) for their meetings.[329] Indeed the dissatisfaction with the provision for county quarter sessions at the Town Hall was the reason for much of its rebuilding.

LAW COURTS   79

County quarter sessions, held here once a year, were discontinued under the 1971 Act and Marlborough was not chosen as the location of a crown court. The county court was still sitting in 1952[330] but probably did not survive here for long thereafter. Borough petty sessions were replaced by county petty sessions in 1951 and these continued as a magistrates' court sitting at the Town Hall until closure under the 1991 revisions,[331] after which Marlborough has been without any courts.

Marlborough Town Hall, the ground floor converted into a court room for the quarter sessions in the 1902 rebuilding. Trap doors in the centre of the floor lead to cells below

Melksham

The Manor House, later **Place House**, was used as a court house at some date after its construction, probably in the middle of the 16th century. It stood at the north end of the Market Place where Place Road now is but was demolished in 1864.[332] The front was of four gables, the left hand one perhaps an extension and believed to have been the courtroom, with a substantial round-arched window in the centre of the end wall.[333]

The petty sessions were in being by 1820 if not before but it is not known where they met before the *Town Hall*, described in Chapter 2, opened in 1847. It is, though, known that they were meeting alternately at Melksham and Trowbridge during this period.[334] The county court, founded in 1847, met at the Town Hall from the start.[335] Both magistrates' and county courts continued at the town hall until at least the mid-1950s[336] and probably until the court was closed under the 1991 revisions.[337]

Mere

Hundred and manor courts are believed to have been held in, amongst other places, the **Guildhall**, described in Chapter 2.[338] After this was demolished in 1863 some further meetings, perhaps of the courts of the Duchy of Cornwall, were held in the Talbot Inn, now *The George*, immediately adjacent.[339]

Mere was in the Hindon division for petty sessions, from the 1850s and very probably earlier.[340] In the 1880s and 1890s a revision of petty sessions divisions resulted in the creation of one for Tisbury and Mere but there were still no meetings in Mere until 1897.[341] In that year the disused former schoolroom at the **Workhouse**, described in Chapter 7, was leased from the board of guardians and infrequent meetings were held there thereafter.[342] The lease was given up in 1935 and the court then met for a few years at the former offices of the rural district council, noted in Chapter 7.[343] The sessions were only meeting in Mere four times a year and, the cost of maintaining a room for such infrequent meetings being considered disproportionate, it was decided in 1941 to cease meeting here and instead to meet only in Tisbury.[344]

The town was in the Shaftesbury county court district and it seems that no meetings of that court were held here.[345] Therefore the closure of the petty sessions in 1941 meant the end of court hearings in the town.

Salisbury

Salisbury is distinguished from other towns in the county by the role the bishops played in the exercise of the law. The bishops' courts were dominant from the city's foundation, declining after the corporation gained a commission for the peace in the 15th century and substantially overlapping in their jurisdiction by the 17th century.[346] Although the bishops' jurisdiction over the Close was not removed until the Municipal Corporations Act of 1836, it seems that court sessions had been abandoned well before that, possibly with the destruction of the **Bishops' Guildhall** in 1785 (see Chapter 2).[347]

Salisbury Guildhall, the Oak Court

By the middle of the 19th century the city had what might be regarded as a complete set of courts: the assizes visited once a year and the county quarter sessions likewise; there were separate city quarter sessions, both city and county petty sessions each held weekly, and a county court held monthly.[348] All these courts sat at the *Council House*, later renamed the *Guildhall*. This is described in Chapter 2 which also describes how improvements were made to guard against the risk of losing the assizes, first to Devizes and later to Trowbridge.

Salisbury Guildhall, the Crown Court.

The Guildhall maintained this role over a remarkably long period. Assizes and quarter sessions were replaced after 1971 by the crown court, but the courts remained there until the 1980s. Eventually pressure of space required a larger building and in 1981 plans were drawn up for the conversion of *Alexandra House*, at the corner of New Street and St John's Street and built originally as a NAAFI, into a new combined court centre for the crown and county courts.[349] The conversion was carried out in 1984-5 to designs by C R Hardy of the Property Services Agency, the main exterior change being the introduction of more substantial doorways on both frontages, that to St John's Street with the royal arms freestanding above the columned porch.[350] The exterior is plain neo-Georgian ashlar in two storeys under a mansard roof, the New Street façade of 13 bays, and behind is a substantial block with the added courtroom to the rear.

Despite its substantial size this building also became too small and in the early 2000s the decision was taken to build a combined crown, county and magistrates'

Salisbury, the Law Courts

courts complex on the north side of Wilton Road. After delays the new building, designed by Feilden and Mawson, opened in 2009.[351] The *Salisbury Law Courts** contain six courtrooms with ancillary meeting rooms and offices and are amongst a new generation of large buildings constructed with such facilities as solar heating and heat recovery in efforts to reduce their environmental impact. The façade to the street has considerable presence, a long central section of glass with strong metal banding flanked by substantial buff brick walls, that to the right with the royal arms applied in metal and 'Salisbury Law Courts' in incised lettering, the whole beneath deep eaves on long brackets. The ends have buff brick and more utilitarian glass, and a block to the rear is in glass and white render.

After 2009 Alexandra House was converted to solicitor's offices. The only other remaining court building in the city is the coroner's court at *26 Endless Street*, described in Chapter 7 and previously used first by the rural district council and then as council offices before conversion in 2011. The coroner's previous premises were at *6 Castle Street*, a three-storey building of brick with rusticated stone dressings under a hipped roof, probably of early 19th century date and in 2023 an estate agent's premises. The offices here were considered inadequate, with jury inquests having to be held at Trowbridge town hall: a move to Devizes was considered in 2011 but instead the court moved to the Endless Street building which already had a suitable room for the court.[352] It remains the sole coroner's court for the county.

Swindon

Swindon became the head of a county petty sessional division c1829, probably as a result of the 1828 Act.[353] By 1833, and very probably before, the magistrates were meeting in an assembly room at the *Goddard Arms Hotel*[354] on the High Street in the Old Town. The room seems to have been a small one – 'small and crowded with just eight or ten people in it'³⁵⁵ - and may now have been absorbed into the hotel's general accommodation although a meeting room remains across the first-floor front. They remained until the *Town Hall*, described in Chapter 2, opened in 1853 and soon afterwards moved there.³⁵⁶ A county court district centred on Swindon was set up in 1847 and the meetings of that were also held at the Town Hall.³⁵⁷

In 1857 the quarter sessions were already considering whether to add a courtroom for petty sessions to the existing police station³⁵⁸ but the sessions actually remained at the Town Hall until 1873 when the new police station on *Eastcott Hill*, described in Chapter 8, opened:³⁵⁹ this contained a substantial courtroom. The county court stayed at the Town Hall but by 1899 had transferred to the *new Town Hall* in Regent Circus which had opened in 1891 (see Chapter 2).³⁶⁰

Swindon, the County Court.

In 1899 the soon-to-be unified town was considering an application to have its own quarter sessions but the application, if made, was unsuccessful. However, in 1906 it was granted its own petty sessions and thereafter county and borough petty sessions were held in parallel at the police court on Eastcott Hill.³⁶¹ The county court, also in 1906, left the new town hall for its own *County Court** building on Clarence Street just south of Euclid Street.³⁶² This is in 17th century style in brick and stone, three-storey bays under gables brought forward at both ends and the centre, the remaining bays two storeys plus attic, all with mullioned and transomed windows and strong stone platbands. There were three entrance doors, two now blocked, and that at the north end has a hood covering the royal arms above the door. Originally the building extended around a further three sides to enclose a courtyard at the rear but these extensions were demolished at some time after 1942.³⁶³ Drainpipe heads dated 1935 suggest other alterations prior to that date.

The Eastcott Hill police station and magistrates' court were demolished in 1973 but it seems that the magistrates moved out some years before that. They used the *Central Club and Institute* on Milton Road on a temporary basis from 1962, a building which itself only then survived into the 1970s before it was demolished,³⁶⁴ and in 1964 moved into the new *Magistrates' Courts* in Gordon Road. These were designed by J Loring-Morgan, the borough architect, but the appearance was substantially altered when they were re-faced in brick by the Kendall Kingscott Partnership in 1989-90 and extended on the Islington Street side by the County Council's property services department in 1994.³⁶⁵ The building is of substantial size

Swindon, the Magistrates' Court as built, very 1960s before its later refacing in brick. (Local Studies (Swindon Library & Information Service)).

but low, patterned with different shades of brick, the entrance front on Gordon Road with brick pilasters separating green-framed windows of graduated height either side of the entrance, the royal arms above. In 1978 part of the recently closed **Queenstown**

Swindon Magistrates Court in 2005, behind it the tower of the Princes Street police station, soon to be demolished (see Chapter 8). (Courtesy of D & M Ball).

Infants' School was remodelled as an additional magistrates' court and used as such until 1990, subsequently being demolished in 1993.[366]

In 1962 a separate court of quarter sessions was granted to the borough and this, later the crown court, is believed to have met alongside other courts in one of the existing court buildings. In 1985 it moved to the new crown and county court, now the **Combined Courts**, on Islington Street near to the magistrates' courts.[367] The county court, which had continued to meet in the 1906 building, joined it there and the 1906 building was later converted into apartments. The combined courts are also in brick but monochrome, the only interest a steep metal roof above the courtroom and an entrance front cut on the diagonal.

Trowbridge

Petty sessions were meeting in Trowbridge by 1722 if not earlier and by 1814 the magistrates were meeting alternately at Trowbridge and Melksham, using the **Woolpack Inn** in Trowbridge.[368] This was on the south-west side of Fore Street but by

Trowbridge, the Court Hall.

1922 it was replaced by a variety hall which then became a cinema.[369] The sessions were still at the Woolpack in 1855 but soon afterwards moved to the new **Police Station** on Stallard Street, described in Chapter 8.[370] From there they moved again to the **Town Hall**, described in Chapter 2, after that opened in 1889, and remained there.

As well as being the head of a petty sessions division, Trowbridge became in 1847 the centre of a county court district.[371] Meetings were held initially in the

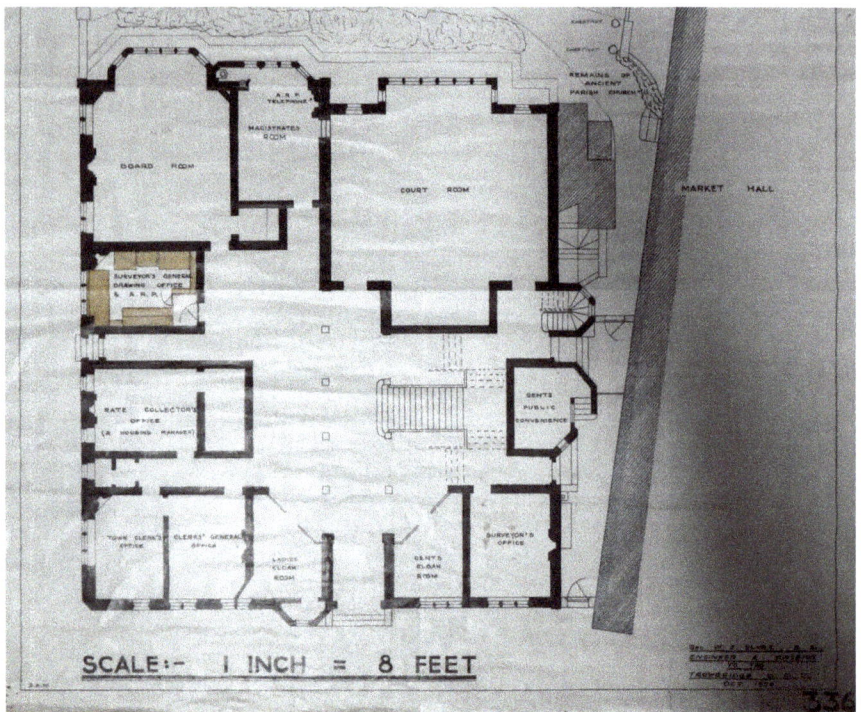

Trowbridge, 1938 ground floor plan of the Town Hall showing the single court room of that period to the rear overlooking the gardens. (WSA).

Woolpack Inn[372] but in 1854 moved to the new ***Court Hall****, built for that purpose, on Castle Street facing down Market Street. By Charles Reeves, surveyor to the County Courts,[373] the simple but pleasing front is in ashlar under a hipped slate roof. A large triple window above has pilasters and a segmental pediment to the centre; below is a smaller arched set. The ground floor and pilasters are rusticated and doors are set in one-bay porches either side. Volutes above the porches joined to the main building but one of these has been replaced by an ill-matched lavatory block and the other is much worn: the owner of the building in 2023 had expressed an intention to restore them to their original condition.[374]

The Court Hall was built by a group of leading townspeople who intended it to have shared use by the county court and the mechanics' institute. On the ground floor were a reading room, committee room, classroom and judges' room; upstairs was mainly taken up with the large hall used as the courtroom.[375] The court did not remain here long, however, for by 1874 the building was in use as a cloth warehouse[376] and by 1875 the county court was meeting at ***Hill's Hall***, described in Chapter 7.[377] After the ***Town Hall*** opened the county court joined the petty sessions there.[378]

Both courts remained at the Town Hall for much of the rest of their lives although the petty sessions are believed to have met for some years in the **Victoria Institute**, described in Chapter 6.[379] The Town Hall was altered in 1997 to provide one court on the ground floor and two on the first floor but the magistrates' courts eventually closed in 2003, when Trowbridge cases were transferred to

Chippenham.³⁸⁰ The county court survived until 2013, at which date cases were transferred to the Chippenham and Trowbridge Court in Chippenham, itself later closed and demolished.³⁸¹

One other building here should be mentioned. Called **Court House** and located at the north end of Court Street, its origins could be traced back to at least 1450 but it seems never to have had a court function in the modern sense of the word.³⁸² It was demolished to make way for the Shires shopping centre.

Warminster

The summer quarter sessions for the county were held at Warminster from the time of the Restoration if not before.³⁸³ It is not clear when the first formal petty sessions were held but they were certainly in place by early in the 19th century.³⁸⁴ As with many other Wiltshire towns, the county court here was established in 1847.³⁸⁵

The quarter and petty sessions met in the new *Town Hall*, described in Chapter 2, from its opening in 1832, joined there in 1847 by the county court.³⁸⁶ The quarter sessions had previously used the predecessor **Guildhall**, also described in Chapter 2, and it is possible that the petty sessions did likewise, although they are also recorded as meeting in 1822 at the *Bath Arms* hotel in the market place.³⁸⁷ It is not clear where else in the town, if anywhere, either court met before the construction of the town hall.

The courts remained at the town hall through to the late 20th century. Quarter sessions were lost in 1972 following the creation of crown courts. The town's petty sessions, since 1949 designated a magistrates' court, lasted until 1991 when the business was transferred to Trowbridge.³⁸⁸

Westbury

There was a court house here in 1599, though nothing more is known of its history, and a house called Whitehall at Chalford, south of the town on the Warminster road, was reputedly once used by local magistrates who had caused cells to be erected there.³⁸⁹ It may be that this was in fact a manor court and later a meeting place for estate tenants, though it is possible that magistrates might have come from Westbury for local cases.³⁹⁰ Whitehall has been identified as one of a row of three cottages immediately to the north of the Bell inn; they were demolished sometime after 1941.³⁹¹

There were petty sessions in the town from an early date, before the 1828 Act which established the Westbury and Whorwellsdown petty sessional division, and in 1847 Westbury also became the centre of a county court district.³⁹² Both courts sat in the *Town Hall*, described in Chapter 2, until well into the 20th century,³⁹³ although concern was expressed at quarter sessions in 1859 that Sir Massey Lopes was now demanding payment for the petty sessions when previously they had had the use of the building for free.³⁹⁴ This apparently did not deter them from remaining there and it was not until 1938 that concern was expressed that the Town Hall was too cold and damp: by 1939 they had moved to the *Laverton Institute*, described in Chapter 7.³⁹⁵

The county court ceased in the late 1930s when Westbury was included within the Trowbridge district.³⁹⁶ The petty sessions, later termed the magistrates' court, lasted until closure under the 1991 revisions.³⁹⁷

Wilton

Although Wilton had courts in earlier times, by the 19th century its relative decline was such that it had no courts normally sitting there. By mid-century it was in the Salisbury and Amesbury petty sessions division and the Salisbury county court district.[398] It seems that, for a brief time in the late 1870s and early 1880s, the Salisbury petty sessions were held on occasion in Wilton.[399] The magistrates are likely to have met during that period at the *Town Hall*, described in Chapter 2.

Royal Wootton Bassett

Wootton Bassett was in the Swindon county court district and the Cricklade and Wootton Bassett petty sessions division, the meetings held in both places. It also had borough petty sessions in the later 19th century and these were active until 1886.[400] The *Town Hall*, described in Chapter 2, was the favoured meeting place for petty sessions but for a period around the end of the century, and perhaps at other times also, the *Royal Oak Hotel*[401] was used: most of this was later demolished but its remaining section, later a bank, is on the corner of High Street and Station Road. This lacks the impact of the tall and multiple-gabled original but it still has a presence, the upper storeys in red brick with horizontal banding in black, the ground floor retaining the rusticated stone dressings added to make it appear appropriately solid when it was converted from a shop into a bank.

The *Police Station* rebuilt on Station Road in 1912 (see Chapter 8) had a *Sessions Hall* constructed at right angles alongside it[402] and the petty sessions moved to this building on its completion that same year.[403] It is a strange construction, more like a scout hut than a significant civic building, single-storey with wood framing and

Wootton Bassett, the Sessions Hall alongside the Police Station c1900. (Royal Wootton Bassett Town Hall Museum).

panels under a shingle roof. There are side gables at the mid-point of each side; the windows and doors, now mostly blocked in, are rectangular to fit the framing, and there are round ventilators at the gable heads. It was reported to be more convenient and comfortable than the previous one, with 'decorative wood panelling.'[404]

It is likely that the petty sessions closed at around the same time as the Police Station in the early 1980s. There appears to be no evidence to suggest the Swindon county court ever met here.

5
Museums and Art Galleries

Introduction

THE TWO MOST substantial museums in Wiltshire date from the third quarter of the 19th century, at the start of a period when the number of museums across the country was expanding rapidly: in the 15 years from 1872 around 100 were opened in Britain.[405] There had been public or semi-public museums before – the Ashmolean in Oxford (founded 1683) and the British Museum (founded 1759) are quoted as two of the earliest examples – but these were places for the well-connected and, as such, not that different except in their much larger scale from the private collections of 'curiosities' which members of the gentry had accumulated for many years past.

Now, though, a combination of factors produced an upsurge. The causes varied by place but chief amongst them were a growing educated middle class, an increasing interest in the past and particularly the discoveries then being made by fossil-hunters and archaeologists, a civic pride in the larger industrial towns and cities which produced the wish to keep up with their neighbours in this respect, and finally a paternalistic wish to keep the working classes safely occupied in their slowly increasing leisure hours. Acts of 1845 and 1891 gave local authorities powers to support museums from the rates, although the early museums in Wiltshire were privately funded.

Those early museums were the county museum of the Wiltshire Archaeological and Natural History Society (WANHS) in Devizes (founded 1874) and the Salisbury and South Wiltshire (1861) and Blackmore (1867) museums in Salisbury, the latter two separately founded but run under single management from the start. These three were very much dominated by the county gentry and the clergy and remained so for many years, though both Salisbury and Devizes made some efforts to open up to a wider public. To these should be added the annual three-day summer meetings of WANHS in which they based themselves in one or other Wiltshire town – for example Chippenham in 1869 and Marlborough in 1879 – and held a series of lectures and visits, with a temporary museum set up each time containing loans from nearby.

There was probably no feeling in the county's smaller towns at that period that they needed or could justify a museum, but it might always have been expected that the rapid growth of Swindon after the arrival of the railway would lead it eventually to copy Salisbury and Devizes, though in the event this did not happen until 1920. Museums in other towns did follow, but only a couple between the wars and many of the remainder of quite recent date. Again there were several reasons for this late flowering, including a widening interest in more recent history, a resentment at locally-found treasures from Roman or prehistoric times being sent away to Devizes, and a growing number of retired professionals who had the time and the energy to devote to such matters.

The focus of early museums was limited, with fossils, prehistoric relics and stuffed natural history specimens much to the fore, though most contained a library from the start. The nature of the displays – objects in glass cases – meant that they could be fitted without difficulty into many types of building, so there seemed to be no need to build specifically for this purpose. As a result, of all the general museum buildings noted here only the Blackmore in Salisbury was purpose-built. Over the intervening period, but particularly in the last 50 years, the nature of museum displays has changed greatly, with much more emphasis on the context of objects, and a widened focus bringing the history displayed right up to the mid-20th century. This means that the requirements for buildings are now much more demanding: the Wiltshire Museum, for example, which currently makes imaginative use of its warren of small rooms, will look for much larger display spaces in its proposed move to the Devizes assize courts.

This chapter covers only what might be termed general purpose museums: there are other more specialist ones such as the Rifles museum in Salisbury and the Steam museum in Swindon but these are not described. Most museums have plenty of pictures on display but there were also in the county two specially constructed picture galleries, in Salisbury and Swindon, and these are recorded. Finally, mention is made of the county records service, initially at Trowbridge and now in the Wiltshire and Swindon History Centre at Chippenham.

The Buildings

Amesbury

As early as 1823 Henry Browne, who became the first keeper of Stonehenge after Sir Edward Antrobus purchased the site in 1824, is described as having a museum in Amesbury.[406] This presumably contained items relating to the monument, including examples of the watercolours and cork models which he made for sale, but could have been just a display in his own home. He died in 1839 so his museum, at an unknown location, presumably closed before then.[407] By the turn of the century a Mr. Edwards had a museum in the town and, on his death, many books and other artefacts were bought from the estate by the Salisbury and South Wiltshire museum. Mr. Edwards's museum, believed to have been in Edwards Road, survived him but was destroyed in the fire of 1911.[408]

One of the town's finest buildings, *Antrobus House* on Salisbury Road, initially contained a museum on its first floor. This housed mainly the furniture and art of Lady Antrobus, the donor; people could visit by appointment and it may have been open as well on set days in the week. Interest waned in the second half of the 20th century and most of the collection was sold in 1974 to pay for repairs to the building.[409] Antrobus House is described in Chapter 6.

The former Melor Hall in Church Street was taken over as a history centre in 2011 with the aid of the town council. In 2019 it was closed in anticipation of reconstruction as a purpose-built history centre to designs by Larkham Design of Salisbury. The building was completed and the first two phases of reopening completed in 2023. The new *History Centre* is of substantial depth, steel-framed and timber clad, the sides with lines of square windows on each of its two floors and the gable end facing the street mostly of glass, the window-heads following the angle of the gable.[410]

Bradford on Avon

Though the industrial history of Bradford has become a subject of wider interest only in quite recent times, artefacts from the Roman period and before have been unearthed over many years and it is perhaps surprising that thought was not given to a museum at an earlier date; indeed a number of finds ended up in the Wiltshire museum because there was no suitable place in the town for them.[411]

The earliest initiative was probably that of the Wiltshire Archaeological and Natural History Society, which had acquired the town's tithe barn in 1914 and from 1935 used it to house what was originally H Rivers Pollock's collection of agricultural implements.[412] After the war, ownership of the tithe barn having transferred to the Ministry of Works in 1940, the collection was gradually transferred to the Lackham School of Agriculture, which had begun its own collection; the last implements left Bradford c1977.[413] This was followed in 1982 by the use of the barn for a different collection of agricultural instruments, that belonging to Mr R D Croker of Bromham, who had leased the space. He charged a fee for entry and remained there until the 1990s.[414]

There was a suggestion in 1956 that the tithe barn might be used for a conventional museum[415] but this came to nothing and the prompt which led finally to progress was the announcement in 1986 that the Christopher pharmacy in the

Calne, the Carnegie Library converted into a museum.

town centre was to close. This contained a historic collection of medicine bottles and other equipment and the wish to stop this being split up led to the formation of the museum society and the eventual incorporation of the pharmacy as the centrepiece of the society's displays.[416] Their home was in the *New Library* of 1990, described in Chapter 6, where the museum is well displayed but confined to much too small a space on the first floor.

Calne

A working party to establish a heritage centre was set up in the early 1990s and eventually leased the *Carnegie Library* after the library service moved to its new building. The heritage centre opened there in 2004.[417] The Carnegie library is described in Chapter 6.

Chippenham

The use of the Yelde Hall as a museum was first discussed in 1909.[418] Nothing further happened until a temporary museum was set up in there to celebrate the 1951 Festival of Britain.[419] This seemed to spark renewed interest and by 1954 plans were being drawn up for renovation, to include demolition of the ramshackle buildings adjacent to the hall.[420] The *Yelde Hall*, described in Chapter 2, was finally opened as a museum in 1963.[421]

Chippenham, the Town Museum.

The museum was successful and by 1999 the Yelde Hall was proving too small, prompting a move in 2000 to its present home at *9-10 Market Place**, the so-called 'Palace,' named such after medieval remains discovered there c1820 and then thought to indicate the site of a former royal palace.[422] The building, formerly used as council offices and courts, is of c1770, with a four-bay ashlar front containing tripartite windows under depressed arches – a later alteration – either side of a pedimented doorway.[423] To the right is an archway, now the entrance to the museum, and above are three Venetian windows, with a single window above the door. There are four dormers in the mansard roof and to the rear are two wings, that to the left in brick and rubblestone of the late 19th century, that to the right the former *County Court*, now a registry office, originally free-standing but now linked to the front building. This is described in Chapter 4.

Inside, the museum makes good use for its displays of the building's set of relatively small rooms, many with original plasterwork. An education room is on the first floor at the end of one rear wing and on the opposite side is the main entrance to the County Court, accessed via stairs from the rear courtyard but perhaps originally entered through the archway which now forms the entrance to the museum. The adjacent building, *11 Market Place*, has long been owned by the town council and the first floor used as a store, and in 2023 there were plans to expand the museum displays into the ground floor. 11 Market Place is of similar date, of seven bays in coursed rubblestone with ashlar dressings, the doorway asymmetrically placed with Tuscan columns and pediment. The roof is hipped at the Timber Street end where the return is of one bay.

Chippenham, the Wiltshire and Swindon History Centre.

Chippenham has also been, since 2007, home to the *Wiltshire and Swindon History Centre.* This succeeded the previous record office in Trowbridge (see below) and acts both as a record office for the county and Swindon and as headquarters of the county museums service. It is by Atkins with Kendall Kingscott,[424] the west end of two storeys sharply defined in white with a substantial overhang to the entrance corner and continuous glazing to the first floor front. Some of the public space is contained within a single-storey front extension and at the east end is the more utilitarian and windowless two-storey archive store.

Corsham

There is currently no museum in Corsham.

Cricklade

The museum at Cricklade opened first in 1950 in the former *Weighbridge Building* on High Street immediately north of the town hall.[425] This is a tiny rubblestone single-storey building as befits its previous role, though the roof was raised at some point, perhaps when it was converted to a museum. It is of probably mid-19th century date and was in use as a weighbridge until at least 1920 and probably longer.[426]

The museum moved to a new home in 1986, larger if only in comparison with its first premises. This is the former Baptist chapel of 1852 at *16 Calcutt Street.* It is small and plain in coursed rubblestone under slate with round-arched window and a door in a porch to front centre. The chapel closed in 1937, was used by the Women's Royal Voluntary Service as a canteen until 1955 and was then taken over as a church by Roman Catholics until 1984 after which it was bought by the town council, leased to the Cricklade Historical Society and opened as a small but well-stocked museum in 1986.[427]

Devizes

The Devizes museum, unlike every other in the county, was intended from the outset to serve all of Wiltshire. The Wiltshire Archaeological and Natural History Society (WANHS), formed in 1853, was as its title implied a countywide society and chose Devizes as its base because 'it was the geographical centre of the county,' although other motives have also been suggested.[428] Unable initially to find a place for their museum, they used a room at the Devizes Savings Bank, *15 High Street**, for a period but this was too small and much of their collection had to be stored elsewhere.[429] 15 High Street faces down Long Street alongside the town hall and has considerable presence. It is mid-19th century, of two-storey ashlar Bath stone with large mullioned and transomed windows, three at the first floor and one either side of a substantial doorway below, the parapet with moulded coping either side of a central ogee-headed gable.

Eventually the Society was able to buy land and the former grammar school building in *Long Street* in 1872 and the first permanent museum opened there in 1874.[430] It is now known as the *Wiltshire Museum**.

The museum expanded into the adjoining two 18th century brick houses, Nos.40 to the left and 41 to the right, in 1902 and 1945 respectively. No.40 is perhaps of the 1760s and of two storeys plus an attic with a mansard roof and a pedimented Tuscan porch inscribed 'Museum'. No. 41 is larger, perhaps of c1740, of three storeys and five bays, with raised stone quoins but otherwise modest decoration though with a narrow pediment above the central bay. During the 19th century both were at different times a boarding school for girls.[431] No. 41 was also a grammar school previously and a reminder of this use is the neo-Gothic schoolroom erected behind it in mid-century; this is today used as a lecture and meeting room.[432]

Nothing could be more symbolic of the earnest scholarship of WANHS than the stone Gothic facade between the two houses, designed by Henry Weaver in 1872

Devizes, the Wiltshire Museum, the original squeezed between the two 18th century town houses which it later absorbed.

to form the entrance to the first museum and complete with cusped windows and an oriel above the new two-centre arched doorway, as if to wipe out with one small addition the memory of the unserious 18th century provided by the houses either side. Weaver, by the way, was instructed by the town council to add rainwater spouts to prevent pedestrians underneath the oriel from being soaked: if he ever did, they are not there now.[433]

There were initial complaints from the Salisbury and South Wiltshire museum that Devizes was trying to steal the first position in the county from them, but good relations were restored by the time of the opening.[434] Only a hundred years later was there any threat to that harmony, when the future of both museums was under review and it appeared for a time as if the county museum might be moved to Salisbury with Devizes retaining just a local museum function.[435] The threat passed and in 1982 the new gallery by the Wyvern Partnership, containing stained glass by John Piper, was opened in a wing extending behind No.40 and parallel to the Victorian schoolroom.[436]

The museum opened with a narrow entrance between the adjacent houses leading to the broader space at the rear, with room for just three display rooms below and a library on the first floor. It has expanded greatly since, but the numerous small rooms on different levels are far from ideal and it has long been evident that better premises would be necessary at some point. The choice has fallen on the former Assize Courts as offering an opportunity to transform not only the museum but also that quarter of the town. The courts are described in Chapter 4, which also summarises progress to date in planning the new museum.[437]

Highworth

Highworth has had from 2019[438] a small museum display in the strong room of the *former Lloyds Bank* on High Street on the south side of the market square, forming part of the town's information centre. The building has two sets of two bays, slightly stepped and of three storeys, in coursed and squared rubble. It has projecting eaves, as does the two-bay building attached to the left which is of similar date and appearance but in ashlar with two platbands.

Malmesbury

It may be a sense of the historic importance of the town which led to the relatively early foundation of a museum here, called the Athelstan Museum from the outset.[439] It opened in the *Town Hall* – described in Chapter 2 – in 1932[440] and remained there until, coming under the control of the new North Wiltshire District Council in 1974, it was moved to *20 Gloucester Street* in 1975. The floors of that building, one of a pair of perhaps early 19th century date, were soon deemed to be not strong enough to take the weight of proposed display cases: the museum moved back to the town hall in 1979 and has remained there since.[441] In 2007 there was a major refit following the takeover of the town hall by the town council and in 2017 the former *Moravian Church** in Holloway was acquired and refurbished to be used for events, for hiring out and for a museum store.[442] Renamed the Julia and Hans Rausing building, this is of 1770, extended in 1859, with a long rendered east front having three round-headed windows, one curtailed by the door beneath.[443] To the rear is a long staircase wing at the north end; inside, though the interior has been stripped for its new use, the gallery retains its distinctive curved dip at the centre.

Malmesbury, Athelstan Museum, the Rausing Building.

Marlborough

There was already a museum at Marlborough College by the 1860s but no museum in the town, nor for many years afterwards despite the stimulus of a temporary museum set up for the three-day visit of the Wiltshire Archaeological Society in 1879.[444] By the 1930s the lack of a museum was being felt – one proposal was that the old George Inn in George Lane could be saved from demolition and turned into a museum - but again there was no action.[445]

The town's small museum was eventually set up in 2018 as part of the *Merchant's House Museum** at 132-3 High Street. This house, now grade 2* listed, was substantially rebuilt after the fire of 1653 and subsequently much altered, extended and subdivided. W H Smith owned No.132 from 1926 and the town council bought it from them in 1991 and leased it to the Merchant House Trust at a peppercorn; the trust subsequently bought No.133 in 1999. An extensive programme of renovation preceded the opening of the house to the public and this was followed in 2018 by the addition of the town museum in one room.[446]

Marlborough, Merchant's House Museum. (Courtesy of the museum)

The building is one of the most striking and most important on the High Street, in three and a half storeys and three gables, with pentice roofs sheltering both the two ground floor shop-fronts and the three first floor oriels, the centre oriel roofed by two miniature gables. The front above shop level is entirely hung in shaped tiles and the whole is lively in the extreme and entirely vernacular. The interior contains much else equally interesting, all well restored from 1993.[447]

Melksham

By 1956 there was some interest in creating a local museum for Melksham[448] but no museum appeared and the nearest equivalent in the town is the private Well House collection on Spa Road, which has local books, photographs and artefacts.

Mere

The Mere Historical Society was founded in 1972 and has established a small set of displays in the town's *Library*, described in Chapter 6.[449]

Mere Library and Museum (see also Chapter 6)

Salisbury

Museums

Salisbury's original network of open water channels along its streets was replaced with sewers in the 1850s and the work revealed a medieval treasure trove of discarded and lost pottery and other artefacts. These were seen as the basis of a new museum; the artefacts were purchased at auction, a committee formed and by early 1861 the Salisbury and South Wiltshire Museum had opened to the public for the first time in a large rented room at the new *Market House*, described in Chapter 3.[450] The new museum was popular but the premises unsuitable and in 1863 benefactors, Dr & Mrs Fowler, bought and presented to them the buildings at *40 St Ann Street** which were to be their base for more than 100 years. Mrs Fowler had the frontage altered by John Harding to that which still exists, and the museum opened at the beginning of 1864. Inside were two display rooms, the inner one being the ornately plastered round dining room erected in 1825 for a previous owner.[451]

The building is of brick and considerably older than its mid-century conversion. There are gables at either end and, between them, two more bays with 18th century sash windows. The right-hand bay has 19th century mullioned and some transomed windows and the left hand one likewise but also diaper pattern brickwork and a Tudor-style doorcase with 'Museum' in stone above it. The diaper patterning and mullioned windows continue down the side return, which was originally of four bays.[452]

Three years later, in September 1867, the Blackmore Museum opened to house William Blackmore's collection of archaeological finds, from various parts of the world but principally the USA.

Salisbury, the Museum building entrance at 40 St Ann St

Salisbury Museum, displays in the 1933 extension at 40 St Ann St. (Salisbury Museum)

This was in a new building, also by John Harding, making it the only purpose-built museum in the county. It contained a single large room, 70ft by 35ft, with a hammer-beam timber roof, display cases round the walls with wooden cornicing over, and large multi-light pointed-arch windows at both ends with two more, gabled, on either long wall. The door was central on the north side.[453] The new museum was managed from the start by the staff of the Salisbury and South Wiltshire Museum.

The *Blackmore museum* was situated, in effect, at the back of the garden of the Salisbury and South Wiltshire, and over succeeding years both museums expanded until an extension to the South Wiltshire in 1933 joined the two together, creating a large new display room with a segmentally arched ceiling. Despite this addition, and

Salisbury, the Blackmore Museum, carefully posed with a woman carrying a tray of ancient bones in the doorway, a gardener mowing the lawn and two worthies in earnest discussion on the path. (Salisbury Museum).

Salisbury, the Blackmore Museum with a curator, perhaps Dr Blackmore himself, in contemplation of a table full of bones. (Salisbury Museum).

the fact that the original Blackmore collection was dispersed in the 1930s and 1960s, the size limitations remained and there was also a growing sense that the museum's out-of-centre location was unhelpful.

It was proposed in the late 1960s that the Devizes and Salisbury museums should be combined into a single county museum. The town mill in Salisbury was identified as a suitable site and progress was made through the 1970s towards this end, though the idea of combining the museums was soon dropped. In the end the impracticality of the mill building defeated the initiative[454] and, although in later years there were repeated proposals to create a new combined county museum, these also came to nothing.[455]

Salisbury Museum at the King's House.

The new site finally chosen for the Salisbury museum was the **King's House*** in the cathedral close, grade 1 listed, which was opened as the new museum in 1981, the conversion having been designed by the Brandt Potter partnership.[456] This far larger building had 11 galleries originally and there have been many improvements and refurbishments since, including the new Wessex archaeology gallery in 2014, based on the Pitt Rivers Wessex collection acquired in 1975. The 'Past Forward' project for further improvements was under way in 2023 and due for completion in 2024.

At the core of the building, running north to south, is the remains of the original prebendal house of the abbots of Sherborne, a great hall with a later two-storey porch, rebuilt in Elizabethan times with an inserted floor, mullioned and transomed windows and three attic gables inserted, the whole now in flint and rubblestone. To the north end is the taller brick cross-wing added shortly afterwards, the east end of which has a gable over a canted bay with spectacularly generous glazing. The north-east wing started as a 15th century outbuilding, later raised in height, and to the south-east a wing added for a school by T H Wyatt in 1851-2 was later raised to two storeys and extended further.[457]

MUSEUMS AND ART GALLERIES

Salisbury Museum, the Wessex gallery. (Salisbury Museum)

The Wessex gallery is mainly housed in a flat-roofed extension at the south west of the site. The 'Past Forward' project will produce three new galleries in the ground floor of the north wing together with a first floor events space, as well as restoration of the building's fabric.

The original buildings for both museums in St Ann's Street were threatened with demolition and with unsympathetic change but in the end have both been converted with some success, the Salisbury and South Wiltshire Museum into sheltered housing and the Blackmore into flats.[458]

The Young Art Gallery

The City's *Young Art Gallery** was founded in 1913 after Edwin Young, a talented amateur artist, left his collection of paintings to the city along with an endowment and the funds to build a gallery to house them in; he also wished the endowment to be used for adding to the collection. The gallery replaced an

Salisbury, the Young Art Gallery. See also image in Chapter 6

earlier building in Chipper Lane, immediately adjacent to the new library, and was designed by George Blount.[459] There was a gallery on each of the two floors and the narrowness of the façade is emphasized by full-height half-octagonal pilasters breaking out into crenellated turrets at the roof. Below the parapet is a full width plaque 'The Young Gallery', in best Arts and Crafts script and below that an equally exuberant large panel of carved roses. At the base is a long inscription about Young and his donation and above that the two levels of six-light mullioned and transomed windows, the lower set with blind gothic top halves, bring a jumbled completion to this eye-catching front.

The art gallery moved with the library to the *Market House* in 1975, where it occupies the first floor; the art gallery and library in Chipper Lane have since been subdivided into offices.[460] The market house is described in Chapter 3.

Swindon

The Great Western Railway seems to have been aware of the significance of its railway works development from an early stage and may have created some sort of small museum of its products, presumably within the works, from as early as 1848.[461]

It was 50 years or more later before there were significant moves towards a general museum for the town.[462] The major initiative here came from C H Gore, the museum's first honorary curator and a main inspiration for both its foundation and the acquisition of exhibits. He donated his own collection to the town in 1913 and this formed the basis of the first museum opened in the *Victoria Hall* in 1920.[463] The hall, built for the Free Christians as a chapel in 1874, became the Roman Catholic Holy

Swindon, the Apsley House Museum, 1964 Art Gallery extension to the right.

Rood chapel in 1878 and had been kept by them until 1912.⁴⁶⁴ It had two gables to fit its corner site; one had three Gothic windows, the central one larger, for the chapel and the other was substantially larger with two storeys and an attic of domestic-looking windows; the main door was in the angle.⁴⁶⁵

The collection grew rapidly and it was soon apparent that the building was too small as well as being otherwise unsuitable – it was recorded as having serious damp problems when used as a church.⁴⁶⁶ In 1930 the museum moved to *Apsley House** on Bath Road and the former premises were soon afterwards replaced by the art deco building which still stands there opposite the new library.⁴⁶⁷

Apsley House, at the junction with Victoria Road, is an ashlar villa of the 1830s, built for a prosperous coal and seed merchant,⁴⁶⁸ with a rusticated ground floor, round-arched windows either side of a Greek Doric portico below and 12-pane sashes above; a short windowless extension to the left looks like an afterthought but may not be. The 1964 extension to the right to create an art gallery extends round into Victoria Road above the shop fronts in a triple row of windows articulated by dark vertical boards. It was designed by the borough architect, J Loring-Morgan.⁴⁶⁹

The museum is attractive but small and from as early as 1938 the curator was calling for larger premises; indeed not long afterwards he was forced to adapt two attic rooms to accommodate no less than 50 cases of stuffed birds from Grittleton House.⁴⁷⁰ The addition of the art gallery may have relieved some pressure and allowed a considerable local art collection to be put on display, but no move happened.

There is the sense that the Swindon museum was always embraced more closely by its community than others, perhaps more austere, elsewhere,⁴⁷¹ and it is therefore perhaps not surprising that there was an outcry when the borough council, having been forced to close the museum at the start of the Covid 19 outbreak in 2020, decided to keep it closed. The building was up for sale in 2022⁴⁷² and plans at that date were to relocate the museum and art gallery on a temporary basis to the first floor of the council offices in Euclid Square pending a longer term move to the town's new 'cultural quarter'.⁴⁷³ The Euclid Square offices are described in Chapter 7.

More widely known is the town's railway museum, which opened in a former Methodist chapel in 1962 and relocated as 'Steam' to the former railway works in 2000. It is a specialist rather than a general museum and so is not described further here. Other specialist museums include the Railway Village Museum at 34 Faringdon Road, set up as a 19th century worker's house, and the Richard Jefferies Museum at Coate.

Trowbridge

The Wiltshire Archaeological and Natural History Society made its summer visit here in 1872 and a temporary museum was set up in the *Court Hall* (described in Chapter 4) for the duration of the meeting.⁴⁷⁴ There was an early move to establish a town museum in 1880, which came to nothing, and by 1938 the question was under consideration again and the council was accepting donated pictures and other artefacts for display in the *Town Hall* (described in Chapter 2).⁴⁷⁵ The one-room display here remained until 1977 when it transferred into the Garlick Room at the *Civic Hall*, described in Chapter 7.⁴⁷⁶

Trowbridge, the Home Mills building now housing the Town Museum.

With the development of the Shires shopping centre an approach was made for the use of the former Baptist chapel there but the solution eventually agreed was to use the first floor of the *Home Mills* building. The new museum here, still run by the town council, opened in 1990. In 2018 it closed for a major refurbishment using money from the Heritage Lottery Fund, Trowbridge town council and others, and reopened in 2021 with an extra floor of display space. Difficult to see from outside, Home Mills is an industrial building of 1862 by Charles Underwood of Bristol in brick and stone.[477]

The county council, concerned at the damage done to archives in the late war, established a record office in 1947.[478] At first the storage was in the small lodge at the north end of *County Hall* which had been built for that purpose. This was soon outgrown and provision was made in the basement of the main building but in 1971 the search rooms and storage were moved to the former *Airsprung* building to the east, described in Chapter 6. There were concerns that the storage facilities here were not suitable and the Wiltshire County and Swindon Borough Councils agreed to the creating of the new *History Centre* in Chippenham, described above, which opened in 2007.

Warminster

By 1939 the council had accumulated enough objects of local historical interest to fill a display case in the council chamber at the *Town Hall*. The display was removed during the Second World War but reinstated in 1951 and in 1973 was taken over by the town's history society, which set up a museum in the *Sexton's Cottage,* a small brick building immediately to the rear of the Chapel of St Lawrence in the High Street. Since 1982 it has had a small area, with changing displays, in the town's *library*, described in Chapter 6.[479]

Westbury

The Westbury Heritage Society maintains a small museum, with changing exhibitions, in a first-floor room in the town's *Library*, described in Chapter 6.

Wilton

The Wilton Historical Society, formed in 1977, set out to establish a small town museum. Summer displays in the town council's council chamber were followed by the creation of a museum in the premises of the carpet factory, set up in 1985. This moved to various places in the factory, was closed for a period in 1997, and eventually closed finally in the early 2000s.[480]

Wootton Bassett, the Town Hall Museum

Royal Wootton Bassett

There were the beginnings of a museum in the *Town Hall* – described in Chapter 2 – from the 1890s as various people donated portraits and other artefacts to be held on display there.[481] The Town Trust took over the hall in 1909 and the collection was added to gradually until it was boosted by being taken over by the town's historical society in 1971.[482] It continues to mount changing displays on the town's history.

6
Libraries and Reading Rooms

Introduction

FREE PUBLIC LIBRARIES were late in arriving, not appearing in most Wiltshire towns until the 1920s. Before that, a variety of literary societies, mechanics' institutions and reading rooms provided access to books for some in an often pioneering fashion. In addition to these, and continuing in some cases right up to the 1960s, were the commercial circulating libraries.

Circulating libraries are not discussed in the following analysis but had an important role to play. They started at an early date: a circulating library of 5000 books covering the south Wiltshire area is mentioned in 1741 and another, in Salisbury High Street, in 1822.[483] Right through the 19th century the borrowing fees were probably affordable only by the middle classes but that gradually changed as working class people acquired more disposable income and the books on offer increasingly catered for the taste in popular fiction not often served by the more earnest literary institutions and other libraries. Some of the largest, such as Mudie's (founded 1842) and WH Smith's (founded 1860), with their bulk-buying of books, exerted a considerable influence on the publishing industry.[484] The circulating libraries faded out in the 20th century in the face of the falling cost of books and the availability of the new free public libraries, though Mudie's lasted until 1937 and WH Smith's until 1961.[485]

The Lending Library, Cruickshank print. (Open domain image from the Yale Centre for British Art, Paul Mellon Collection).

Reading Rooms

A number of Literary and Scientific Institutions and Literary Societies are described below, many set up early in the 19th century as a type of gentleman's club whose

The Warminster Literary and Scientific Institution of 1838. (WSA)

existence was justified by a commitment to intellectual enquiry. They typically had reading rooms, libraries and often a small museum and were aimed at the middle and professional classes, as the two guinea annual subscription at the Warminster example in 1838 illustrates. Lack of funds and declining membership led to short lives for most but they have left behind at least two interesting buildings, in Salisbury and Warminster.

Mechanics' Institutes and other reading rooms for the working classes were equally common, though most of these suffered the same problem of lack of funds leading to frequent closures and re-openings, often under a different name. They were almost all founded in paternalistic fashion by middle and upper class people guided partly by altruism, partly by the wish – as in the GWR case at Swindon – to have a better-skilled workforce, and partly by the view that giving working class men something more useful to do in their leisure hours would keep them out of the pubs.[486] Most set out to ensure that they were non-sectarian and avoided any discussion of politics.

Many attracted the skilled manual workers for whom they were intended but the existence of most, Swindon Mechanics' Institute always excepted, seems to have been tenuous, usually for financial reasons. Salisbury Mechanics' Institute, for example, proved unattractive to the working class and closed as early as 1840; the Literary Institution in Swindon Old Town moved towards a more middle class membership in the 1880s with subsequent benefit to its finances, and the Trowbridge Mechanics' Institute failed to attract working class members and closed in 1866. Nearly all appear to have fallen by the wayside by the late 19th century, despite many being used increasingly for more general leisure pursuits such as billiards rather than for reading and lectures. One consequence of this precarious history is that only in Swindon was it possible for the Institute to acquire purpose-built premises.

Mechanics' Institutes offered a library, a reading room and often lectures and tuition, particularly in English and mathematics. The books were often donated so subject matter tended to be hit-and-miss depending on what was given. A footnote to their history is provided by the Penny Readings movement, which thrived from about 1860 to the end of the century. The readings were very often associated with the institutes and generally included extracts from 'improving' literature in a mixed programme which also contained poetry and song.[487]

Many reading rooms, mechanics' institutes and the like had a short life and left little trace, so the analysis of these in the following pages cannot be guaranteed to be comprehensive.

Public Libraries

Early moves to legislate for free public libraries, starting in the 1830s, resulted eventually in the Public Libraries Act 1850. The motivations of those supporting this movement were similar to those supporting reading rooms, namely the benefits of a better-educated workforce and a reduction in drunkenness. Those opposing were concerned about the costs, the risk of undermining the private enterprise effort involved in running reading rooms and circulating libraries and, bearing in mind that this was the period of revolutions throughout Europe, a fear that a more educated working class would be more easily provoked to rebellion. In the event, the legislation had to be so compromised to get it past the House of Commons that the powers given applied only to boroughs with over 10,000 population, only after a plebiscite had voted in favour and only within the funding provided by a half-penny on the rates, which could not be used to buy books.[488]

Although these restrictions were eased later in the century there was little progress in the provision of free libraries. Salisbury, the only place in Wiltshire which qualified under the 1850 Act, eventually held a poll in 1877, which was lost. Calne Literary Institution had converted into a free public library in 1871, without local authority involvement, and that was it until Salisbury held another poll in 1890 which was narrowly won; its first library was opened that year.

From the turn of the century Andrew Carnegie, the Scots-American businessman and philanthropist, donated public libraries in large numbers in the United States, Britain and other countries. Generally he paid for the buildings and the local authority was responsible for the site and for running costs; and all libraries had to be free. Four towns in Wiltshire were offered libraries: Devizes and Trowbridge turned the offer down but Calne and Salisbury accepted; two very different libraries resulted but both are amongst the most interesting in the county.

The Calne library was an example of the 'closed' system, common for many years. In this, the book store was kept separate and borrowers had to select from a list of titles without seeing the books themselves. This was useful for minimizing the space taken by the book stock in early libraries and also met concerns about potential theft of or damage to books, but the disadvantages from the borrower's point of view became increasingly evident. In Calne's case the closed system allowed the main space to be given over to the reading room, which was open for much longer hours than the library itself with its small stock of books.

The Public Libraries Act 1919 reformed the provision of libraries by giving the powers to county councils. Wiltshire was quick to take up these powers and indeed had already set up a scheme using an eight-year grant from the Carnegie United Kingdom Trust.[489] Under this, the county libraries committee, an offshoot of the education committee, supplied boxes of books to various outlets, replenishing them at regular intervals; it was up to the recipients to provide space and to staff the library during opening hours. Schools were the top priority followed by 'library centres' in villages but by the early 1920s offers were being made to the towns as well and the first public libraries there date from this time.

The early libraries were mainly in ad hoc premises many of which were unsuitable, like the cupboard first used for this purpose in the entrance to Trowbridge town hall. They had small book stocks of usually under 1000 volumes and, staffed by volunteers, were open for only short periods, typically one or two evenings a week to meet the required minimum of three hours a week total.[490] Such provision may seem pitiful compared to modern standards but this was a service established from scratch and there was some doubt at first as to whether it would catch on. The county council took over the funding after the initial eight year period elapsed and the service steadily developed during the inter-war period, with its headquarters and main book store in Trowbridge. The history during this time was of steady expansion, a constant search for larger and more suitable premises, and pressure for reference libraries and reading rooms in addition to the basic lending facility.[491]

A modern library interior, in this example Melksham

In the post-war period the county council assumed full control of not only the book supply but also the premises, its responsibilities being defined eventually in the Public Libraries and Museums Act 1964. In 1947 there were only 17 public libraries in the county and only six of these had paid librarians; about half of the one million books circulating each year were issued from village halls, schools and other such locations.[492] The county council responded to this by expanding both the scale and the scope of the service, and also constructing many new libraries, some in adapted buildings, some entirely purpose-built. More recently, new libraries have been provided in the community campuses which bring together local government services in one building in a way not seen since the early days of town halls.

The Buildings

Amesbury

A '*Reading Room and Men's Club*', paid for by the vicar, opened in Church Street c1903 and was used until at least 1923; it is possible that it closed in 1925 on the opening of the library at Antrobus House.[493] The reading room was probably the small extension to the east of the parish rooms, now all the Dunkirk Social Club, the extension single storey with two large segmentally arched windows.[494]

Antrobus House* in Salisbury Road was designed by Geoffrey Fildes and opened in 1925 as a public building in memory of an Antrobus son killed in the First World War.[495] The main purpose was to house the furniture and other possessions of Lady Antrobus, perhaps inspired by a spiritualist belief that keeping her possessions together would keep her in touch with her dead son. As well as some 540 possessions which formed the upstairs museum, described in Chapter 5, there was her library

Amesbury, Antrobus House. (Courtesy of Antrobus House Trustees).

of approaching 3000 volumes. There was public access to the library but its use as a lending library may have been limited, the access being mainly for reference. The library, with the museum, declined after the Second World War and late in the century both the upstairs and downstairs rooms were available for meetings, including those of the town council. In 2023 it was still run by a trust but now hired out for weddings and other events.

It is a building of remarkable quality, in neo-Wren style, all in brick, the central block flanked by pavilions either side originally containing accommodation for a curator and a caretaker. The ground floor is tall, with a central doorway and fanlight flanked either side by a pair of 28-pane segmentally arched windows, and above that a string course ties together the three elements of the whole below a row of 12-pane, almost attic-like, windows. The hipped roof of the main block is topped by a square cupola and the pavilions each have a pair of tall panelled chimneys reminiscent of Lutyens.[496]

In the late 1940s there were plans to open a county library in premises off High Street,[497] and these may have been used for a brief period before a move in 1950/1 to a prefabricated youth club hut at the top of Kitchener Road.[498] The library moved from this inconvenient location in 1959 and from then until 1973 was in the former *Fire Station* at the corner of Earls Court Road and Edwards Road.[499] This tiny gable-ended building in brick and flint, the original fire engine door replaced by a shopfront, faces the *New Library* of 1973 which occupies part of the site of the former Amesbury House, demolished when the town centre bypass was made. Designed by Wiltshire County Architects, it is in front of and linked to the health centre of 1970 and is octagonal with walls of chequered flint and ashlar and a low-angled pyramidal roof of sheeted metal. The windows are mostly at clerestory height and the interior, consciously or not, harks back to the 'panopticon' model of some early libraries.

Bradford on Avon

In 1835 there was a public circulating library in the town with 295 members but it is not known where this was based.[500] Other later commercial libraries included Dotesio and Todd's at 28 Silver Street from 1899 or earlier, known as 'The Library' when it was offered for sale in 1934; and James Randell's, a bookseller at 44 St Margaret's Street, recorded in 1890 and advertising his library in 1913.[501]

A literary institution was formed in 1852 and was closely involved in the building of the *Town Hall* in 1855.[502] It was allocated two rooms there for a reading room and library, and membership was by subscription, it seems mostly from the town's growing middle class. It acquired a library of 400 books but by 1881 had too few members to remain solvent and the institution closed that year. The town hall is described in Chapter 2.

A working men's reading room was opened in 1863 near the churchyard and with the support of the clergy; it may have been in the Old Church House.[503] In 1869 it was open six nights a week and apparently successful but perhaps had only a short life because in 1875 attempts were made again to raise funds for a 'Working Men's Reading Room'. No more is heard of this.[504]

Bradford on Avon Library.

A temperance tavern was opened in 1879 at the bottom of what is now Market Street, on the site of the former White Hart inn and bearing the same name. Amongst its facilities was a first floor reading room. Around 1907 it was converted into a shop which lasted until the 1960s but was then demolished as part of road improvements.[505]

The town received a county public library in 1923, the first such urban branch library to be established by the county library committee.[506] It was located in ***Westbury House***, described in Chapter 7, and subsequently, following a short and unhappy spell in an ante-room to the **swimming baths**, moved to a room in the Church Army Social Centre in Church Street.[507] This was at ***No. 17***, now the Dutch Barton dental practice, an early 18th century rebuilding of a previous house, re-fronted with five bays c1830 in ashlar with raised quoins.[508] The next move, in 1944, was into a room in what was previously the Constitutional Club, then the Conservative Club, and was in 2024 the ***Timbrell's Yard*** restaurant by St Margaret's Hall.[509] It was probably located in the small rubblestone extension to the right of the 17th century main building, 18th century in date with a Venetian window and a semi-hipped roof. It stayed there until 1966 when it moved to a double **Portakabin** opposite the entrance to St Margaret's Hall in what is now a car park, remaining at this site for much longer than had been intended.[510]

The town at last obtained a purpose-built library in 1990, designed by Bob Broadhead of Wiltshire County Architects and located on ***Bridge Street*** on the site of the former swimming baths.[511] It is in ashlar stone, to fit the predominant building material of the town, and has a pyramidal roof and tall windows either side of each corner angle; the front is canted in slightly behind full-height pillars. The prevalence of blackened glass panels to disguise the mezzanine floor gives it a sombre look but the inside is toplit, full height and airy. The town's museum is located upstairs.

Calne

There was a 'Society for the Cultivation of Useful Knowledge' in Calne from 1840, based originally in the market house and then in the church house. This soon became known as the Literary and Scientific Institution (usually just the Literary Institution) and by 1852 it had a room in the building at *13 Church Street* originally intended for the earlier society but then owned by Calne Savings Bank and later to become an Oddfellows Hall before conversion to a shop.[512] The Literary Institution started off in the usual way of such bodies, with a library and lecture series aimed at the town's more prosperous inhabitants, but in 1870 took the decision to make the library free, opened on three evenings a week and aimed specifically at working class men; comments at the opening ceremony in early 1871 made clear that the stated intention was to improve the education of the workers.[513] The library, expanded to 2000 volumes, was supported by subscriptions and gifts from the gentry, particularly the Lansdowne family, and was well used for a number of years, but by the end of the century it was struggling to survive.[514]

13 Church Street is a terraced building in ashlar, the doorway in an angled bay at the north end, with four sash windows above. The main part of the ground floor has been replaced by a late 20th century shopfront.

The Town Council noted the state of the Literary Institution, their own powers to fund a public library and the availability of Carnegie grants.[515] They applied for a grant and received £1200 on condition that they manage land purchase, and equipment and running costs, in such a way that the library did not become a white elephant. The resulting new building, designed by C H Smith of Smith and Marshall, opened in March 1905. The *Carnegie Library** on New Road, of modest size, has considerable charm, the front elevation of generally 17th century appearance with two large mullioned and transomed windows to the left and the segmentally arched doorway to the right under a portico containing the Calne borough arms. The whole is much decorated, with fluted pilasters continuing through the parapet and terminating in heavy stone finials. The front block contains the entranceway and

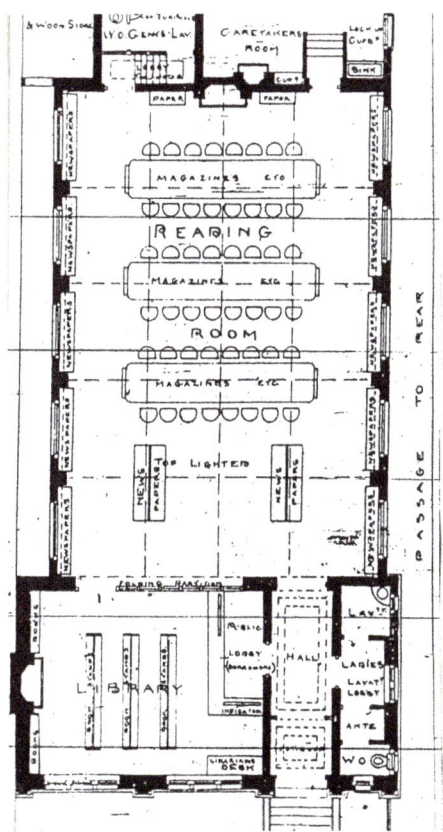

Calne, Carnegie Library floor plan as set up in 1905, much more space given to the reading room than to the library. (Courtesy of Sue Boddington).

Calne, the Carnegie library

Calne, the New Library.

a small room to the left; behind this the main hall is set at right angles to the road, attractively top lit and with iron roof girders and 5 bays of diocletian windows.[516]

In early days the main space was given over to the reading room, with reading slopes and tables, which was open for long hours while the library, with only 200 books initially and no open access, was squeezed into the smaller room at the front and staffed for very limited hours. The library's later history was one of struggle until in 1948 the town council reluctantly agreed to hand it over to the county library service.[517]

Better managed as part of the county service, the library was nevertheless much too small for a town of this size, though it took until the end of the century to produce a replacement. This is the *New Library*, on The Strand opposite the town hall, which opened in 2001 to designs by Aaron Evans.[518] Part of a wider redevelopment of this important corner, the library is a large ashlar drum with incised bands to match those on the adjacent buildings. The main illumination for the interior is provided by a wide full-height window facing The Strand, with four tiers of horizontal metal shutters giving protection from direct sunlight but doing little for the building's appearance. The main interior space is also circular and is of full height. The Carnegie library was later converted into the Heritage Centre described in Chapter 5.

Chippenham

The town's Literary and Scientific Institution, which seemed as elsewhere to be an organization for the more affluent inhabitants, was founded in 1833 and soon acquired a small library; by 1875 it was based in premises in the Market Place.[519] By 1857 there was a 'library and reading room for the working classes' at Landsend, possibly supported by Gabriel Goldney, at that date not yet the town's MP; its location is not known.[520] The new *Temperance Hall* in Foghamshire, opened in 1863[521], also contained a reading room, soon used by a newly established working men's club set up there.[522] Its history thereafter is not clear but in 1886 the reading room was re-established, under the control of the Liberals but not intended to be party political in nature.[523] In 1887 the Conservatives established a reading room, this time explicitly political in intent, in their High Street committee rooms.[524] It is not clear when any of these libraries ceased to function.

The *Temperance Hall* is by W J Stent in his typical coarse Gothic, in appearance not dissimilar to the nonconformist chapels in the design of which he specialized. The front is now despoiled by the insertion of a broad entrance below an all-too-visible steel joist. Inside there were originally the reading room and a committee room on the ground floor and a large hall above, supposedly capable of seating 400.[525]

The *Constitutional Club*, opposite the Temperance Hall in Foghamshire, was built in 1909, a long building of vaguely 17th century appearance with mullioned and transomed windows, rough squared stone blockwork and a balconied central entrance bay of almost town hall pretension. This also contained a reading room.

The overall picture of library provision in the town was moving towards some coherence before this, with the opening in 1889 of the *Jubilee Building* at what is now 32 Market Place, a site given by Sir John Neeld.[526] This was built by the town corporation to celebrate Queen Victoria's golden jubilee, was used from the outset by the Literary and Scientific Institution, and contained their reading room. It is a tall three storeys, perhaps deliberately out of scale so as to dominate adjacent buildings, of coursed rubble with ashlar dressings, the windows, door and roof all much pedimented. The main front is of three narrow bays and a further bay containing the entrance is set back to the south; the tympanum of the main roof pediment contains the town crest and the motto 'Unity and Loyalty 1837-1887'. The cottage to the rear, a survivor probably from the previous town house on this site, is of 17th century date and was later used as a caretaker's cottage.[527] Initial designs for the building by Graham Awdry were rejected as being too expensive and the final design was produced by Messrs. Smith and Light, perhaps members of the corporation.[528] The crowded window pediments may betray the use of amateur designers.

Chippenham, the Jubilee Building.

In 1925 the county library committee approached the town council saying it wished to establish a free library in the town and asking the council to find premises and then manage it.[529] After consideration of a room in the *Neeld Hall* the library opened in 1926 in a room in the *Town Hall*, initially on two evenings a week; it was kept open at first by voluntary effort but from 1928 with a paid librarian.[530] In 1934 the library was moved to the former billiard room at the *Jubilee Building*, where the Literary and Scientific Institution was still based, and remained there for nearly 40 years.[531]

The final move came in 1973, to the *Timber Street* library which is still in use. This is by the

Chippenham, pre-war Jubilee Building sign for the Literary Institute. Note the emphasis on games by this date and the half fees for women, who were presumably expected to use only the library. (Chippenham Town Council).

county architect's department, with tall aggregate panels alternating with windows below a recessed hipped roof, the materials perhaps an unsympathetic choice for a building so close to the town's historic heart but the strong verticals nevertheless giving it a significant presence.[532]

Corsham

A Literary and Scientific Institution was founded in 1839 and a Mechanics' Institute in 1853: it is not clear whether either body had its own premises in their early years but the Mechanics' Institute had rooms in the High Street in the period up to 1882 and both probably maintained some sort of reading room and library for their members.[533] A working men's institute, with reading room, had opened in Pickwick by 1877 in a room donated by Gabriel Goldney MP; its location is not recorded but it lasted until at least 1897.[534]

In 1882, the conversion of the market hall into a *town hall* – described in Chapter 2 - provided a reading room and library on the ground floor to the left of the entrance, let to the Mechanics Institute.[535] This first library seems not to have been long-lasting but by the end of the century the town council was supplying books and in 1926 the library reopened in the Card Room at the town hall as a free library supported by the county library committee.[536]

In 1944 the library acquired premises of its own in a long black prefabricated hut, since demolished, south of *Pickwick Road* and almost opposite the entrance to Oliver Avenue. This, formerly a school, was of substantial size but cold and musty, heated by a small stove which caused much condensation.[537] A move to better premises had to wait until 1969 when the *New Library* opened, located immediately east of the Mansion House on Pickwick Road. Designed by Gordon Luck of Wiltshire county architects, this was single-storey in stone below a low-angled pyramidal metal roof, with an applied modernist sculptural panel to the front adjacent to the doors.[538] The interior was open to the roof.

In 2014 this library closed – it has since been demolished – and a new one opened as part of the *Springfield Community Campus* on Beechfield Road. This, by Alex French architects, contains council and police offices as well as a café and the library, all attached to older sports facilities which include the swimming pool.[539] The main block is tall and clad in grey ceramic tiles, the library spacious and well-windowed though with a lowering timber-clad ceiling.

Cricklade

A reading room was established in St Sampson's parish in the town before 1865 and was still in being in 1908, and a literary institution was established before 1863. It is not clear where either of these was based, nor how long each lasted.[540]

In 1924 the county library service deposited books for lending at the school immediately south of the town bridge, though it seems probable that these were part of the schools libraries scheme rather than for general use.[541] Later a part-time county library service was provided in *37 High Street*, a small 18th century terraced house, rendered, with a first floor bay window and an inserted 19th century shopfront.[542] In 1971 the library transferred to a single-storey prefabricated building behind the fire station on *Bath Road*, in 2023 a pre-school playgroup.[543] Finally, in 2002 it moved to the *Old Town Hall*, described in chapter 2, where it remains. Here it occupies the former council chamber on the first floor overlooking the street.[544]

Devizes

The town's Literary and Scientific Institution, known also for its first 20 years or so as the Mechanic's Institution, was formed in 1833 and at first occupied rooms at *6 High Street*, a two-storey building of the late 18th century with inserted shop windows below and three double sash windows above.[545] It was not there long, moving in 1842 to unidentified premises near St Mary's church on New Park Street which were burned down in 1843; following this it moved first to the Chequer, and then in 1848 to the Town Hall, described in Chapter 2.[546] By late in the century it had a considerable library for which the succession of small rooms was far from suitable, but in 1907 it acquired the former *British School** on the north side of Northgate Street close to the junction with New Park Street.[547] This has a narrow façade, set back from the street and of three storeys in stone cut curiously to the dimensions of bricks, with Tudor Gothic windows and inscriptions '1822' and 'British Schools'; equally curious are the fan-shaped brackets at either end of the cornice, with no apparent function. It would appear to have very little internal space but in fact widens out behind into a substantial two-storey brick block, five bays deep under a hipped roof. The Institute, perhaps a surprising survivor over such a long period, remains at this address although the more earnest parts of its functioning are no more.

In 1903 the Carnegie trust offered funding of between £1600 and £2300 to establish a free library if the town would provide a site and implement the Free Library Act, implying that they would spend from the rates for the library's upkeep; it was suggested that the new library might be combined with that of the Literary and Scientific Institution which at that date had 2500 volumes.[548] The town council took a poll of ratepayers as to whether to accept this offer; the proposal was lost by a two to one majority – presumably because of fears for the burden on the rates - and so the opportunity of Carnegie funding was lost.[549]

A free public library was eventually opened in 1928, the last in an urban area in the county.[550] It shared the premises of the Literary and Scientific Institution in Northgate Street, renting separate space but sharing the Institute's

Devizes, the British School, acquired in 1907 by the Literary and Scientific Institution.

LIBRARIES AND READING ROOMS 121

Devizes, the British School, the side temporarily visible during building works next door and showing how much larger this is than the entrance section to the right.

librarian.⁵⁵¹ The space there was inadequate and in 1936 the library moved to ***33 St John's Street***,⁵⁵² described in Chapter 4, and eventually in 1968 to the present premises in ***Sheep Street***.⁵⁵³ The new library is by Wiltshire county architects, two storey with grey aggregate panels and a white-rendered triple entrance alongside plentiful glazing which gives good light to the double height interior.⁵⁵⁴ Its other feature, of no relevance to its main function, is the former cold war bunker in the basement.⁵⁵⁵

Highworth

There was a circulating library from at least 1830, still active in 1842.⁵⁵⁶ The town had a Literary and Scientific Society in premises in Swindon Street by 1855 and a 'Mechanics' Athenaeum and Working Men's Club' by 1863.⁵⁵⁷ The Working Men's Club, which appears to have changed its name subsequently, had a library and lasted probably until the turn of the century;⁵⁵⁸ the history of the Literary and Scientific Society, and the location of its premises, are not clear. The Working Men's Club's reading room opened in an unidentified central location in 1874 and by 1884 was said to have had an annual income of over £300.⁵⁵⁹ There was also a Young Men's Institute and Reading Room⁵⁶⁰ which was in existence by 1901 and lasted until at least 1936. It had rooms initially in the High Street and later moved to Gilbert's Lane.⁵⁶¹

By 1939 a branch of the county library was located in one of the town's schools.⁵⁶² It seems that this may not have lasted long because in the early post-war period the town was served by a mobile library based in Marlborough.⁵⁶³ This lasted until the start of 1963, after which a room was rented in ***Inigo House, 24 High Street****.⁵⁶⁴ This, described by the Buildings of England as Highworth's finest house, is early 18th century in brick, four bays wide by 3 storeys high, finely detailed in ashlar with a conspicuous doorway with Corinthian pilasters and a stepped-back curved pediment. It is now grade 2* listed.

The library was not in this splendid building for long, however, because in 1970 it moved to a temporary building at the junction of Eastrop and Brewery Street.⁵⁶⁵ The final move came c2000 when the new library, designed by the Coleman Hicks Partnership, opened on the first floor above the Co-operative store off *Brewery Street*.⁵⁶⁶ The building is of brick under tile, sprawling with hipped roofs and semi-dormers typical of fake-vernacular supermarket design, though the library inside is spacious and light.

Malmesbury

There was a circulating library run from a bookseller's in the High Street in 1830 and a second, from another bookseller in the High Street, by 1842.⁵⁶⁷ A Literary Institution was in place by 1838⁵⁶⁸ and a Mechanics' Institute was founded in 1851 and had a library of 900 books: nothing more is known of its location nor how long it survived.⁵⁶⁹ A new Literary and Scientific Society was founded in 1855; it was still in existence in 1864 but it is not clear where its premises were nor when it ceased to operate.⁵⁷⁰ A reading room was established before 1866 but closed because of declining support and was replaced by one paid for by Walter Powell, the town's MP. The building he constructed at *4 Silver Street* was equipped with several hundred books.⁵⁷¹ The facade is small and neat in ashlar with a large three-part mullioned sash window to the right of the doorway; it stretches a long way back. Powell died in 1880 and the library was

Malmesbury, former library at 44 High Street, a noisy brick intrusion into a row of older stone buildings. (Athelstan Museum).

sold off, but the building was bought back for the town by the new MP Charles Miles and reopened, with a coffee room to the back and also a room in which evening classes were held twice a week. The reading room was still operating in 1888 but probably soon thereafter the building started to be used by the town council and then by a day school.[572] It subsequently became a Pentecostal church and later a day nursery.[573]

There was said to have been a reading room adjacent to the old Prince and Princess hotel in the late 19th century,[574] and the YMCA took over the old cottage hospital in 1897 and was able to expand its reading room as a consequence.[575]

Malmesbury was amongst the last to join the new county library scheme, and there seems to have been some reluctance on its part.[576] The library was set up in 1926 and was soon, if not immediately, located in the *Town Hall*, described in Chapter 2.[577] After the Second World War it relocated to *44 High Street*, with the county council now taking full control from the borough council.[578] 44 High Street is strikingly tall against surrounding buildings in its assertive red brick, with two storeys of segmentally arched windows and much brick detailing above ground floor shop fronts. A strong cornice is topped by a pedimented attic storey, with more ornamental brick and the date 1901. It was built in that year as the business premises of J E Ponting, a prominent local retailer.

Malmesbury Library.

In 1972 the library moved finally to larger premises in the former *Church of England Primary School* in Cross Hayes, which had closed in 1966.[579] This is of 1857, by John Shaw,[580] single-storey rubblestone with generous segmental-arched sash windows, its coped gables and ball finials giving it something of a north country look. It was altered and extended on becoming a library.

Marlborough Library.

Marlborough

There was a circulating library run from a bookseller's in the High Street by 1830.[581] A Reading and Mutual Improvement Society, supported by some of the town's 'respectable inhabitants', was formed in 1844 and met first in the schoolroom of a school belonging to one J Brown; it is not clear which building this was.[582] In 1854 they opened their reading room, with a library of 800 books, in the Savings Bank, a building which has also not been identified.[583] The society closed in 1905 due to a falling off in demand, an imminent rent rise and the poor state of the book stock: one suggested reason for the declining usage was that newspapers and books were then much cheaper than they had been 50 years before.[584]

This society was aimed at the town's middle class but a Working Men's Hall, promoted with typically patronising intent and clearly intended to deter men from drinking, opened in late 1864; it was at the south end of High Street near St Peter's church.[585] It was still in use in 1906 but it is not clear when it finally closed.[586]

LIBRARIES AND READING ROOMS

The town council joined the county library scheme in 1925, hosting the library initially in the court room in the *Town Hall*, though this brought protests from the volunteer librarians when the library could not open on one of its two nights a week because the room was booked by another body.[587] In 1936 it was moved to the building at *1 The Green* newly taken over by the town council and described in Chapter 7.[588] In around 1946 the county council took over the running of the premises as well as the supply of books and in 1964 the library was moved to the former *St Peter's school** at the south end of High Street, where it remains.[589] This is Tudor Gothic of 1853, by John Gould,[590] in pale brick with two gables joined by a much smaller central gable containing the doorway. The gables are coped, with finials, and each has a large mullioned window below with square head and hoodmould, and an oculus of complicated shape above.

Melksham

A reading room and lending library was opened c1815 at 'Mr. Ward's printing office'; it may have been associated with the spa and it is not known how long it survived.[591] A circulating library was being run from a bookseller's in Bank Street in 1830.[592] A Mechanics' Institute was active in the town in 1837/8 but it is not known where it was based nor for how long it existed.[593]

The town's main reading room was that belonging to the Mutual Improvement Society, which was founded in 1849 and opened its premises on the east side of Bank Street, in a building now called *Prospect House**, in 1852.[594] The design and construction were apparently all undertaken by members of the society and it contained initially a large lecture room, a reading room, classroom and committee room.[595] It is interesting if naïve, classical in style with two storeys and a cornice below a hipped roof, the ground floor rusticated. Surprisingly for a building designed for a club, there are two doors to the front, at either end with the two windows between placed oddly at a higher level and three windows above. The doors have fanlights, the windows are round-arched and the sides, of three broad bays, are of rubblestone. The society lasted until at least 1949.[596]

Melksham joined the county library scheme in 1924,

Melksham, Prospect House, Bank Street, premises of the Mutual Improvement Society

Melksham, view north up Bank Street, the Old Bank House 2nd building on the right. (Melksham and District Historical Association)

with the county library committee supplying the books and the urban district council renting a room in the former **Quaker Meeting House** in King Street.[597] The meeting house, much altered over the years, has an ashlar front below a hipped roof, with two, originally three, segmentally arched windows.[598] In 1954 the library, now being run by the county council directly and with much longer opening hours, was transferred to the **Old Bank House** in Bank Street against the protests of the district council which had not been consulted and which said having the library on the first floor there made it inaccessible to elderly people.[599] The justification for the move appeared to be that the county's 'reading scheme' store of 50,000 books could no longer be accommodated in premises in Ashton Street, Trowbridge because the lease had run out: they were taking over these premises for the book store and could accommodate the library as well, with consequent cost savings.[600] Old Bank House was the former Capital and Counties Bank, next to the George Inn on the corner of Bank Street and Lowbourne. In ashlar, its four large three-light windows divided by multiple pilasters, it was an asset to the town but both it and the inn have now been replaced by shop units.

In 1964 the new library on **Lowbourne** opened, the first to be built by the county council and designed by its architects' department.[601] A long main block has four low-angled gables, fully glazed above, looking out over a lower flat-roofed block in front. This library closed when the new **Community Campus**, also containing a swimming pool and other facilities, opened in 2022 on a site set back behind the town hall. The campus, boxy and flat-roofed as would be expected of a building of its period, signals its different purposes by the external materials. The largest box, in vertical grey metal cladding, contains the swimming pool; the large library, open and well lit, is contained in a lower section of reconstituted stone, and brown panelling clads the first floor walls of the reception area, with glass below. The building also contains the offices of the Melksham Without parish council (see Chapter 7).

Mere

A literary and scientific institution was started in 1856 in unidentified premises in Salisbury Street; it was defunct by 1862, apparently because of difficulty in finding suitable rooms.[602]

The temperance movement was strong in the town and a *Temperance Hall* was built in 1865 on the site of the former Swan Inn in Salisbury Street, promoted jointly by John Farley Rutter, a Quaker, and Charles Jupe, a silk merchant and leading Congregationalist.[603] The hall, later a Liberal Club and then the town's library (see below), had a large committee room on the first floor and a reading room below. It is built of the badly eroding local stone, a triple mullioned sash window on the ground floor illuminating the former reading room, with a narrow doorway alongside to the right. On the first floor is a four-part mullioned sash window, the central pair round-arched. In 2023 the ground floor was used as a shop and the first floor housed a snooker club.

In 1883 a cottage next to the Talbot was set up as a temporary reading room; this was replaced the following year by a part of the Angel hotel, on the corner of Church Street and Angel Lane, which was sold off and used as a Church Institute and reading room.[604]

Mere took advantage of the county library scheme in 1927 with a branch library opening in a small room in the junior school in *Boar Street*.[605] This was the former Congregational chapel of 1853, of rock-faced local stone, five tall lancet windows to the side between buttresses and to the front a porch of 1868 added on its conversion to a British School.[606] By the 1940s this room was in a poor state and in 1947, now under full county council control, the library was moved to the Liberal Club in Salisbury Street, formerly the temperance hall, where it presumably occupied the former ground floor reading room.[607]

Mere, the former Temperance Hall.

The next move came in 1970, to the former *National School* in Church Street where it remains, sharing the space with the town's museum. The school was built in 1840 to designs by John Ford of Mere, single-storey in coursed and squared rubblestone with five tall windows to the street, all mullioned with cusped flat heads below hoodmoulds, the middle one shorter above a blank inset oval plaque. The building was extended to the north in 1892 and there is a 20th century addition to the rear which provides the modern entrance.[608]

Salisbury

It is unsurprising that there should have been early moves to establish libraries and reading rooms here. In 1735 the Rev Samuel Fancourt established a library at his home in Salt Lane and by 1741 his New Circulating Library had over 5000 volumes.[609] A commercial circulating library was established in Ann Fowler's milliner's shop in Silver Street in 1779 and in 1826 there was an early attempt at bringing library facilities to the working classes with the establishment of the 'Salisbury Lending Library', although this had a short life because of the poor choice of books made available.[610]

More successful was the Salisbury and Wiltshire Library and Reading Society, established by William Bird Brodie in 1819 to provide a library and reading room and to promote discussion amongst its members.[611] It had premises on the first floor of a shop in Blue Boar Row and in 1847, following Brodie's bankruptcy, was sold to George Brown who reopened 'at the printing office on the Canal.' Brown died in 1853 but the business continued as 'Brown & Co' and the Salisbury and Wiltshire Library and Reading Society was renamed 'Brown's Public and Subscription Library'. It survived in this form until at least 1915.

In the meantime a Mechanics' Institute had been established in 1833, its library and meeting room in the Methodist Sunday school room in *Salt Lane*.[612] This, built for Presbyterians, sold to the Methodists and later to the Salvation Army, has early 18th century fabric within it but much concealed by later alterations.[613] The

Salisbury, the Assembly Rooms

LIBRARIES AND READING ROOMS

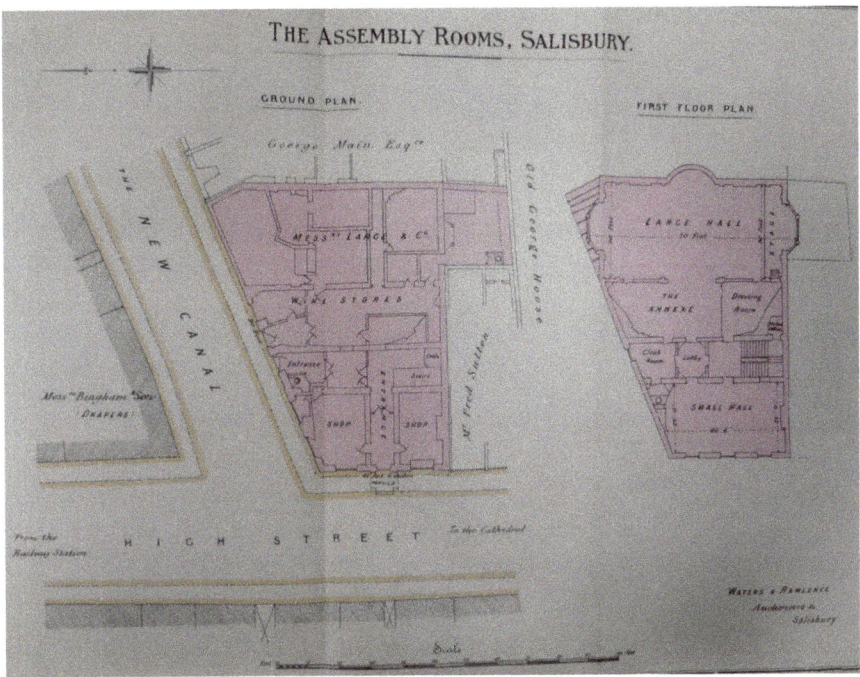

Salisbury Assembly Rooms, 1911 floor plans. (WSA)

Mechanics' Institute was not here for long, growing numbers forcing them to move in 1834 to meet in the **Assembly Rooms***. A library and reading room was set up there by 1839 but the focus was increasingly on subjects unattractive to the working class members the institute was designed to attract and in 1840 it was dissolved.[614]

The Assembly Rooms, at the corner of High Street and New Canal, were of c1803 but much altered by W H Smith when taken over for a bookshop c1923. There were large and small halls on the first floor with three tall round-arched windows from the small hall overlooking High Street and the tile-hung end of the large hall overlooking New Canal; the High Street end is now rendered under a hipped roof with a clock turret above; the entrance on New Canal is part of the W H Smith conversion.[615]

The Literary and Scientific Institution was founded in 1849 and met initially in the basement of the Assembly Rooms;[616] indeed it seems to have had no permanent premises of its own until in 1871 it opened **Hamilton Hall*** on New Street.[617] This was built on the site of a former theatre and incorporated a re-building of that to create an 800 seat concert and lecture hall, together with reading room, library and other rooms.[618] Designed by John Harding, its Gothic front is in brick with bands and patterns of other colours including much use of glazed pale blue, a brave choice.[619] It has three narrow bays, three storeys high, with Gothic-arched doorways either side of a heavily mullioned window on the ground floor with 'Literary and Scientific Institution' in stone script above it. The top floor was designed to accommodate a School of Science and Art, which had moved there by 1875, and in 1889-90 an extension was added to the left, by Michael Harding, again of three bays and three storeys but in

Salisbury, Hamilton Hall, New St.

highly contrasting domestic revival style with half-timbering to the top two floors and brick and stone, with mullioned and transomed windows, below.[620]

A further reading room was set up in St Martin's in 1876 under the chairmanship of the parish priest. The building, at *50 St Ann Street*, has a gable to the street with a double door between narrow pointed-arch windows, a first floor window asymmetrically placed above and pierced shaped bargeboards. It was extended in the early 20th century, perhaps when it became a Conservative Club, and has in more recent years been converted into a private house.[621]

Salisbury was the only urban area in the county which qualified immediately under the 1850 Library Act to support a public library from the rates, but there appeared to be little enthusiasm to do so: a poll of ratepayers in 1877 was lost and it was not until 1890 that a second poll produced a small majority in favour (984 for, 856 against).[622] In December of that year the first library was opened in the former Congregational chapel in *Endless Street*, now the Royal British Legion Club, its replacement façade hiding what may be original fabric of 1810.[623] The library prospered and better premises were soon required, and duly delivered with the aid of an offer in 1903 from the Carnegie trust to provide £4000 towards the cost.[624] The chosen site was in *Chipper Lane**, the architect A C Bothams,[625] and the building of three storeys in a Tudor Gothic style of three broad ashlar bays, the large windows mullioned and transomed, the Tudor-arched doorway to the left with decorated spandrels and 'Public Library' incised above beneath a row of miniature mock crenellations, and the outer bays with gabled heads. The building opened in 1905, was added to by the *Young*

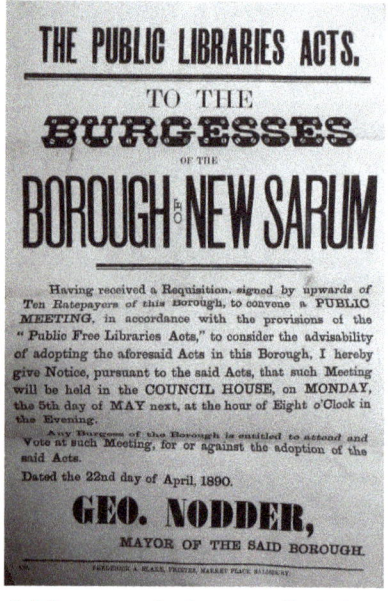

Salisbury, poster for the 1890 poll which produced a small majority in favour of a public library. (WSA)

Art Gallery next door in 1914 (see Chapter 5), and variously adapted over later years until the increasing demands outstripped its limited capacity and it closed in 1975.[626] It was restored in 1989 by Brewer, Smith and Brewer and is now in commercial use.

There had been co-operation on book stocks with the county council from the late 1920s but it was not until 1974, following local government reorganisation, that the county took over full control of the libraries service. This made Salisbury the centre of a network of libraries in the south of the county and the new library, opened in the former *Market House* in 1975, had to take on this additional role: the building is described in Chapter 3. The city council had had a policy of not supplying branch libraries, wishing to attract people into the city's shopping centre, but a mobile library service was introduced in a compromise when the county council took over.[627] The central library remains in the Market House and the mobile library service continues, though integrated into a countywide network.

Salisbury, the former library, Chipper Lane; Young Art Gallery to the left

Swindon

Swindon is famous for its Mechanics' Institute, both its pioneering first 100 plus years and also, unfortunately, its sad state of increasing dereliction since its closure in 1986. The other main element to the story here is the late appearance of a council-owned public library in the town. As with most other towns, Swindon had at least one circulating library from a relatively early date: the first recorded here is that run from a bookseller's in Wood Street in 1830 and this was still in place in 1842.[628]

Reading Rooms and the Mechanics' Institute

Though the New Town Mechanics' Institute dominates the story, the Old Town also had a sequence of literary institutions, all aimed at keeping 'respectable' working class men out of the pubs. The first of these was the Library and Literary Institute, formed in 1851 with rooms at an unidentified location in the High Street.[629] It seems not to have lasted long because in 1859 the Literary Institute opened, with a room in *Bath Terrace* on Bath Road, described in Chapter 9. It was noted at the opening ceremony that the previous institute had closed through lack of support and that there had been some grumbling from New Swindon that opening another institute in the Old Town might undermine the Mechanics' Institute, an argument that was countered by the claim that no-one was going to walk from the Old Town to the New on a winter's evening.[630]

By 1861 the Bath Terrace reading room had been joined by another based in the **Victoria Rooms** at 8 Victoria Street, and the two were discussing a merger.[631] It is not clear whether the merger happened but the original reading room in Victoria Street (now Victoria Road) seems not to have lasted long because in 1872 it was reopened as the Literary Institute and Reading Room.[632] By 1882 this too was described as having had 'a very precarious existence', having several times been in a state of bankruptcy, but there had been an upturn in its fortunes, by implication because its membership had moved from working class men to those who were better off.[633] It was still in being in 1885 and may have lasted until the turn of the century.[634] It is not certain where 8 Victoria Street was, given the subsequent renaming and renumbering of the street, but it seems likely that it was next door to the former Newspaper House at what is now 100 Victoria Road.[635]

Swindon's status in the later 19th century as a major industrial town naturally gave rise to a number of working men's clubs, many of which had libraries though their main emphasis was on other things. The first of these may have been the Bridge Street Club, established in 1880, and that was followed by around 20 more by the turn of the century; the number probably peaked at around 27 in 1948 but there were still 20 in 1965.[636]

The *Mechanics' Institute** in Emlyn Square, is of national importance as one of the pioneers in the development of mechanics' institutes and one of the first effectively public libraries in the country.[637] It emerged from an initiative by Great Western Railway employees in 1843, who set up a library within the works which, supported by the management, was soon offering a reading room and a programme of lectures; it was designated as the Mechanics' Institute in 1844. Most people in New Swindon worked for the GWR, or were family members of people who did, so this

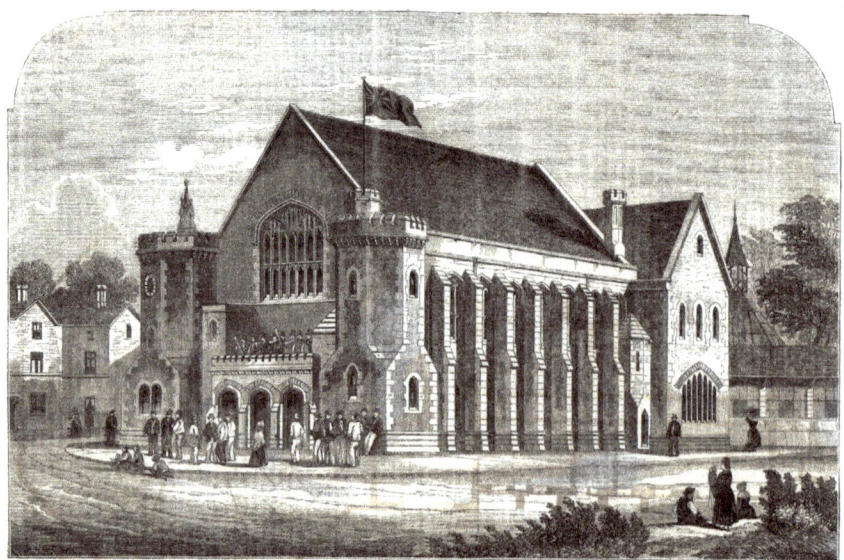

Swindon, the Mechanics' Institute as planned; note the band on the balcony and the octagonal market to the rear. (The Builder, courtesy of Local Studies (Swindon Library & Information Service)).

Swindon, the Mechanics' Institute reading room in its final form: high-ceilinged grandeur. (Local Studies (Swindon Library & Information Service)).

created what was effectively a public library some years before the first library under the 1850 Libraries Act was established in Birmingham: hence the claim that Swindon had the country's first public library.

A recession in the late 1840s slowed the provision of a separate building but in 1853 a site was selected and leased by the GWR to the New Swindon Improvement Company. Here was to be built the new Mechanics' Institute with, at the south end, a covered market to make up for the shortage of shops in the New Town. The architect appointed was Edward Roberts of London and the Institute opened in 1854, the octagonal market having opened six months earlier. The ground floor contained baths, a canteen, offices, and the reading room transversely at the south end; on the first floor was a large hall with a stage.

By 1892 the baths and canteen had been moved elsewhere and the market was deemed to be no longer necessary (see Chapter 3). A large southern extension, to designs by Brightwen Binyon of Ipswich, replaced the market, creating a much larger reading room, more library space and a number of other new rooms. There were further alterations later, including an accumulation of single-storey extensions round the main block, but the last major change came in 1930 when a fire destroyed the proscenium, wings and stage roof: the rebuilding by R J Beswick and Son of Swindon produced a large and conspicuous fly-tower.

The 1855 building is Perpendicular Gothic, a large traceried window facing the railway works between castellated turrets either side of an entrance porch, Gothic windows between heavy buttresses along the sides and a transverse block to the south

Swindon, the Mechanics' Institute 1892 extension, more down-to-earth than the original. (Local Studies (Swindon Library & Information Service))

containing the reading room below and the theatre stage above. The 1892 extension is in a less assertive Jacobethan style with two storeys of coursed rubblestone, ashlar dressings and mullioned and transomed windows. The 1930 block in the centre, making no attempt to respect the previous architecture, is a large rectangular brick slab.

The Institute came into British Railways' ownership on railway nationalisation and suffered declining use and lack of investment until it closed in 1986 with the closure of the railway works. Since then, despite being listed as grade 2*, the building has declined substantially in the ownership of various developers, with no signs at the time of writing that any successful resolution to the problem is imminent. The result is that a building which ought to be the pride of the New Town is instead a boarded-up, graffiti-covered eyesore.

The conspicuous success of the Mechanics' Institute led to demands for branch reading rooms closer to workers' homes in the expanding town. The first, in 1902, involved the former Swindon Waterworks offices of 1876 at what is now **66 Bath Road.**[638] This was two-storey brick with stone dressings, round-arched below and square above, and an open archway through at the centre. Taken over by the Institute, providing a reading room and smoking room, it was used until 1932 but demolished in 1967 to make way for a block of flats.

Two more branch reading rooms were opened in 1904. One was in the former Baptist chapel at the corner of *Cricklade Road* and Ferndale Road. This was of brick with stone dressings, subsequently converted to the Plessey Social Club with a glazed front almost entirely concealing the original. It was still operating in 1950 but probably closed by 1954.[639] The second was at the junction of *Rodbourne Road* and Morris Street, the only one to be purpose-built, dated 1904 and with an inscription 'GWR Mechanics' Institution Branch Reading Rooms'. Designed by R J Beswick in brick with stone dressings, there are three pairs of generously-sized sash windows to each floor facing Rodbourne Road with a shaped parapet above; the front is curved to the street corner and the side facing Morris Street is more plain. This also lasted until the early 1950s and is now the local headquarters of St John Ambulance.

Public Libraries

The dominance of the Mechanics' Institute library may be one main factor explaining the slow arrival of public libraries in the town, but at any event it was not until 1943 that the first one was opened by the borough in a corner of the ground floor of *McIlroy's department store* in Regent Street, now much altered.[640] It had been preceded by a commercially run library in the same location, opened in 1935 but probably not lasting for long.[641]

Despite this apparently unpromising location the library was of some size, but better premises were obviously needed and in 1949 it relocated to temporary prefabricated buildings behind the new town hall. In 1976, after the county council assumed responsibility for libraries in the town, these were replaced by more of the same.[642] Both sets were as unprepossessing as the description implies but it was not until 2006 that the second set was demolished, the long delay apparently because the borough council had prioritized the provision of neighbourhood libraries in the town's new housing areas.[643] The eventual replacement was the *New Library** by Nic Newland and Tony Currivan of Swindon Borough Architects, which opened in

Swindon New Library. (Courtesy of D and M Ball).

2008.[644] This takes the shape of a truncated horseshoe, fitting neatly to the rear of the town hall. The three-storey front, in brick below a notably extended roof containing an attic storey, is punctuated by tapered buttresses below substantial pale blue metal pots forming part of a natural ventilation system. The entrance is in a circular tower and a separate oval tower to the rear contains the stairway; the interior spaces are relatively low-ceilinged and unexceptional.

The great expansion of the town after the second world war was matched with a substantial number of branch libraries in the new housing areas, as noted above. Early planning c1965 matched proposed libraries with local populations[645] and the buildings followed. A small number have since closed but in 2023 ten were open, all but three now run by local bodies – usually the parish council – rather than the Borough Council, and they are often incorporated into community centres.

The Borough ones are at *North Swindon* (2003 - Orbital retail park), *Park* (1964 – in a development by Frederick Gibberd and partners) and *West Swindon* (1985 – in Link Centre, by Thamesdown borough architects, large, metal clad and supported by external masts like a stadium).[646] Of the remainder, those at *Beechcroft* (Beechcroft Road), *Liden* (Barrington Close), *Moredon and Rodbourne Cheney* (Church Walk North), *Penhill* (Penhill Drive) and *Pinetrees* (the Circle - 2011 by Capita Symonds) are unexceptionally of their time. That at *Even Swindon* is in the community centre (1990 by Thamesdown Borough Architects, Jennings Street), of cruciform shape in brick, the front with a long roofline sloping up to a perspex tunnel vault above a tall glass entrance screen.

Finally, there is the *Old Town* library in the Swindon Arts Centre on Devizes Road. This is in the former Bradford Hall, of early 20th century date, at one time a dance hall but opened as an arts centre in 1956, extended in 2002-3 and refurbished in 2010. The Old Town library relocated there at that date from its previous premises in a shop unit at the top of Victoria Road.[647] The original building is in coursed rubblestone, gable to the road, the ground floor much altered but with three windows at the first floor, the centre a pair beneath a lunette, and a clock inset above.

Trowbridge

By early in the 19th century there were lending libraries attached to three Baptist Sunday schools and one in the (nonconformist) British schools, illustrating the leading role played by nonconformists in the town by that date.[648] There was at least one commercial library, run from a bookseller's in Fore Street by 1842.[649] A Literary and Scientific Institution was founded in 1839, meeting in the British school, but it seems likely that it was dissolved in 1841.[650] The town's Mechanics' Institute was more long-lasting: in existence by 1842, it met initially in a former factory at the back of the Market Place though this was destroyed by fire in 1846.[651] There were immediate efforts to raise funds for a replacement building[652] and, having spent some years in unidentified premises elsewhere, the Mechanics' Institution moved into the newly built *Court Hall* – described in Chapter 4 – in 1854, sharing this with the County Court.[653] The Institution remained there until its demise in 1866, the cause, according to a newspaper report, the fact that it was never supported by 'the class for whom it was designed'.[654]

Various private and circulating libraries remained, but the first move towards establishing a free public library came with an offer from the Carnegie Trust in 1903; this, however, was refused, presumably on financial grounds.[655] The decisive initiative came when Trowbridge joined the county library scheme in 1924.[656] To start with, a large cupboard in the entrance of the Town Hall (see Chapter 2) was used, in 1926 open only on Wednesday afternoons.[657] Shortly afterwards the library was moved to the court room there, but again with very limited space for book shelves.[658]

In 1932 the library moved from these inadequate premises into a semi-basement room in the **Victoria Institute**.[659] The institute was built to commemorate the diamond jubilee but Victoria was dead by the time it opened in 1902, by which time cost had gone well over budget principally because of a choice of stone rather than brick for its construction. Designed by T R Davison of London, it stood at the junction of Market Street and Castle Street – indeed its construction fulfilled an

Trowbridge, the Victoria Institute. (WBR).

earlier pledge to create a proper road joining Castle Street to the market place – and had a front of five main bays facing Castle Street. There were classical sash windows with alternating triangular and segmental pediments matched with a central doorway between pilasters and below two successive segmental arches, one for a window, one for a pediment and both with a distinctly Arts and Crafts feel. The project ran out of money and was never completed: the side return to Market Street was of three bays but cut short as a consequence of this, stonework left projecting as if it was planned at some stage to complete it; the third window was almost at the corner making the whole uncomfortably unbalanced.[660]

The Victoria Institute was built as a school; its facilities were criticized but it served various educational purposes for many years before being taken over as a magistrates' court and finally by the newly-formed West Wiltshire District Council (see Chapter 7). It was not thought well of by the planners and was demolished in 1984,[661] to be replaced by a small block of shops.

In 1947 the library moved into perhaps the least appropriate of all its temporary homes, the former **Congregational chapel** in Silver Street.[662] In the mid-1950s there were plans for a new library and museum in Polebarn Road, by the park entrance, but these were abandoned because of lack of funds and the library had to continue in what were agreed to be highly unsatisfactory conditions in the chapel until that was eventually demolished c1959.[663] At this point the library moved into the former county offices in **Hill Street** (see Chapter 7), before a further move in 1984 to occupy most of the ground floor of the **East Wing** of **County Hall** (see Chapter 7).[664] This was a four-storey office block on the east side of Bythesea Road, opened in 1971 and since demolished.[665] From there it moved finally in 2012 to the remodelled western extension of **County Hall**, described in Chapter 7.[666]

Trowbridge, the new library at County Hall.

Trowbridge was also the headquarters for the county library service from 1919, when an old army hut was placed in the grounds of the Adcroft boys' school at **Prospect Place** to act as both office and book store.[667] This was of substantial size but, simply constructed of timber, was not for long considered suitable for the task. It was replaced by another hut in 1925[668] and in 1934 this was supplemented, and some years later replaced, by the *Prospect Place* building which still stands there.[669] This was designed by T Walker, the county architect, in brick with stone dressings under a hipped roof, single-storey with four sash windows either side, the central two contained with the doorway under a broad pediment. The left hand side was given over to the book store, the right hand to offices.[670]

This building remained the county library headquarters until 1969 when it was moved to part of the former Airsprung factory at **Cradle Bridge**, almost opposite County Hall, a large two-storey building in blockwork with metal windows, later demolished.[671] The final move was into County Hall itself.

It is understood that Trowbridge did not have any branch libraries.[672]

Warminster

The town had a 'news room and library' in the premises of a bookseller from at least 1830.[673] A Literary and Scientific Institution was formed in 1834 and, with the financial help of the Marquess of Bath and others, opened its new building in the *Market Place** in 1838.[674] Designed by Edward Blore in Tudor style, its main gabled ashlar façade, of two storeys and an attic, faces Weymouth Street.[675] The asymmetrical front has mullioned and transomed windows either side of a doorway with Tudor arch and elaborately ornamented dripmould above. The front to the Market Place has a single set of 10-pane mullioned and transomed windows, though it is likely that the linked building to the left, with three narrow gabled attic turrets and two shop windows below, was part of the same construction.[676]

The Institution was clearly for the well-off, with an annual subscription in 1838 of two guineas,[677] but seems to have suffered from a chronic shortage of funds: parts of the premises were always let out and by 1866 the institution was discussing letting out more of the building and selling some of the objects they had by then accumulated for their museum.[678] It was wound up in 1875.[679]

Warminster, the former Literary and Scientific Institute (see also print in chapter introduction)

A Mechanics' Institution was formed in 1838, was still active in 1843 but may not have survived for long thereafter.[680] It had a reading room and class rooms in East Street c1842.[681]

The Warminster Athenaeum was formed in 1851 for 'intellectual enjoyment and education'.[682] The promoters considered the Literary Institute to be aimed too much at the more affluent, though they did offer to combine with them, settling in the end for leasing a room on the ground floor of the Literary Institute building. It seems that they moved as early as 1855 to the former **London Inn** in High Street which however was soon demolished to make way for the new *Athenaeum building** on that site, opened in 1858. This was designed by W J Stent to contain a library, reading room and classrooms to the front and a lecture room and committee room to the rear. Stent's front façade, neo-Jacobean, has two storeys plus attic. Doors at either side of a central two-storey bay – the ground floor of this now replaced by a new entrance – have suitably Jacobean doorcases, the windows are mullioned and transomed and the three attic gables are also Jacobean in style.

The building has been very much changed over the years, the two major alterations being demolition of the original lecture hall in 1879 and its replacement by the larger Bleeck Memorial Hall by T H Wyatt, and the demolition of the adjacent Ship Inn in 1901 and its replacement by a building for the new Technical School, part of the original Athenaeum having been already used for that purpose. The Bleeck hall, hard to see but with workmanlike brick at the sides and rear, had a capacity of 500. The school building is in a stripped-back version of Stent's neo-Jacobean, the windows and gables timid but the main door echoing those of the original building.

Warminster, the Athenaeum.

The Athenaeum struggled financially throughout its life and by the end of the 19th century its original function had more or less ceased. It was used subsequently as a cinema and had other uses, and other crises, before the Warminster Athenaeum Trust was formed in 2000 to restore it as a community-owned centre, primarily for theatre and cinema.

The Christ Church reading room and working men's club was established in 1885 through the efforts of the vicar and housed in two converted cottages in **Sambourne Road** provided by Lord Bath.[683] These were at the south end of the road, on the east side close to what is now the junction between Sambourne Road and

Weymouth Street and almost opposite what is now The Beeches.[684] The combined cottages provided a large reading room 35ft by 14ft, match-board lined and with new larger windows. The reading room was still in operation in 1924 but may not have survived for long after that and was eventually demolished, presumably to allow construction of the revised road junction now at that point.[685]

The Urban District Council was invited to join the county libraries scheme in 1924 and, after unsuccessfully approaching the Athenaeum for the use of their reading room to this end, eventually opened in December of that year in the girls' school in *North Row*.[686] This, formerly the Old Meeting and later to be town council offices, is described in Chapter 7. The library was open for one hour on two evenings a week.[687]

In 1949 the library moved to a first floor room in the *school building* adjacent to the Athenaeum[688] and from there in 1957 to *Portway House*, recently acquired by the Urban District Council and described in Chapter 7.[689] In 1982 it moved finally to its first purpose-built home, in *Three Horseshoes Yard*, designed by Wiltshire County Architects.[690] This is in brick with a long tiled roof giving the sides and front a forbidding feel, especially by the doorway which is inset like a gaping mouth, though the rear is more comfortably vernacular.

Westbury

As with other towns, Westbury had a circulating library run from a bookseller's by at least 1842.[691] The Westbury Mutual Improvement Society, later the Westbury Athenaeum, was established in 1840 for 'the diffusion of useful knowledge amongst the working classes' by providing a reading room, a library and a programme of lectures. It operated until c1851 in a room at an unknown location before being leased a site on the bend of Bratton Road opposite to where the Laverton Institute was later built, and here the *Athenaeum* was erected, a single-storey flat-roofed building.[692] The society continued here for another 25 years but declining membership led to its closure in 1876 after which the building was acquired by Abraham Laverton.[693] It was later used as a masonic lodge but was demolished after 1936[694] and the site is now part of a car park.

A Literary Institution was formed in the town, perhaps in the early 1850s. It seems not to have lasted long although the *Laverton Institute*, described in Chapter 7, was intended to include a literary institution when it opened.[695] It is possible that the Literary Institution was simply another name for what became the Athenaeum.

The town joined the county library scheme at the beginning of 1925 and the library was located first in the *Town Hall*, described in Chapter 2.[696] Following complaints about congestion during the very limited opening hours it moved to the larger court room there in 1926.[697] It seems to have stayed in the town hall until 1938, by which time the county education committee was paying rent but objected to a proposed charge of £24 a year from the urban district council; the result was a move that same year to the *Oddfellows' Hall* on Bratton Road where it remained until 1946.[698] The Oddfellows Hall is nearly opposite the Laverton Institute and now converted into a private house with an inserted floor. The building is of brick with stone dressings, the hall end-on to the road, with a gabled end half-timbered above a mullioned and transomed window and an inset coat of arms below that, the door awkwardly to one side in an extension which looks like an afterthought. The bend in the road exposes the side of the building to view and here, the best feature, a massive chimney stack rises above a four-light basement window.

The library was closed for a year during the war but in 1946, after an apparently failed attempt by the county to acquire the Oddfellows Hall by compulsory purchase, it was moved back into the town hall.[699] With more space still needed, alternative locations were considered in the 1960s, including a 1964 proposal for a combined library and clinic in Haynes Road,[700] but in the end the county bought **Westbury House*** on Edward Street in 1969 and it opened as the new library in 1970.[701] The library remains there, joined later by the Heritage Centre in an upstairs room.

Westbury Library in Westbury House, the plain 18th century front

Westbury, Westbury House rear elevation with exuberant mid-19th century detailing, probably by W J Stent

The street frontage of Westbury House is plain late 18th century, in brick with three storeys separated by stone plat bands and a 19th century stone porch. The rear, extended after the house was bought by Abraham Laverton in the 1850s and probably designed by W J Stent,[702] has much more going on. Here, sets of linked arched windows and a columned round-arched porch in front of an inset bay give an almost Italianate feel, despite the brick. It is no surprise to learn that this was from that time the entrance front to the house.

Wilton

A Literary Institution was founded, probably c1853,[703] and met initially in the *National School*, now the community centre, in West Street[704] By 1867 it had premises in *Silver Street*, almost certainly at No. 4, an early 19th century two-storey building of four bays in painted brick, the roof hipped at one end.[705] In 1880 the Earl of Pembroke

LIBRARIES AND READING ROOMS

erected next door the Talbot and Wyvern Hall, for the use of the Institution but also containing a public coffee room.[706] As well as the coffee room this had a reading room, a library, a dining room and a large room upstairs for meetings and concerts; the existing reading room and library in No. 4, now linked to the new building, were to be converted into a room for billiards and bagatelle.[707] The Talbot and Wyvern was constructed in a lively neo-Tudor, the windows mullioned and the first floor half-timbered and jettied forward in a central bay.

In 1911 the reading room was divided in two by a wood and glass screen because of an incursion of card and chess players, and the Institution was still in existence in 1920 though it may not have thrived for long after that.[708] The building was later used by other groups but became derelict and vandalized and was demolished, it is understood, in the early 1960s.[709] It was replaced by a neo-Georgian house, 20 Kingsbury Square.

Wilton Library.

A Literary and Scientific Society is referred to in 1868 and again in 1872 and 1888, and is probably another name for the Literary Institute.[710] The Anglican church also seems to have been involved in similar work, with reference to a Parochial Library and Reading Room in 1855 and, after the turn of the century, a report of 'work of a similar kind' to that of the Literary Institution carried out by the rector.[711]

Wilton joined the county library scheme in 1926 but the location of the first library is not known.[712] Negotiations in the 1940s to move to rooms in the town hall proved fruitless and in 1951 the library moved to the former ***Quaker meeting house*** in South Street, where it remains.[713] This is of 1883, in pale brick with red brick bands and window arches, the gable end facing the street with windows either side of the door and a single window above, the whole simple and giving onto an equally simple single room interior.[714]

Royal Wootton Bassett

A Mechanics' Institute was established in 1838 and a Literary and Scientific Institute in 1839 but it seems likely that neither survived long.[715] An early Mutual Improvement Society was formed around mid-century but seems not to have lasted long.[716] Other efforts followed, including a reading room at Mr. Puce's in the High Street which opened in 1875, but it was the re-establishment of the Mutual Improvement Society c1886 through the efforts of Lord William Fitzmaurice which seems to have had the most impact.[717] The Society met in the British School and in the ***Town Hall*** after that was restored but it too had a relatively short life, closing c1896.[718]

A town library opened in the restored Town Hall in 1890, its collection based on a small library transferred here from the National School and added to by donations from Lady Meux and others; the collection of the Mutual Improvement Society was also handed over when that closed.[719] It was open on one evening per week and had an annual subscription of 2/-.[720]

When the county library service started in the 1920s an offer was made of a joint venture with the town library but this was refused and in 1926[721] the county council went ahead on its own.[722] This left the two libraries in competition and, although the subscription payment for the town library was modest, the competition was such that the town library closed in 1936.[723]

At around this time the county library was transferred to the Town Hall and stayed there until it moved in 1970 to pre-fabricated buildings in what is now **Borough Fields**.[724] Finally, the new library was built as part of the *Borough Fields* shopping centre in 1990.[725] Here it fits in anonymously enough in pale brick with metal-framed windows.

7
Council Buildings

Introduction

Few council buildings predate the 19th century. Earlier local government bodies needed rooms in which to meet but they employed few if any staff in the modern sense of the word, and the meeting room could as well be in an inn as anywhere else. Only the gradual accumulation of extra responsibilities, and the growth in population, led eventually to the purpose-built office buildings which characterise modern local government.

This pattern of growth has produced a very mixed bag of council buildings. The town halls, described in Chapter 2, are generally the most significant but there are also more modern buildings of distinction. And between these a wide variety of other town houses and the like were used, many of real interest and well worth describing.

The history of the different local government bodies and their powers is confusing so a brief sketch follows to complete this introduction.

Origins

By the end of the 18th century there was a mix of bodies with different and often overlapping jurisdiction over aspects of town life. These included the boroughs; the quarter sessions, whose responsibilities by then extended well beyond the purely judicial into county-level administrative activities such as licensing of alehouses; the remaining manorial courts; and the ecclesiastical parishes exercising powers through the parish vestries, for example for the upkeep of local roads.

The counties were becoming more important as the focus of local administration and since 1739 the local taxes levied by the quarter sessions had been unified into a single 'county rate' under the control of a county treasurer. A county surveyor was also appointed, to supervise the building and maintenance of roads and bridges, though local surveyors were still active late in that century. The county surveyor is particularly significant in the description of public buildings for it was very often he who had the responsibility for designing them.

The 19th Century

The same general position applied for much of the 19th century but a series of Acts of Parliament reflected the growing importance attached to securing effective local administration. The Municipal Corporations Act of 1835 was essentially a measure to introduce more democracy into the election of town councils and give them more powers of improvement. The Poor Law Amendment Act of the previous year had allowed parishes to be grouped together into Poor Law Unions, each administered by a local board of guardians, with the intention that the grouped parishes would be in a position to provide workhouses as part of the harsh legislation intended to bear down upon the poor.

More legislation followed. The Public Health Act 1848 provided for the establishment of a local board of health in towns to regulate sewage and control the spread of diseases. Public Health Acts in 1873 and 1875 built on this to regulate better the poor law, public health and sanitation. Urban sanitary districts were created from the previous local boards of health, and rural sanitary districts were also set up. The workhouse board rooms provided a convenient place for many of these bodies to meet.

By late in the century it was clear that the existing arrangements were not coping adequately with a growing population and increasing responsibilities: the local bodies were unco-ordinated and amateurly run and the quarter sessions, their responsibilities already eroded by the creation of the new boards, were still not able to deal with the quantity of administration required at county level. The Municipal Corporations Act 1882 was to some extent a tidying up of previous legislation but provided for transfer of powers to boroughs from local boards and sanitary authorities. More significant was the Local Government Act of 1888 which established county councils. It also established county boroughs, larger urban areas which were to act as counties in their own right and did not come under county council control: there were none of these in Wiltshire although Swindon applied to become one in 1913, without success.[726] The history of the Wiltshire county council is discussed in the place-by-place analysis below mainly under Trowbridge, where its offices were and still are based.

The other significant piece of legislation at the end of the century was the Local Government Act of 1894 which produced a second tier of local government by dividing the county into urban and rural district councils. The municipal boroughs reformed after 1835 (Calne, Chippenham, Malmesbury, Marlborough, Salisbury and Swindon) were brought into this system as special cases, and the remaining urban districts were at Bradford, Melksham, Trowbridge, Warminster and Westbury. The other towns, with all the rural areas, were divided into 18 rural districts.[727]

The previous sanitary districts were absorbed into this new system, their important role one reason why so many rural district councils met at the workhouses for many years, but the poor law unions and boards of guardians remained separate until the workhouses were wound up in the following century. The 1894 Act also established civil parishes, distinct from the ecclesiastical parishes which thereafter lost their remaining civil responsibilities.

These legislational changes did not lead to any great increase in staff numbers. For example, when the Warminster local board of health was set up in 1867 it had 15 members and just four officials - a clerk, a treasurer, a surveyor and a rate-collector - none of them full-time.[728] Even where there were paid officials it was common for them to work from their own offices: in the previous year the offices of the Trowbridge local board were stated to be at the home of the clerk, William Frame.[729] In one later but extreme example Charles Gough, clerk to Calne borough council, worked from his private office rather than the town hall for his whole tenure, from 1911 to the mid-1950s.[730] With the exception of the county's largest towns, it seems that towards the end of the 19th century there appears to have been little requirement for office space which could not be met in either the various town halls or the private offices of the chief officers.

The 20th and 21st Centuries

The system set up by the 1888 and 1894 Acts lasted a surprisingly long time, more or less unchanged until 1974, although a number of the rural districts were combined in 1929 under the Local Government Act of that year, reducing the county total from 18 to 12. This Act also further extended county council powers and finally ended the poor law unions. There were a number of reviews of the system following the Second World War but it was not until the Local Government Act of 1972 that major change was introduced. In a simplified but in some areas controversial restructuring, all previous first and second tier authorities were removed and, in counties such as Wiltshire, replaced by a county council with increased powers and a small number of district councils. In Wiltshire there were five such:

- Kennet (Devizes and Marlborough areas), with main office at Devizes
- North Wiltshire (Calne, Chippenham, Cricklade, Malmesbury and Wootton Bassett), with main office at Chippenham
- Salisbury (Salisbury, Wilton and Amesbury), with main office at Salisbury
- Thamesdown (Swindon and Highworth), with main office at Swindon
- West Wiltshire (Bradford, Melksham, Trowbridge, Warminster and Westbury) with main office at Trowbridge

Since then there have been two further significant changes. In 1997 the Swindon and Highworth area was designated as a separate county-level unitary authority, independent of Wiltshire county, and in 2009 the remaining district councils were abolished and Wiltshire County became a unitary authority.

The creation of the new county council might have been expected to have a large impact on the requirement for office space but it still had only 26 staff in its clerical establishment by 1906, together with a smattering of specialist chief officers.[731] At the next level down, in 1924 when Chippenham borough first felt the need for space outside that provided by the town hall and took offices at 5 High Street, it still had only seven paid officials together with presumably a small number of clerical staff.[732] From then on, however, staff numbers grew at an accelerating pace: the county council had just over 1,000 staff by the early 1950s.[733] The powers and responsibilities of local government have of course increased greatly since then, leading to the large council buildings now found in Salisbury, Swindon and Trowbridge.

It follows from the above that the range of buildings described in this chapter is a wide one. Amongst these, workhouses are given brief mention since they are not truly within the scope of this book but need some description because rural district councils so often met at them. Overall, there are perhaps surprisingly few modern office blocks here, and some of these are appealing. Alongside them is a wide range of urban buildings of the 19th century and earlier which are brought into focus by their role as council offices for part of their lives. Many are well worth a second look.

The Buildings

Amesbury

Although sometimes called a borough in the middle ages, Amesbury had no significant institution for self-government until the end of the 19th century, though it did have both a Poor Law Union and a Highway and Rural Sanitary District. In 1894 it was established as the centre of the Amesbury Rural District Council (RDC), whose meetings were held at the **Workhouse**.[734] This was south of the town, west of the Salisbury road, and was opened in 1837.[735] Constructed of brick and flint, it was a variation on a standard 'square' design for the many workhouses being built at that time and was designed by William Bonython Moffatt.[736] The workhouse was eventually demolished in 1967 and replaced by the houses of Avonstoke Close.

In 1920 the town made an unsuccessful application to the county council to be designated as an urban district. The RDC thereafter continued meeting at the Workhouse, which in 1930 was redesignated as a public assistance institution under its control, until in 1949 it bought **Redworth House**, a large house north of Flower Lane.[737] It remained there until replaced by its successor authority, the new Salisbury District Council, in 1974. Thereafter the building was shared between the district council and Wiltshire County Council until it closed in 2004 and was demolished to allow the redevelopment of the adjacent supermarket.[738]

The lower tier town council seems to have shared Redworth House but the earlier location for meetings is not known. It moved in 2008 to offices at the **Bowman Centre** in Shears Drive.[739] This is in a housing area south east of the town centre and is T-shaped in brick with tall semi-hipped gables, each with a substantial window, one of them balconied.

Bradford on Avon

Until the early 19th century Bradford was governed by the usual mixture of petty sessions, the parish vestry and, from 1834, the Poor Law Union.[740] In 1839 the government of the immediate urban area, in a circle of one mile radius from the town centre, was moved by act of parliament to a new body of town commissioners, and in 1872 Bradford became an urban sanitary district under the public health act of that year.

Previous bodies may have met in the room above the former market house at the east end of the Shambles but that was abandoned in the early 19th century[741] and thereafter they, and their successors the town commissioners, probably met in the **Swan Inn** until the erection of the **Town Hall** in 1855. The various bodies moved to the town hall at once and remained there for the rest of their existence.[742] The town hall is described in Chapter 2.

The 1894 Act created two new bodies, the Bradford Urban District Council (UDC) and the Bradford Rural District Council (RDC), to replace the various predecessors. Both used the town hall for their meetings[743] but in 1911 the UDC decided that **Westbury House*** would be a more cost-effective location for their offices and moved there.[744] The RDC remained at the town hall for some years longer but

Bradford on Avon, Westbury House

eventually joined the UDC in Westbury House in the late 1920s.⁷⁴⁵ The last public body to move there were the petty sessions, needing to leave the town hall at the end of 1954 when it was sold for conversion to a Catholic church.⁷⁴⁶

Westbury House, just south of the town bridge, is a fine early Georgian clothier's house, now 2* listed, the two main fronts of three storeys and five bays and both with balustrades at roof level. The garden front has angle strips to the corners interrupted by string courses, the ground floor windows tall and segment-headed alongside an open-pedimented doorway; the upper windows mostly flat-headed. The south front is in exuberant baroque style, characterised by an ornamented central bay with pilasters of succeeding orders at each level. It remained a private house until 1906 and one owner, Richard Bethell, rose to become Lord Chancellor as Baron Westbury, hence the name.⁷⁴⁷

By 1953 the Bradford and Melksham RDC had moved to *Abbey House** in Church Street, presumably because of the increasing space requirements of the two councils hitherto sharing Westbury House.[748] This is another grand Georgian clothier's house; built in 1774, its three-storey five-bay façade dominates the view down Church Street, the central three bays advanced under a pediment. It also is 2* listed.[749]

Local government reorganisation in 1974 replaced the UDC and RDC with the new West Wiltshire district council, based in Trowbridge, and so led to the end of second tier local government in the town. The successor town council was located in offices built on the north side of *St Margaret's Hall*, by the river south of the town bridge. This is a late 18th or early 19th century dye-house which closed in 1903, in 1917 was converted into a cinema and in 1959 was bought by the UDC and refurbished as a public hall. Expansion of the town council's responsibilities by transfer from Wiltshire Council led to its move in 2022 to *Kingston House*, on the south side of Kingston Road. This is of 1740,[750] ashlar with, at the west end, Palladian pedimented three-bay facades front and back. The eastern section, a later addition in similar style, nevertheless undermines the symmetry of the original.

Calne

Calne was an ancient municipal borough and had a revised charter issued in 1689 which lasted until 1835 when it was replaced under the Municipal Corporations Act.[751] Various local government functions were carried out by other bodies but in 1889 the borough absorbed the local board of health, adopted its wider boundaries and from then on had much wider powers. The corporation is believed to have met at the *Old Town Hall* from the 1820s and was certainly meeting at the *New Town Hall* from its opening in 1886: both are described in Chapter 2. Some staff maintained private offices throughout this period and worked only part time for the council: Charles Gough, for example, town clerk from 1911 until the middle 1950s, worked for the whole period from his office at 28 Church Street.[752]

The Calne Rural District Council was formed in 1894 and met at the *Union Workhouse*, north of Curzon Street close to the cemetery.[753] This was built in 1847-8, designed by Thomas Allom, a long T-shaped three-storey block in neo-Jacobean style.[754] It was demolished c1945.[755] In 1934 the RDC combined with that for Chippenham and its offices were thereafter located in the latter town.

In 1974 both borough council and RDC were replaced by the North Wiltshire District Council under local government reorganisation. This body had its offices in Chippenham so Calne was left without second tier local government. The successor town council still runs the town hall for hire for events and used it for its offices for many years, based in the former police quarters accessed from Patford Street.[756] The offices are now opposite in *Bank House*, a former Barclays bank which it shares with a pub. Dated 1901, this is in neo-Jacobean style, in stone block with round-arched windows below and mullioned and transomed ones above. A substantial central gable, drawn forwards, contains one door with a further door in a columned porch on the angle at the corner with Church Street.

Chippenham

Chippenham became a chartered borough in 1554 and the corporation was restructured in both 1836 and 1889, throughout this period meeting at the *Yelde Hall* and then, from 1841, at the new *Town Hall*, both described in Chapter 2.[757] A separate body of commissioners was set up in 1834; this was replaced by a local board in 1870 and this in turn was absorbed into the corporation in 1889.

The Chippenham Rural District Council, formed in 1894, met at the *Workhouse* on Rowden Hill, now the Chippenham Community Hospital. This replaced a previous building in 1858-9 and was designed by Christopher Creeke in Dutch Renaissance style. The long entrance block has a central two-storey gatehouse and the main block behind, of two storeys, has a large hall and a central octagonal cupola. There were further service buildings to the rear, now largely replaced by modern additions.

The corporation, meanwhile, continued to meet at the town hall until a move in 1907 to the town clerk's office in the *County Court* building (see Chapter 4) and the attached *9 Market Place*, now the museum (see Chapter 5).[758] It moved back to the town hall in 1924 and, in the face of a growing requirement for office space, took six offices and a committee room at *5 High Street*: there were just seven paid officials at that date.[759] This had been built at the same time as the Town Hall but was not part of it; it was used initially as a bank and then for various other purposes before being taken over by the corporation.

To ease pressure on space the town hall was used from 1935 for committee meetings and in 1942 the council bought the offices at *9-10 Market Place*, (later the museum) together with *No. 11* alongside, big enough to provide also a council chamber and a mayor's parlour.[760] The borough council's final move was in 1967 to a new eight-storey concrete office block in *Monkton Park*, at the top of Monkton Hill.[761] Designed by Burrough and Hannah,[762] this was on the site of the future larger block which still stands there (see below).

Chippenham RDC, in 1934 combined with that for Calne, had meanwhile moved c1938 from the workhouse to *Bewley House* on Marshfield Road.[763] This was just north of the railway arches but adjacent to the former alignment of the road which is now in the middle of the circulatory system there. There were claims that it was built by Brunel for his residence while working on the Great Western Railway and it was of substantial size, of three bays and three storeys with string courses between, ashlar fronted and with a large pillared porch extending out over the pavement.[764] This became too small and in any case had to be demolished to make way for the new road layout there in the 1960s. The council was based temporarily in the former police station nearby (see Chapter 8) until it could move into the new *Bewley House*, set a short way further west. This opened in 1968, five storeys of concrete and glass, the council chamber in a two-storey front projection. The building was designed by A D Kirby of Wyvern Design.[765]

Both the Monkton Park and Bewley House buildings arrived late in the lives of their respective owners, for the 1972 Local Government Act led to the demise of both councils and their replacement by the new North Wiltshire District Council which was set up in the same Monkton Park offices and also maintained the offices

Chippenham, Monkton Park offices, the stepped entrance front

in the Market Place. The former were demolished and replaced in 2002 by the new **Monkton Park** offices by DKA of Bath,[766] a long five-storey block in concrete panels and glass, the entrance front facing Monkton Hill stepped out in glass boxes with some imagination. As with the 1960s buildings, this arrived late in the life of the owning council and from 2009 it was taken over by the new Wiltshire unitary council, with later shared use by the police. DKA returned in 2013 for refurbishment work here.[767]

There was no immediate successor town council after the abolition of the borough council in 1974; instead a body of charter trustees was set up with very limited consultative powers, and they met in the ***Jubilee Building***, described in Chapter 6.[768] In 1984 the body gained the status of a parish and town council, remaining for the time being in the Jubilee Building, but in 1986 they bought replacement offices at ***12 The Causeway***, a double-fronted early 19th century villa of substantial depth under a hipped roof.[769] The town council agreed to acquire the freehold of the Town Hall in 1994 and moved there in 1996. It remains there.

Corsham

The town was not incorporated and was not the base for any significant local government body, coming under the Chippenham Rural District Council when RDCs were formed in 1894. It did have a parish council under the Local Government Act 1894[770] and by March of 1895 the town hall trustees were proposing to the charity commissioners to vest the ownership of the town hall in the parish council;[771] it is believed that this went ahead.[772] The parish council, used the ***Town Hall*** (described in

Chapter 2) for its meetings thereafter, interrupted by the hall's use as a VAD hospital during the First World War.[773] Redesignated as a town council in 1999,[774] it continues to use the town hall for both offices and meetings.

Cricklade

Before the late 19th century, public services in Cricklade town and parish were provided by several bodies: Cricklade manor court, the parish vestries, the borough and Wayland's charity.[775] The 1894 Act produced a rural district council – for Cricklade and Wootton Bassett but meeting at the workhouse in Purton and then in Wootton Bassett – and two parish councils, covering the St Mary's and St Sampson's ecclesiastical parishes.[776] The two parish councils were combined into one in 1898 at the request of St Sampson's and against the opposition of St Mary's.[777] In 1974 the parish council was redesignated as a town council.[778]

The parish council met in the former *Town Hall* and subsequently in the *1933 Town Hall*; both are described in Chapter 2. There was no parish office until the museum moved out of the former weighbridge building in 1986 (see Chapter 5) and that was then taken over as an office until the final move back to the former town hall in 2002.[779]

Devizes

Devizes functioned as a borough from an early date and was already managing its affairs through committees in the 17th century.[780] It was reincorporated under the Municipal Corporations Act 1835 and in 1867 a local board for health was set up. In case this gives an impression of an active bureaucracy requiring significant office space it might be noted that the borough treasurer and town clerk remained part time roles until 1948 and 1965 respectively. Throughout this period the borough council met at the various town hall buildings described in Chapter 2.

The borough council first took central offices in 1959 when it moved to *Northgate House**, used as judge's lodges from 1869 to 1956.[781] Opposite the *Assize Court* on Northgate Street, (see Chapter 4) this, now grade 2* listed, was originally the King's Arms, a coaching inn of 1766[782], a fine building. The main part is of five bays and three storeys, in brick with strong stone string courses and a pedimented Ionic porch. To the west end is a further generous bay, canted to both front and rear, and indeed the rear elevation is almost as fine as the front. The borough council offices remained there until abolition in 1974.

The Devizes Rural District Council, established under the 1894 Act, met initially at the *Union Workhouse* to the west of what is now Sedgefield Gardens just south of the canal.[783] This was what appears to have been a particularly gloomy example of the type, designed by George Wilkinson and erected in 1836-7 as a variant on the standard 'square' plan, with three-storey accommodation blocks either side of a low central tower with pyramidal roof.[784] It was used as a geriatric hospital until around 1990 but then demolished.

By 1931 the RDC had moved to *Maryport Chambers*, at the south end of Maryport Street and fronting onto Sheep Street in what is now a partly open space.[785] This was a 19th century building with a steep gable on the east wall at the north end and a subsidiary gabled dormer with an exceptionally tall window on the north face.[786] In 1947, however, the RDC acquired **Browfort**, a large if plain red brick house of the 1860s just off Dunkirk Hill, and remained there until abolition.[787]

Both borough and rural councils were replaced by the new Kennet District Council in 1974. The new council took over the RDC's offices at Browfort and in 1985 added a substantial new block of offices by the Fitzroy Robinson Partnership, of three storeys in brick with a canted corner doorway. The district council was itself abolished with the introduction of the Wiltshire unitary authority in 2009: Browfort has since been demolished and the offices replaced by sheltered accommodation.

Devizes, Northgate House.

The town has had a lower tier town council since the abolition of the borough council in 1974. This has its offices in the *Town Hall*.

Highworth

As well as having a school board and membership of the Board of Guardians for the Swindon and Highworth Union, Highworth appears in the later 19th century to have had an active parish vestry.[788]

Under the 1894 Act it both gained a parish council and became part of the Highworth Rural District Council. The RDC was abolished on local government reorganisation in 1974 and the area then became part of the new Thamesdown district. RDC meetings were held initially at the Highworth and Swindon *Workhouse* in Stratton St Margaret, described below under Swindon, but by 1939 they had moved to the council offices at *17 Bath Road, Swindon*, described under that place.[789]

The parish council, which was meeting in the school in the early 20th century,[790] continues as Highworth Town Council, with offices at *3 Gilberts Lane* in a long two-storey rubblestone and brick building, formerly outbuildings to premises in the High Street.

Malmesbury

Malmesbury was a borough from an early date but in 1886 was incorporated as a municipal borough under the 1882 Act, a status it maintained until 1974.[791] The old corporation met in earlier years in **St Paul's Church** and perhaps at *9 Oxford Street*, as described in Chapter 2, although such use had ceased by 1794.[792] The new borough council met initially at the reading room at *4 Silver Street* erected by Walter Powell in the 1870s and described in Chapter 6.[793] In 1920 it bought the *Town Hall*, started to hold meetings there in the following year, and stayed there until abolition.[794]

The Old Corporation continued after the 1886 changes, with residual responsibilities for managing the borough lands and some charities. Since then known as the Warden and Freemen of the Borough of Malmesbury, they continue to meet several times a year in the *Court House*, described in Chapter 4.[795]

The Malmesbury Rural District Council, formed in 1894, met first at the workhouse board room.[796] The **Workhouse** of 1837-8 was on the Sherston Road, designed by George Wilkinson with a typically long range across the front though taller than many, the central section of three storeys plus an attic, the ranges either side of two plus attic, the whole in rubblestone with brick dressings.[797] Initially converted to flats after closure, it was demolished in 1971-2 and the houses of Bremilham Rise now occupy the site.[798]

In 1927 the RDC moved its offices to *10 High Street**, a fine early 18th century building, remodelled as a bank c1870, of three storeys and five bays in brick with stone dressings and rusticated quoins.[799] The middle window to each floor is round-headed; the door on the right, under a bracketed swan's neck pediment, leads to a through passage and there is a coved cornice and balustrade above. The RDC was there until abolition.[800]

The corporation and the RDC were replaced in 1974 by the North Wiltshire District Council, which had its offices in Chippenham. The replacement town council, founded in 1974 on the dissolution of the borough council, has always had its offices at the Town Hall.[801]

A claim in the Historic England listing that 22 Cross Hayes, the former school house, was once used as municipal offices does not seem to be backed up by other evidence.

Marlborough

Marlborough was a borough from ancient times, lately coming under the oligarchical control of the Ailesbury family before reform in 1835. The various versions of the town hall were used for meetings and in 1936 the borough added *1 The Green** as offices.[802] This is a large early-Georgian townhouse, three storeys high and seven bays wide, in chequered brick and little ornamented except for a stone columned porch with broken pediment. It was used until the borough's dissolution in 1974 and now remains as offices.

The Marlborough Rural District Council of 1894, combined with that of Ramsbury from 1934, met at the ***Workhouse***. The Marlborough workhouse of 1837, by the Common at the north end of Hyde Lane, was by William Cooper and in ashlar, of two storeys with a three-storey block at the hub of the radiating arms. This gives it a less forbidding appearance than many and may help to explain why, after closure and a period as a hospital, it survived to be converted into flats in 1999 by Sidell Gibson.[803]

The RDC was still at the workhouse in 1931 but by 1939 had moved to the ***Town Hall*** and is believed to have remained there for meetings until its dissolution in 1974.[804] It maintained offices for a period up to 1974 at ***47 London Road***, an early 19th century brick villa under a hipped roof, the bays at each end projected forward with a first floor balcony between providing a porch.[805]

From 1974 the new Kennet District Council was based in Devizes. The replacement town council continues to use the town hall but also has offices at ***5 High Street***, a four-bay three-storey building in chequered brick directly opposite the town hall on the south side of the street.

Melksham

Melksham appears to have had no substantial organisation for local government until an Act of 1816 set up a body of 32 commissioners to control matters to do with the highways in the town.[806] This was replaced by a local government board in 1878 and this in turn was replaced by the Urban District Council, with much wider powers, in 1894.

Early meetings may have been held at what is now ***St Michael's Church Room*** at the south-west corner of Canon Square.[807] This is small, of one storey plus attic under a stone slate roof, the brick gable facing the road and the north wall of stone. The local board used the ***Town Hall*** at first but by 1889 were meeting at an unidentified building in Lowbourne.[808] The UDC, perhaps surprisingly, also used a

Melksham, Semington Workhouse, the entrance front. Entrance buildings often presented a less grim face than the accommodation blocks behind.

separate building from its formation: it is suggested that this was at *3 Spa Road*, a villa to the right of what is now the entrance to the Rachel Fowler Centre.[809] Despite buying the town hall in 1914[810] the UDC seems not to have used it for meetings and offices until the mid-1920s.[811] It remained there until absorbed into the new West Wiltshire District Council, based in Trowbridge, in 1974.

The Melksham Rural District Council, also formed in 1894, met in its early years at the *Melksham Workhouse* at Semington.[812] This was built in 1836-9 by H E Kendall to a standard commissioners' pattern, the barracks-like three-storey ranges relieved only by the nine-bay entrance block on the north side, which has Classical ornamentation including a three-bay central pediment. On St George's Road in Semington, it was nearly equidistant between Melksham and Trowbridge and indeed was shared by the latter from 1898. It was later a hospital until 1988 and was converted into housing in 2002-3.[813]

In 1934 the RDC combined with that for Bradford on Avon and thereafter met in the latter town.[814] The successor town council from 1974 continues to use the town hall. The Melksham Without parish council, created in 1894 and serving the outer parts of the town, now has its offices in the *Community Campus* described in Chapter 6.

Mere

The Mere Poor Law Union was formed in 1835 and built the *Workhouse* on Castle Street in 1838-9, to designs by George Gilbert Scott and William Bonython Moffatt.[815] The Rural Sanitary Authority, formed in 1872, and the successor Mere Rural District Council, formed in 1894, also met here. The workhouse had a central archway at the front with single-storey buildings to either side; behind these was a three-storey accommodation block with more single-storey buildings to the rear.[816] It was still open, at least for RDC meetings, in 1931 but closed soon afterwards and, after various uses, was largely demolished in 1968 and replaced by a garage; much later this in turn was replaced by housing, becoming St Michael's View.[817] Only a forecourt wing at the front and part of the service buildings to the rear remain, the former in a cheerful and pleasing Tudor style.

In 1934 the Mere RDC joined with that for Tisbury and thereafter met alternately in the petty sessions hall at Tisbury and in the *Lecture Hall* here.[818] The lecture hall was built in 1863, on the south side of Salisbury Street, and combined a hall with a Quaker meeting room and, from c1927, a further small meeting room.[819] The building is of modest size, single-storey in stone with doors either end separated by a triple mullioned sash window with 'Lecture Hall' inscribed above. By 1949 the RDC had offices in *The Square*, perhaps the substantial 18th century building on the north side, now Nos. 1 and 2, and remained there until abolition in 1974.[820] The replacement Salisbury District Council had its offices in Salisbury.

Mere Parish Council was created in 1894. It appears to have met at either the Lecture Hall or the Board Room of the workhouse, both described above, for almost all of its life.[821] It was later designated a town as well as parish council and since 2005[822] has had offices at *Duchy Manor* on Springfield Road, separate from but in the same building as the school.

Salisbury

The city's government was in the hands of the bishops from its foundation but lay people gradually gained more influence until a charter of 1612 incorporated Salisbury as a free city and confined the jurisdiction of the bishops to the cathedral close.[823] Amended from time to time, it remained the city's governing charter until 1836 and during all of this period the council met in the **Council House** described in Chapter 2.

After the Municipal Corporations Act of 1835 the corporation was remodelled to cover a wider area but with initially very similar responsibilities, and it was not until 1852 that it took over responsibility for the increasingly critical area of public health, acting thereafter as both town council and local board of health. During this period the local board rented offices in Chipper Lane. From 1882 a house in Endless Street, left to the city in 1880, was used as public offices for both board and council. This was very probably the building at *13/13a Endless Street*, described in Chapter 8, which was certainly in council use by early in the 20th century.[824]

Continuing growth thereafter led to the purchase of St Edmund's College in 1927, described below: the council must have moved to here from 13/13a Endless Street before the police moved from across the road into the Endless Street building in 1930. The exchange with the police was completed by the council taking over the police's previous premises at the *Endless Street/Salt Lane* corner, also described in Chapter 8. This building carries the date 1935 with the city's arms on the new canted corner and must have served as additional accommodation to that at St Edmund's College.

Salisbury, Endless St/Salt Lane offices as rebuilt for council use. Compare with photograph of same location in police use in Chapter 8

When the city council bought St Edmund's College in 1927 they renamed it the **Council House***, and so the former Council House in the Market Square had to be renamed the Guildhall. St Edmund's College, a fine building on Bourne Hill, grade 2* listed, has a long and complex history[825] and was previously the largest and finest private house in the city. It now presents a main south front of two storeys and nine bays in brick with stone dressings, with Gibbs-style rusticated windows and rusticated quoins. The previous front had corner stair-towers and a row of gables together with mullion and transom windows but all this went in the early to mid-18th century alterations: the stair-towers are now encased as projecting end bays and the gables are replaced by a cornice and parapet with balls. A previous storeyed central porch was replaced by the present one, perhaps slightly later than the rest of the front, with a frieze and pediment above triple Doric columns.

A north wing was added in 1790, to the modified plans of S P Cockerell, and produced a nearly symmetrical east front in brick with two big canted bays and a central tripartite window; only the different fenestration to the bays reveals that this

Salisbury, Council House, the front elevation.

Salisbury, Council House, the east elevation

is partly the refacing of earlier work. Further extensions northwards were added in the 19th century but were demolished in recent years.

In the meantime the Salisbury Rural District Council had been created under the 1894 Act. It met first at the East Harnham **Workhouse** of the Alderbury Poor Law Union, off Coombe Road.[826] Salisbury had had its own workhouse for more than two centuries but in 1869 it joined, with a number of others, the Alderbury Union. The Harnham (Alderbury) workhouse was built originally in 1836-7 to designs of Edward

Hunt but rebuilt in 1877-9 to designs by G B Nicholls, presumably to cope with the extra demand. The main block was two-storey, T-shaped and typically glum in appearance. After various other uses it was all demolished in the 1970s, bar the chapel which remains in use locally, and the houses of Hawksridge now occupy the site.

The RDC was still meeting at the workhouse but transferred to the *Guildhall* for its meetings between 1931 and 1935, perhaps when it combined with Wilton RDC in 1934.[827] In 1953 it bought for its headquarters the building at *26 Endless Street* which it kept until abolition in 1974.[828] This is all in painted brick with to the right a double-fronted house with a full height canted bay to one side and a central porch with thin paired shafts, the whole of substantial depth under a hipped roof, extended further back under RDC ownership. The RDC also added the Georgian-style addition to the north.

The 1974 local government reorganisation replaced both the city council and the RDC with the Salisbury District Council, and this council in turn was abolished with the creation of the Wiltshire unitary authority in 2009, at which date the new lower tier city council was created. The building at the Endless Street/Salt Lane corner has remained in public ownership as has 26 Endless Street, and the new Salisbury City Council continues to use the Guildhall.

The previous Salisbury City Council had commissioned a new extension at the Council House in 2006, after a competition won by Stanton Williams.[829] Completed in 2010, this replaced the Victorian extensions with a rectangular building cased in vertical panels of alternating glass and dark grey metal. On the north and west sides, lines of 12 metre high stone-faced fins stand proud of the glass wall and just clear of the overhanging roof. The council house was taken over by the new Wiltshire unitary authority and is now shared by them with the police.

Salisbury, the 2010 Council House extension

Swindon

From the late 17th century the only effective organ of local government in the Old Town of Swindon was the vestry.[830] This remained the case into the 19th century, the New Town in its early years being in effect run by the Great Western Railway. In 1864 however, under some pressure, both Old and New Towns set up local boards of health under the Public Health Act. That for the New Town was meeting at **6 Albion Buildings** by 1889 and perhaps before, a building whose location has not been identified. The Old Town board met, perhaps from its inception, at *Villetts House, 42 Cricklade Street**.[831] This fine house, now grade 2* listed, is of 1729, in

Swindon, Villetts House: 'The best house in Swindon by far'.

brick with ashlar dressings, of two storeys and five bays. The front façade makes a considerable impact: the central bay is all of stone with a doorway between pilasters under a segmental pediment and above that a Venetian window. Windows either side have heavily ornamented keystones, at the corners are giant pilasters and above is a three-bay pediment between balustrades. The curved bays added at each end are later but overall it is no surprise that Pevsner described this as 'the best house in Swindon by far'.[832]

In 1891 the New Town board built offices in Regent Circus, the *New Town Hall* described in Chapter 2, and in 1894 the local boards of health were abolished and both Old and New Towns became Urban District Councils, that for the Old Town continuing to use the Cricklade Street offices.[833] The UDCs were short-lived for, despite the fractious relationship between the Old and New Towns, the case for combination into a single entity was sufficiently strong to persuade them, particularly the previously

Swindon, Euclid Street council offices soon after completion. (Local Studies (Swindon Library & Information Service))

reluctant Old Town, to accept the creation of a single municipal borough in 1900. From that date forwards the offices were concentrated into the new town hall.⁸³⁴

By 1936 the growth of local government services had put heavy pressure on space in the new town hall and offices had to be spread out in various other buildings. The solution to this problem was the new office block on a site in **Euclid Street***, in a former children's playground adjacent to the Clarendon Street schools. The architects were Bertram, Bertram and Rice of Oxford, who had won the commission in open competition. It was built in 1936-8, the front a long two-storey block in brick, the central section broken forward and raised with some ashlar detailing and first floor balconies, the squared roofline of its period. The whole building is a hollow square with a similarly sized block at the rear facing Beckhampton Street, the two joined by 10-bay linking sections at either end. The five-bay central block at the front extends through to the rear, thus dividing the interior courtyard into two halves. The whole

Shades of the Cunard liners – a committee room in the Euclid Street council offices, Swindon. (Local Studies (Swindon Library & Information Service))

building, though unassuming, must surely be considered a considerable achievement of the 'Moderne' style and was granted overdue listing in 2020.⁸³⁵

The Highworth Rural District Council, established in 1894 and covering the rural district to the north, east and south of Swindon, met initially at the **Workhouse** at Stratton St Margaret.⁸³⁶ This was east of the Highworth Road at a location just south of what is now the A419. It was built in 1845-6 as a replacement for an earlier building elsewhere and was T-shaped in two-storey brick with various subsidiary buildings. It followed the typical pattern of later conversion to a hospital and was demolished between 1990 and c2002.⁸³⁷ The site has since been redeveloped for housing.

The RDC continued to meet at the workhouse until c1924, at which date it moved to offices at **17 Bath Road**.⁸³⁸ This is a three-bay three-storey terraced house of

COUNCIL BUILDINGS   163

Swindon, Euclid Street council offices in 2023.

1860-70,[839] rendered with raised quoins, the ground floor with door to one side and next to that four engaged columns supporting an entablature, the large windows later. Above are two tiers of sash windows, the central ones pedimented, and above that a cornice with raised central attic, the whole of some pretension. The RDC remained there until abolished in 1974.[840]

The new Thamesdown borough council, formed in 1974 and taking over from both Swindon borough and Highworth RDC, had its main base initially at the Euclid Street offices but soon needed additional space. It provided this with a new four-storey block facing *Beckhampton Street* and just north-west of the 1938 block. This is c1975 by the Harry Weedon partnership with Thamesdown borough architects[841] and is in brick with strong horizontals of continuous glazing.

This was followed in 1985-6 by *Wat Tyler House** by Thamesdown borough architects, adjacent but facing Princes Street. The new building is again in brick with strong horizontals in glazing, but this time enlivened by the blue and green window trim, the roofline detail and the curving metal roof to the porch on Princes Street. In a complete takeover of this block of land, in the late 1980s the borough also converted to its use the *Clarence Street Schools* of 1895 and their *Annex* to the north added in the early 20th century.[842] The schools are particularly demonstrative in brick with stone detailing and highly ornamented gables, the annex in similar style but more restrained.

In 1997 Thamesdown became a unitary authority and moved outside the control of Wiltshire County Council, renamed as Swindon Borough. It continued to use the same offices.

Swindon, Wat Tyler House.

Trowbridge

Trowbridge has a unique position as the home of Wiltshire County Council, now Wiltshire Council. Before that, it had a local board of health from 1864, followed by an urban district council from 1894 which was in turn replaced by the West Wiltshire District Council in 1974. This was based in the town until its demise in favour of the Wiltshire unitary authority in 2009. There was never a Trowbridge Rural District Council – the town's surrounding area was covered by the Bradford, Melksham and Westbury RDCs – but it has had a successor town council since 1974.

The County Council

The County Council was established in 1889 and, there being no recognised county town in Wiltshire, it was initially seen as sensible to follow the pattern of the quarter sessions and meet in turn in Devizes, Salisbury, Marlborough and Warminster.[843] However, the council was already meeting in Trowbridge by late 1889 and, with much debate continuing amongst the competing towns as to which should have the offices, a policy of concentrating premises in Trowbridge seems already to have started. The reasons for the choice are not entirely clear although good rail access is quoted as one, coupled with the unsuitability of the *Assize Courts* at Devizes, used by the county council for its first meeting in 1889. It is also suggested that one of the motivations for building the new *Town Hall* at Trowbridge was that it might be used as an incentive to persuade the county council to come here. The county council's meetings were in fact peripatetic for the first ten years, with two meetings a year in Trowbridge and one each in Salisbury and Swindon. But a further acrimonious debate in 1899 led to a decision to hold all meetings in Trowbridge, in the town hall.[844]

In 1893 the county council took a seven year lease on *56 Stallard Street*. Two years later it was agreed that the staff of the county clerk's office should move to Trowbridge, a lease was at once taken on a floor of *Arlington House, 72 Fore Street*, and in 1896 the house was bought. A final consolidation, bringing all the then offices and a council chamber under one roof, was achieved in 1900 with the completion of the '*1900 Building*', barely visible from the street, behind Arlington House: this, of substantial height in brick, has now been replaced by a modern block of flats, also in brick and of similar bulk. At this point the Stallard Street office was given up and it was also resolved that all council and committee meetings should be held in Trowbridge from that date forwards.

Expanding county council functions soon outgrew the available accommodation and a series of leases and acquisitions followed: adjacent property in 1905, rooms in Fore Street in 1908 and another adjacent house in 1912. It was then decided that even this was not enough and in 1913-14 the *Hill Street* office block was constructed. Thereafter further acquisitions were made including a house in Back Street by 1919 and, in 1921, the purchase of *Polebarn House*. Finally, amongst various other short term leases, they bought *8 Wicker Hill* to add to the substantial block of property already held in that part of the town.

Not all this collection of buildings can be described but the five highlighted above are all worth mentioning. *56 Stallard Street* is part of a warehouse and office building for the former Studley Mills, Italianate in ashlar by William Smith in 1878.[845] The façade to Stallard Street is of five bays and four storeys, with an uncomfortable mix of paired arched and broader segmental windows in the middle floors and the top floor flat-headed. *Arlington House, 72 Fore Street*, is a five-bay early 18th century house, two tall storeys plus an attic, with a heavily corniced doorway. *8 Wicker Hill*, two doors west, is late 18th century ashlar, uncomfortably set out with four windows and a door below facing the street but only four windows above; there is a similarly uneven split on the side elevation and decoration is restricted to three narrow pilasters, a string course at first floor level and a cornice.

The *Hill Street** offices, though dismissed as 'Banker's Georgian' in the listing, are appealing,

Trowbridge, Hill St offices.

if too constrained on their tight corner site, made even more tight when the front steps were cut off for a later road widening. By George Powell, the county surveyor,[846] the front to Hill Street is stepped back to fit the site, with four bays to the right and two more set back to the left, all of three storeys plus a rusticated basement, in brick but with dominating ashlar dressings, many heavily rusticated. The former entrance, now cut off by the road widening, is inset to the left as an elaborately decorated curved ashlar bay, the door in an almost fantastical Baroque surround with 'Wiltshire County Council' inscribed in it. The offices were later used partly as a library and were eventually sold in 1983.

Polebarn House*, Polebarn Road, is of 1789, confidently composed in ashlar with canted bays either side of a pedimented doorway with Ionic columns, itself under a Venetian window and the whole separated from the bays by Corinthian pilasters. The quoins are rusticated, there is a parapet with balustrades and urns, but the face to Roundstone Street is more plain with numerous blind windows. The building is now 2* listed and was kept by the county council until c1978 after which it was converted into a hotel.

Trowbridge, Polebarn House.

Spreading staff around a variety of buildings in this way hardly made for efficient working and there was soon pressure to find a single headquarters. In 1929 the choice of town for the headquarters, again under debate at that date, was seen to come down to either Devizes or Trowbridge. Devizes offered Southbroom House and its park, already owned by the council, whereas the initial proposal for Trowbridge was based around the existing block of council-owned buildings and would have involved the demolition of many of the historic buildings on Fore Street.[847] Devizes was chosen but the recession delayed further action and when the matter was again considered in late 1933 a former football ground on Bythesea Road, Trowbridge was put forward as an alternative. This was accepted, after further controversy, in 1934. P D Hepworth was appointed as architect and the new county hall authorized at an estimated cost of £150,000. Construction begun in 1938 and it opened in 1940.

County Hall* achieves an impressive but uncomfortable Classicism in a way typical of large civic buildings of the period. Its long front is rusticated at basement and ground floor levels and above this the tall first floor windows are alternately pedimented in rusticated surrounds. The second floor contains smaller windows below a hipped roof with dormers, this an alteration from the original proposal which contained no attic storey. The two ends are drawn forward by one bay and at the centre is a broad columned porch with rooms either side of the central opening. There are narrower wings at each end, the council chamber is a half-octagonal extension centrally behind the main block, and committee rooms were provided along the first floor front.

Trowbridge, County Hall.

A fire in 1958 saw the roof burnt off. A western extension was provided in 1972-5 by Alex French and Partners, generally respectful of the shape and materials of the original. In 2012-13 this was altered by Stride Treglown and the linking section to the main building replaced by a full-height glass entrance hall in boxy panels, linking the two buildings and giving access to a new library space in the western extension.[848]

Trowbridge, County Hall, the 2013 linking block

The county council had kept the old offices until the late 1950s when Arlington house and the 1900 Building were sold; the Hill Street building remained in use until 1983 as offices and also as the Trowbridge public library. Further expansion took place around County Hall, however, with buildings on the far side of Bythesea Road, all now demolished: a 1964 pre-fabricated two-storey building for the planning department called **Brook House**, in 1968 the use of part of the former **Airsprung** factory and in 1971 the construction of the '**East Wing**', a four-storey block.[849]

Town and District Government

Town government in the 18th and early 19th centuries was mainly undertaken by the local magistrates and the vestry.[850] The local board of health, established in 1864, had its office at the home of the clerk but met in its early years at *Hill's Public Hall,* established by the 1860s as a main social centre for the town.[851] This is on Silver Street, just east of the town hall, a substantial brick building with multiple arched windows under a hipped roof, set back behind a shop. The board did not use this for long, however, because by 1876 they are recorded as meeting at 'the board room' at an unidentified location in Fore Street.[852]

The *Town Hall*, described in Chapter 2, opened in 1887 and the board, and from 1894 the urban district council, met there thereafter[853] and indeed right up until abolition in 1974.[854] The successor West Wiltshire District Council incorporated five urban areas, including Trowbridge, and two RDCs. It was based in Trowbridge and commissioned new District Council Offices in 1974 at a site on the corner of *Bradley Road* and Wiltshire Drive; it also used the **Victoria Institute**, described in Chapter 6, for a few years. Designed by John Sharpe Associates,[855] the new Bradley Road offices were in brick of two storeys, metal panels extending down from the roofline to the first-floor windows. Disused after the abolition of the district council in 2009, they were demolished in 2013 and replaced by a small housing estate c2020.[856]

The new lower tier town council immediately commissioned a *Civic Centre* in St Stephen's Place at the bottom end of Castle Street. Designed by John Simmons Associates, it opened in 1974 as both town council offices and a community centre with events spaces. It was re-clad in 2011 by John Wilde[857] and now presents a confusing but lively mix of brick, timber cladding and green metal sheeting to balance out the large ashlar panel, with the town's arms on an inserted window, hanging menacingly over the north entrance.

Warminster

Warminster's local board of health was set up in 1867, before which the town was governed by the vestry and its various committees, the turnpike trusts, and ad hoc boards of health set up to deal with specific outbreaks of disease.[858] The local board, of 15 members, appointed a clerk, a treasurer, a surveyor and a rate-collector, none of them full-time. Each of these would have operated from their own premises but the board itself met at the *Town Hall*, described in Chapter 2.[859]

The successor Warminster Urban District Council, formed in 1894, also met at the town hall until at least 1939 and probably until 1955.[860] At some date before 1953[861] they had acquired premises at *36 Market Place*, presumably just additional

Warminster, Portway House.

office space in the three-storey terraced building which contained the Warminster Journal printing works. This is of four bays with two tiers of sash windows above a 19th century shop front with a service door to the side.

In 1955 the UDC acquired ***Portway House*****, sharing it from 1957 with the public library (see Chapter 6). This clothier's mansion of 1722, grade 1 listed, was originally of seven bays and three storeys plus basement but was added to with well-matched three-bay two-storey wings in the early 20th century.[862] The building is of fine ashlar with modest decoration, the door originally set in a three-storey pilastered and pedimented central section but moved to the left-hand wing when that was built, and replaced by a five-sided canted bay. The rear is fine but unsurprisingly simpler in design and there are also fine railings and gates of c1760.

Portway House had been an estate house for Longleat prior to the UDC's occupation. The council stayed there until abolition in 1974 and the successor West Wiltshire District Council, based in Trowbridge, sold it in 1978, though the library remained there until 1982.[863] It was later divided into flats.

The Warminster Rural District Council was also created under the 1894 Act and met initially at the ***Workhouse*** on Sambourne Road south of the town centre.[864] This was designed by Sampson Kempthorne, a prolific designer of workhouses, and opened in 1837.[865] It was hexagonal, though the main blocks – three-storey and seven and eight bays long – formed a Y at the centre. The entrance block, two storeys and nine bays wide, had a rusticated ground floor but the remainder was in rubblestone with brick dressings and typically forbidding in appearance. The workhouse followed the usual process of change into first a public assistance institution and then a hospital, closing finally in the mid-1990s after which the entrance block and the three blocks forming the Y were converted into housing as The Beeches, the remainder being demolished.

In 1934 the Warminster RDC was combined with that for Westbury; the new council met first at Westbury workhouse (see below), then alternately at the Laverton Institute in Westbury and the town hall in Warminster.[866] In 1947 the combined RDC acquired *Craven House*, at the junction of Silver Street and Vicarage Street.⁸⁶⁷ Of the 1780s and 2* listed, this is brick-fronted with stone dressings and canted bay windows on two floors neatly either side of a pedimented doorway. The main house was built onto an earlier hip-roofed building to the rear and side and this had to be adapted so as to be able to accommodate meetings of the full council, which was only achieved in the late 1950s. The UDC was abolished in 1974 and replaced by the new West Wiltshire District Council based in Trowbridge. Craven House was sold.

Warminster Town Council was formed as a successor lower tier authority in 1974 and had a small office in Portway House for two years.⁸⁶⁸ It was then in temporary offices until it moved in 1981 into the former Old Meeting chapel, and later school, in North Row, naming it *Dewey House* after Harold Dewey, a longstanding teacher and beneficiary of the town. This is of 1704, double pile in two-storey brick of five bays under a hipped roof, with stone dressings, much altered over succeeding years.⁸⁶⁹

Assembly rooms were built off Sambourne Road in 1973 and remodelled by BTA of Warminster as the town's new *Civic Centre*, opened in 2011 and providing both meeting rooms for hire and the town council's main offices.⁸⁷⁰ The tall brick hall is partly concealed behind a flat-roofed single-storey white office block, the whole fronted by a pyramidal-roofed porch on thin steel supports like a latter-day porte-cochere.

Westbury

Westbury had a corporation from an early date but it seems to have exercised almost no powers; the vestry, though, does seem to have been increasingly active in the early part

Westbury, the Laverton Institute

Westbury, the Laverton Institute before alterations to the roof. (Westbury Heritage Society).

of the 19th century.[871] The corporation was abolished in 1886 under the 1883 Municipal Corporations Act and town trustees were appointed to take over the remaining corporate property. It is not clear whether any other body was acting for the next few years but following the 1894 Act both a parish council and a rural district council were elected.[872] Many in the town were upset that Westbury had become merely a part of a rural district council area whereas adjacent towns had their own urban district councils;[873] they agitated for change and in 1899 the Westbury Urban District Council was formed and the parish council abolished.[874]

The UDC, and the parish council during its short life, met at the **Laverton Institute*** on Bratton Road, the gift in 1873 of Abraham Laverton, a dominant employer in the town and a considerable philanthropist.[875] It was designed by the prolific W J Stent in a Venetian Gothic style, the lively front in brick and stone offering two floors of generously sized arched windows under a hipped roof. The tympana of the ground floor windows have incised scrollwork, those either side of the door carrying Laverton's initials and the date. The door is contained in a heavy ashlar porch, with pillars, a pelican crest at the centre – part of Laverton's arms - and above that a balcony in front of the paired central windows of the first floor. The Institute was built with a more elaborate central bay carried up past a clock to a French-looking pavilion roof but this was removed sometime after 1920.[876]

Westbury, the Laverton Institute, stained glass in the main hall

The Institute had committee and meeting rooms on the ground floor and there was a large hall across the front of the first floor, containing at one end a notable four-light stained glass window by Horwood Bros of Frome[877] depicting Shakespeare, Newton, Watt and Landseer. It may be noted in passing how much this layout echoed those of many town halls elsewhere even though this building, nominally at least, was not one. From 1874 to 1925 a boys' school occupied part of the ground floor and the Institute has had many different uses over the years. Indeed it is perhaps amongst the most successful of all the county's town halls or equivalents in retaining a viable range of uses up to the present day. It has certainly been much used by local government: the UDC stayed here until abolition in 1974, the rural district council, discussed below, was back here holding meetings after the closure of the workhouse, and the successor town council continues to be based here.

The UDC took for its offices *Westfield House*, almost opposite the Laverton, a substantial double-fronted brick villa of mid-Victorian date with a pillared stone porch. Previously owned by the son-in-law of W H Laverton, it was used by the council from c1930 until abolition in 1974.[878]

The Westbury Rural District Council was formed in 1894 and, as was usual, held its meetings at the workhouse. The Westbury and Whorwellsdown Union *Workhouse*, (Whorwellsdown being the name of the ancient Hundred adjacent to Westbury Hundred), was an 1836-7 rebuilding and enlargement of a previous building at the junction of what is now Springfield Road and Eden Vale Road.[879] Designed by T L Evans, it had a front range linked to a parallel rear range by a spine building with an octagonal supervisory section at its centre. The spine, and perhaps the rear range, were typically forbidding in their three-storey brick construction but the front range was softened by its Classical proportions, the middle three bays of five advanced slightly and the three tiers of windows well proportioned. The workhouse closed around 1930 and by 1936[880] the rear range, the rear half of the spine and all the ancillary buildings had been demolished, leaving only the front range and half of the spine. These still stand and, after a long period as a building yard, have now been redeveloped for housing.

The RDC, combined with that for Warminster, met alternately at the Laverton Institute and Warminster town hall for some years and in 1947 moved to Craven House in Warminster, as noted above. Both the UDC and the RDC were replaced in 1974 by the West Wiltshire District Council.

Westbury town council, the successor lower tier authority created in 1974, took over the Laverton Institute from West Wiltshire District Council in 2003 as sole trustee of the trust which runs it,[881] having rented rooms in the building for some years previously. It is understood that they met at the town hall for a time after 1974.[882]

Wilton

Wilton was chartered in the 12th century and for long had all the trappings of borough government, but the town's long decline meant that, although its constitution was redefined in 1832, many of the nominal functions were by then more or less meaningless.[883] There was, however, a local board of health, formed in c1854,[884] and this was seemingly well thought of.[885] A petition in 1884 for incorporation under the 1882 Municipal Corporations Act was successful and in 1885 a new charter creating the municipal borough was granted; this led to the abolition of both the previous corporation and the local board. The new borough council remained in being until its abolition in 1974 when it was replaced by the Salisbury District Council established under the 1972 Act.

The local board was meeting in the *Town Hall*, described in Chapter 2, from at least 1862 and quite possibly from the start of its existence.[886] It is uncertain, but likely, that the previous borough council did likewise. The new borough council met there

Wilton Town Council offices, the council chamber. Photograph courtesy of Wilton Town Council

and continued to do so until it eventually moved, in 1948/9, to the former chapel and masonic hall in *Kingsbury Square*.[887] This has a narrow late 18th century façade of painted brick in three storeys under a hipped mansard roof, the windows large and round-arched with prominent imposts, altered when it was converted into a Methodist Reform chapel in 1872.[888] The main room on the first floor is long and narrow with exposed tie beams and rafters, well suited as both chapel and council chamber, but the chapel did not last long, closing by 1896. The building had various other uses including a period as a masonic lodge before being taken over by the borough council.

The Wilton Rural District Council, formed under the 1894 Act, met at the *Workhouse* throughout its life until its eventual combination with Salisbury RDC to form the Salisbury and Wilton RDC in 1934, after which meetings were held in the city.[889] The workhouse, alongside the Warminster road just north of the first railway bridge, was built in 1836-7 to designs of Edward Hunt, using a standard design of cruciform three-storey central blocks, a similar three-storey block at the end of one arm for the entrance, and lower buildings around the perimeter.[890] In brick, the entrance block is of typically softer appearance while the main blocks do little to hide their grim purpose. After closure it was used by a storage and removal company for many years but was converted into housing by a housing association in 2007-8.

A lower tier town council was formed in 1974 after the abolition of the borough council. It took over the borough council's offices in Kingsbury Square shortly afterwards and remains there.

Royal Wootton Bassett

Wootton Bassett had been a borough since the 14th century but by the early 19th the borough had virtually ceased to have any function; in 1886 it lost this status as a result of the 1882 Act.[891] A town trust was established by the Charity Commissioners in 1889 to administer its remaining property.

The Cricklade and Wootton Bassett Rural District Council was established under the 1894 Act and held its meetings at the *Purton Workhouse* until at least

Wootton Bassett, former council offices at 141 High Street.

1931.⁸⁹² The workhouse was built at the west end of the village in 1837, to designs by George Wilkinson based on the standard cruciform plan.⁸⁹³ In the 1930s it was converted into a mental hospital and at a much later date, perhaps around 2000, all but the front entrance block was demolished and replaced by the housing of what is now Willis Way. The entrance block is in brick of two storeys and 10 bays, the middle four advanced slightly under a pediment, the whole under a hipped roof.

The RDC moved for its meetings to the *Institute* in Purton between 1935 and 1939.⁸⁹⁴ This is the former workmen's institute of 1879-80 by Orlando Baker of Swindon, at the corner of High Street and Station Road.⁸⁹⁵ It fits its corner site neatly, tall but compact in stone, Gothic in detail with a neatly designed wing containing the doorway to one side and, above, a bellcote on the ridge. It had not lasted long as a workmen's institute, being let to the parish council by 1902.⁸⁹⁶ It is now used as a library, museum and parish council offices.

The RDC established offices in the High Street, Wootton Bassett, perhaps between 1906 and 1911,⁸⁹⁷ and at some date thereafter leased *141 High Street** for this purpose.⁸⁹⁸ This building, of about 1700, stands at the corner of Station Road though it formerly had a further house to its right. It presents a grand if slightly uncomfortable front to the street, in ashlar of nine bays and two storeys and an attic. The central three bays are advanced slightly below a semicircular gable, the windows are tall and narrow, arched in the gable and in the middle of the first storey, and the doorway has a shell hood on carved brackets. Grade 2* listed, it is now used as solicitor's offices.

The meetings of the RDC later transferred to Wootton Bassett alongside the offices. In 1952, the 141 High Street offices having become too small, the RDC bought *Manor House* at the north end of the town centre and moved there in 1954.[899] The original building here, of the later 19th century and previously called Troy House, was of modest size, two-storey brick with ashlar dressings under a hipped roof, with a three-bay front facing north and canted bays either side of a round-arched porch with pillars. It was much extended later, perhaps when occupied for a period by a boys' school, and by the time the RDC moved in was said to have had '20 lofty rooms'.[900] The RDC remained there until abolition in 1974 and the building was then owned successively by the North Wiltshire District Council and Wiltshire Council, though the former had their main offices in Chippenham.[901] The police subsequently moved their local headquarters to new buildings alongside and the Manor House itself was let out for a variety of different uses.

The parish council was formed in January 1895 and met in its early days at the *British Schoolroom*,[902] now forming part of the Infants' school and much altered but with its brick front still visible, complete with ogee-arched window in the gable. Around the turn of the century the council had its own parish room, presumably rented, though it is not clear where this was.[903] It was said to have met later at the *Cemetery Lodge*, off Downs View,[904] large for such a building and untypically not Gothic with its cross-windows set into rubblestone walls below a semi-hipped roof.

The parish council was redesignated as a town council in 1974 and in 1981 took over the former *National School* on Station Road. This had opened in 1861 but by the mid-20th century its inadequacies were becoming obvious – the classrooms were described as small and ill-lit and the stone staircase as dangerous – and in 1973 it closed.[905] Designed by E W Mantell,[906] the school is surprisingly tall with three storeys

Wootton Bassett, the National School, later town council offices. Remarkable scale for such a building.

of rubblestone like a mill building, five bays of irregularly spaced mullioned windows facing the street and buttressed against the slope at the bottom corner. A house for the headteacher is attached to the north end and there were other later extensions.

The building was restored to provide meeting spaces as well as offices, becoming the town's civic centre, but in 2015 it closed, deemed no longer suitable or cost-effective; it was sold and converted into housing.[907] The town council took over *117 High Street* for use as offices, the end of a neat terrace of four small houses in brick with stone dressings, each with a small canted bay on the ground floor and seemingly early 19th century in date. Council meetings since leaving the National School have been held in various places, including Manor House.

The town council bought Manor House from Wiltshire Council in 2020 and by 2023 plans were well advanced to convert this into a much improved replacement for the civic centre, containing community space as well as council offices, though the project would require substantial additional finance.[908]

8
Police Stations

Introduction

UNTIL THE EARLY 19th century the county was policed by the ancient system of parish or petty constables under the control of the quarter sessions. They were 'unpaid, untrained and usually unwilling,'[909] and their duties encompassed not just matters of law and order but also the collection of local rates and other tasks such as keeping standard weights and measures and completing census returns[910]. Local lock-ups were used, as well as the county gaol, but the dispersed and minimal nature of local policing meant that police stations were not needed. Not surprisingly, the system did not work well and was increasingly inadequate in the context of the rapid population growth and growing urbanization associated with the industrial revolution.

The 1820s and 30s slump following the Napoleonic wars put particular pressure on the old system. General unrest and the rise of chartism from the late 1830s produced a sense of crisis: as just one example it was said in 1832 that in Devizes burglary had become so common that 'most families keep fire-arms in their bedrooms'.[911] The problem was recognized explicitly at the county's Easter 1839 quarter sessions at which a resolution was passed that '…a Body of Constables appointed by the Magistrates paid out of the County rate and disposable at any point of the Shire where their Services might be required would be desirable as providing in the most efficient Manner for the prevention as well as detection of offences for the Security of person and property and for the constant preservation of the public peace.'[912]

In the meantime the establishment of the Metropolitan Police in London in 1829 was followed by the Municipal Corporations Act of 1835 which allowed some boroughs to establish police forces. Salisbury did so the following year, and retained an independent force until the Police Act of 1946 required its merger with the county force. Devizes did likewise but merged with the county force in 1847.[913] There seems to have been some degree of independence elsewhere as well, perhaps more theoretical than practical: Wilton, for example, did not enter into a 'formal consolidation' with the county force until 1887.[914]

The County Police Act of 1839 provided the opportunity the Wiltshire quarter sessions had wished for and this became the first county to use the new powers, establishing its force that same year: it still boasts of it in its motto, 'Primus et Optimus'. The force started with a chief constable, 13 superintendents, 10 inspectors, 25 sergeants and 152 constables, close to the maximum of one officer per 1000 population allowed by the legislation but even so an insubstantial force to spread across the county.⁹¹⁵

Many of the earliest premises used by the new force are not recorded but it is clear that most were improvised, for example the London Inn in Warminster, used by the inspector there for two years from 1840.⁹¹⁶ For long afterwards some local forces made use of existing houses but at the same time the purpose-built station began to emerge. Some of these were built as part of new town halls - Bradford on Avon and Melksham are examples - but as early as the 1850s free-standing police stations were being put up with an internal layout which remained basically unaltered until well into the 20th century.

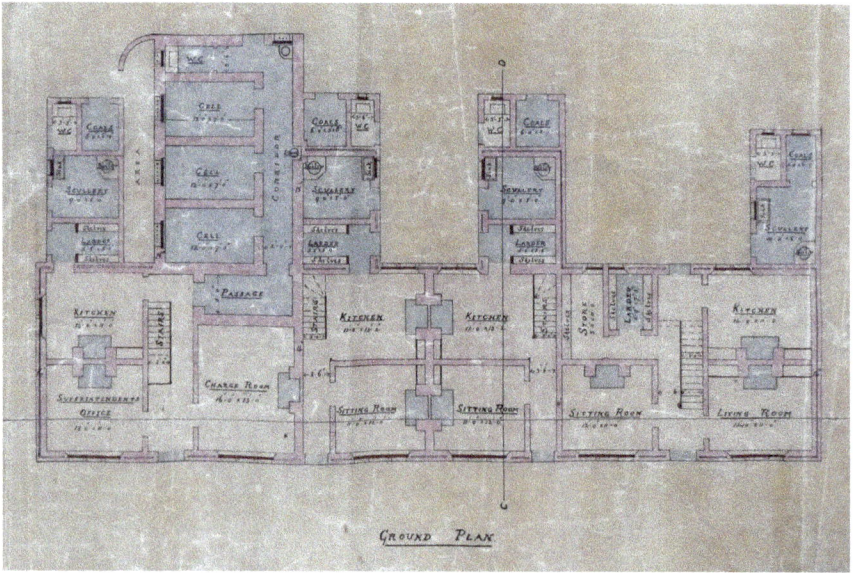

Plan of the 1899 police station at Marlborough, showing how domestic accommodation took the lion's share of the space. (WSA).

The front elevation of the same building, thoroughly domestic bar the central pediment. (WSA)

The first characteristic of these early buildings is that they are largely given over to residential accommodation for police officers. The main reason for this, apart from the necessity for some newly appointed officers to live away from home, was probably security. The new police were often resented and officers would have been vulnerable if living alone in the community: sharing accommodation within a secure police building would have given some protection. So the police stations might have provided accommodation for four or more officers but only one room for an office or charge room: prisoners being taken to the cells at the rear would have passed the living rooms of off-duty officers in a strangely intimate setting. As one example, the substantial 1899 police station in Marlborough, of two storeys and six bays, provided only two offices – a charge room and a superintendent's office – with a block of three cells attached to the rear. Officers in the early days were usually single, and indeed required the permission of the chief constable to marry.[917]

The second characteristic is their domestic appearance. It might seem natural for buildings which were essentially houses to look like houses but an obvious alternative was to make them look more like small-scale gaols. Instead, they were almost all built with the appearance of semi-detached dwellings, or sometimes short terraces, with multiple doors as if to separate houses although these usually opened to

Ash Walk police station at Warminster, an earlier example of domestic scale

interconnecting corridors. 19th century examples were usually modest in appearance, as if to be less visible in the streetscape, and there was a strong emphasis on symmetry. As a consequence most are at least dignified and some, like the pair on Ash Walk in Warminster, are attractive. Later ones, like that on Station Road in the same town with the long terrace of police houses beyond in the same style, can appear overbearing. Only in rare cases, like the flamboyant 1911 building in Wootton Bassett, was this general pattern broken.

Police stations were located close to town centres for obvious reasons, though constraints on land availability led some later buildings to be less well positioned, like the 1929 set in Melksham way out on the Semington road. One noticeable point, however, in the descriptions which follow is how many were located on the town's 'Station Road'. This may have been coincidence but a possible explanation may be offered in the comment made by the chief constable at the 1925 public enquiry into moving the Trowbridge police station from the station approach to Polebarn Road: he said that prisoners were now usually conveyed by road so it was no longer necessary for the police station to be close to the railway station.[918] In passing, it may be noted that the 1920s produced a set of new police stations in the county, as is evident from the text below: perhaps coincidence but perhaps also a reflection of the belief that modern policing required better facilities than had had previously been deemed necessary.

Early police stations, particularly those attached to town halls, were often leased rather than owned outright, and some also contained court rooms. A further general point to note is how many stations had a substantial yard to the rear of the main building, usually with stables, cart shed and hay store. A main purpose of these yards was to allow the constables to parade, a required part of daily duty for many years.

By the 1950s and 1960s police stations were no longer being built to provide living accommodation as well as offices and their general appearance was, and has remained, that of contemporary office buildings. A programme of station closures was announced in 2017, for reasons of economy, and in 2021 eight former town stations were offered for sale, at Calne, Cricklade, Highworth, Malmesbury, Marlborough, Warminster, Westbury and Wilton. In an apparent return to the shared use which characterised early town halls, the police in Chippenham, Corsham and Salisbury now share Wiltshire council premises. Village police stations, not covered in this review but of which there were many, had almost without exception closed by this time.

The Buildings

Amesbury

A *lock-up* was built in the north-east angle of Salisbury Street and High Street in 1827, its front curved to follow the corner, and this was followed by a **police station** towards the east end of Salisbury Street, on the north side.[919] This was part of a large building, probably of jettied and timber-framed construction, the police quarters showing just a door with a window alongside. There was a similar disposition of door and window at the far end but the two dwellings were separated by a tall pair of double doors, as if for a barn.[920] The police were certainly using this building by the 1880s and quite possibly much earlier.[921] By the turn of the century there was criticism of both buildings, the lock-up because it was so insecure a policeman had to be on continuous guard outside and the rented police station because it was too small.[922]

The new police station was in *Back Lane, now School Lane**, on a site bought from Sir Edward Antrobus,[923] and opened in 1912. This is in brick with entertainingly assertive stone dressings and an equally assertive portico at the entrance below a date stone in the style of the period; a small stone pediment with a representation

Amesbury, former police station, Back Lane

Amesbury, the Back Lane police station when newly built.

of Stonehenge once stood above the portico.[924] Three gables punctuate the roofline, the outer two brought forward above crenellated bays, but the windows and doors are unevenly divided for no seemingly good reason with what Pevsner called 'ham-fisted asymmetries.' Inside, the central section contained the charge room and superintendent's office, with four cells behind. By the 1920s the superintendent occupied the right hand wing, with bedrooms above, and the sergeant likewise the left, with constables' bedrooms above the offices: strangely intimate living arrangements but for what was intended to be an all-male environment.[925]

The 1912 building was in turn replaced in 1976 by the current police headquarters, on *Salisbury Road* some way south of the town centre. This is in brick with vertically paired windows separated by concrete panels. There are two police houses of similar date behind the substantial rear yard.

The lock-up probably went out of use when the 1912 building opened[926] but still stands, in use in 2023 as an estate agent's. The Salisbury Street building remained in place until probably the 1970s[927] but has since been demolished and replaced by modern shop premises, in 2023 an undertaker's and a building society.

Bradford on Avon

Bradford's Town Improvement Act of 1839 gave it the power to appoint a police force[928] and it seems to have done so promptly, although merged almost immediately into the county force.[929]

Bradford on Avon, the Town Hall wing stretching up Market Street contained police accommodation on ground and second floors.

POLICE STATIONS

There was an inspector of police in an office at **Bridge Foot**, at the north end of the town bridge, by 1842.[930] This was in a single-storey building immediately by the bridge on the east side; it was demolished and replaced in the early 20th century.[931]

The construction of the town hall in 1855, described in Chapter 2, gave the opportunity to consolidate several functions into a single building and police offices were provided for in the wing stretching up *Market Street*: the lease with the private company which built the town hall was signed in 1858 and this seems to be the date at which the police moved from the Bridge Foot office.[932] Doors to the street

Bradford on Avon, the Bridge Foot police station, single storey behind the marching soldiers immediately north of the town bridge. (Courtesy of Pamela Slocombe).

have stonework scrolls above, the lower one 'Police' and the upper 'Superintendent'. Nearly all the ground floor rooms were given over to staff living accommodation with only a single room on the superintendent's side used as an office, and corridors led through between these to a yard at the rear and beyond that three cells. Bedroom accommodation was provided in the attic floor, the intermediate floor being allocated for a library and reading room, for the town rather than the police.[933]

By the late 1920s the accommodation at the town hall was said to be 'unsatisfactory in every way'[934] but the police were not able to move out until 1936.[935] The new police station and housing was at **5 – 11 Avonfield Avenue**, in a new estate off the Trowbridge road south of the town centre. This is a long block, typical of police housing of the period, with projections at both ends and two points between, containing four doors to the houses and a central door to the station office; a rear extension probably contained the cells. Construction is of good ashlar with well-detailed door and window surrounds.

The final move, in 2003, was to a small single-storey office at the rear of the town's fire station off the *Station Approach* road, supposedly to make the police more visible in the town centre.[936]

Calne

The Wiltshire county force policed Calne from 1850 and the borough in response provided a police station at what is now *12 High Street*, a narrow 18th century building in coursed limestone rubble, altered with a Venetian window in the 19th century and with the later insertion of a shop front.[937] It was a DIY store in 2023.

Construction of a *Town Hall* in 1886, described in Chapter 2, gave the opportunity for consolidation, as in Bradford on Avon albeit 30 years later. The police

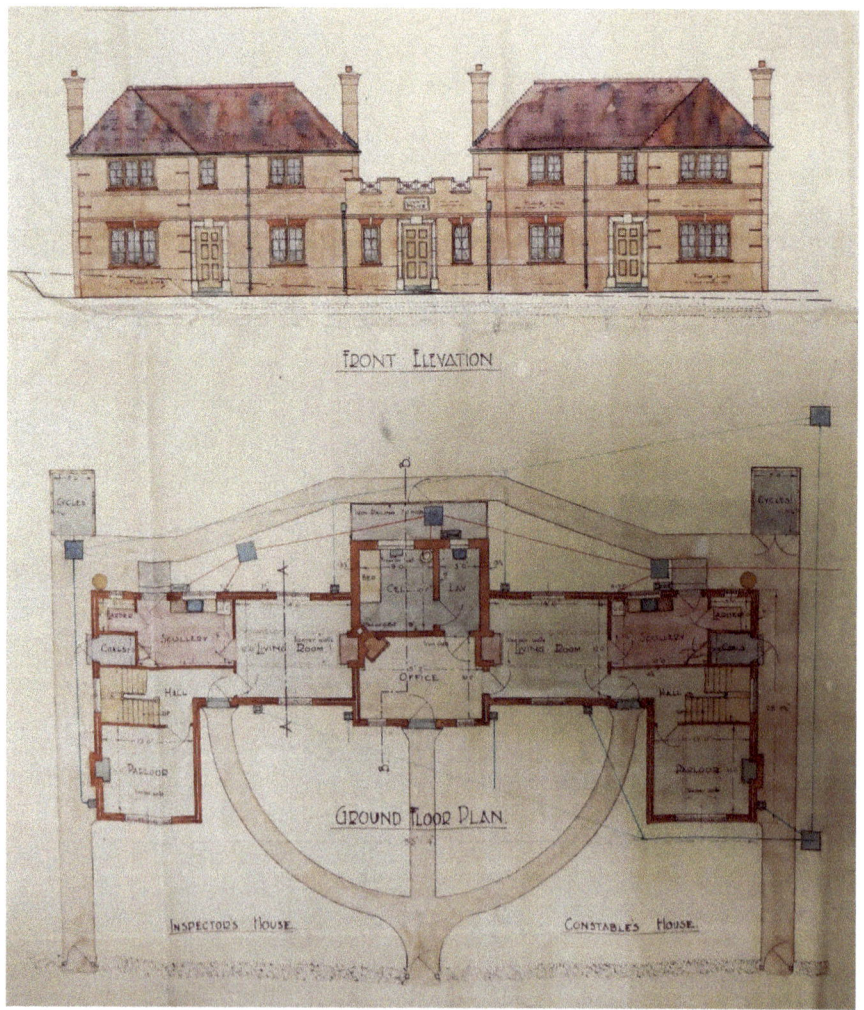

Calne, 1929 police station in Silver Street. Two comfortable villas linked by a minute office block, crenellated to give it a serious air. (WSA)

moved there in 1886 or shortly afterwards and the station occupied the right hand two bays seen from the front. The space was not generous, with one office, a kitchen and two cells on the ground floor and a living room and bedroom above.[938] Nevertheless they stayed there until 1929 when they moved to new premises on the west side of **Silver Street**, some way out of the town centre,[939] having previously considered moving to a site acquired by the county council in London Road.[940]

The Silver Street offices were much the most ambitious of the town's police offices, and lasted until 2010 before demolition and replacement.[941] The whole was in brick under a hipped roof with, to either side, three-bay villas with projecting wings at the outer ends, one being for the inspector and the other for constables. Between was a narrower single-storey section with crenellated roof-line containing an office and a single cell behind.[942] Their replacement on the same site in ***Silver Street***, nearly square in single-storey brick, was closed in 2020 but in early 2023 reopened as the base of a rural crime team.[943]

Chippenham

The Borough had a police force of two officers from 1836 but, following the establishment of the county force, agreed in 1841 to pay them to police the town instead.[944] Relations between the two bodies were not always harmonious and in 1854 there was criticism from the chief constable as to the state of the lock-up in the Yelde Hall (see Chapter 2). In 1857 the quarter sessions ordered the construction of a new police station and lock-up in the town: this is the one still standing at ***41-42 New Road****, immediately north of the railway bridge.[945]

Chippenham, former police station at 41-42 New Road: more semi-detached villas

Similarities with the station at Warminster of the same date suggest this was designed by J M Peniston, the county surveyor.⁹⁴⁶ It presents externally as a semi-detached pair of double-fronted villas in limestone ashlar under a hipped slate roof with prominent chimney stacks, with a string course at first floor level broken forward over the two doorways. Sash windows are 6x6 below and 3x6 above, most probably original, and the whole is consistent with the development of other houses in the street of generally similar design. Behind the façade, the police station proper occupied only the more northerly half, with a block of three cells behind; the other street door led to one of two police houses with the other accessed by a side door, since blocked. A substantial yard to the rear had a stable block at the back corner.⁹⁴⁷ The interior layout has since been much altered in its various commercial uses.

By the 1930s the New Road premises were seen as inadequate and a site was bought on Dallas Road for a replacement, but this was later deemed too small and is now occupied by the town's fire station.⁹⁴⁸ The search for new premises continued during the war years and in 1952 a site in Gypsy Lane was identified and a public inquiry held over plans to place a new police station there, but in the end the new station was created at **34 Marshfield Road** and opened in 1956.⁹⁴⁹ The Marshfield Road station consisted of a late 19th century house, dated to 1898 over the doorway, in coursed rough stone with ashlar dressings and twin front gables. A newly-constructed extension was connected at the rear: the house contained the offices and the new building contained cells and a lecture/recreation room.⁹⁵⁰ The police were not there long, moving out in 1965; the buildings were then occupied temporarily by the Rural District Council while waiting for their new offices to be built⁹⁵¹ (see Chapter 7) and since then all but the original house have been replaced by a new block, in 2023 housing the probation service. Not many years later the police moved again, to a former NAAFI⁹⁵² on **Wood Lane**, which itself closed in 2013⁹⁵³ and has been replaced by a care home. They then moved into the Wiltshire Council offices at *Monkton Park*, described in Chapter 7.

Corsham

Police were stationed in Corsham from 1847 if not earlier.⁹⁵⁴ The first police station is said to have been on the south side of **Post Office Lane** and later became the home of a family of coal merchants before demolition, perhaps as late as the 1970s. It may have been in use from at least 1870,⁹⁵⁵ and perhaps from as early as the 1840s, until the next century.⁹⁵⁶ It was replaced by that still standing at *62 Pickwick Road**, which was probably built in the 1860s but taken over by the police, with a cell added at the rear, around 1910.⁹⁵⁷ This is a double-fronted villa in ashlar with rubble-stone sides under a hipped slate roof, with a string course and an open wrought iron porch, above which is the inscription 'County Police Station'. The only non-domestic parts of the building were a charge room at the right-hand rear leading to a cell. The cell, and a stable block at the rear of the yard, have since been demolished.

In 1943 further police premises were provided on **Westwells Road** for the use of Special Branch, probably associated with the army base nearby.⁹⁵⁸ These were likely to have been wooden huts and demolished in 1998 if not before.⁹⁵⁹

The Pickwick Road station was replaced in 1952 by one on the corner of **Priory Street and Kings Avenue**, designed by the office of the County Architect, F I

POLICE STATIONS

Pickwick Road police station, Corsham

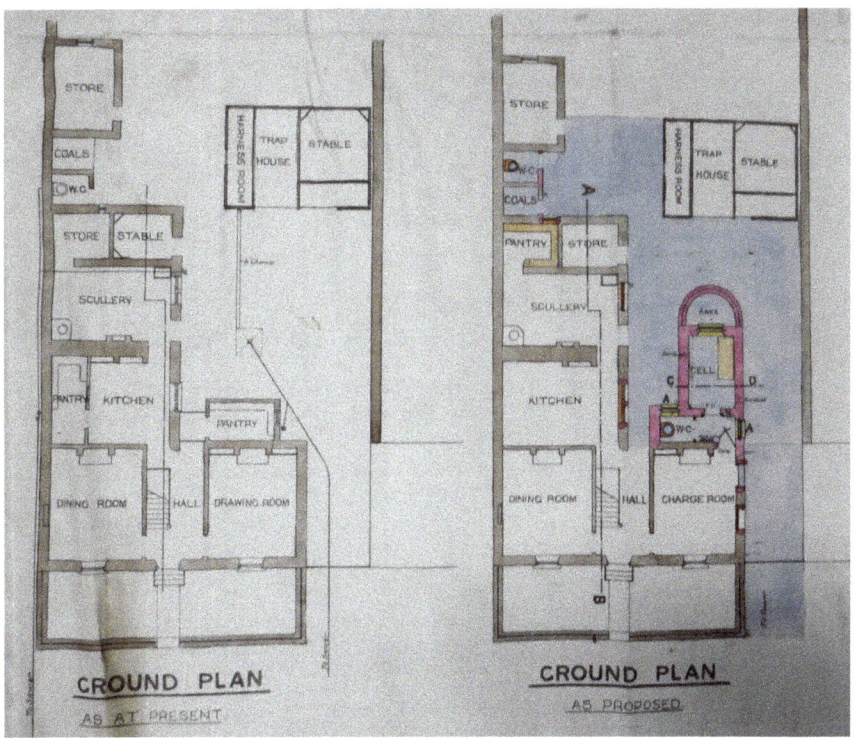

Corsham, Pickwick Road, plans showing how minimal were the changes needed to convert from house to police station. (WSA).

Bowden.⁹⁶⁰ The choice of location followed a dispute between the chief constable and the County Council housing committee.⁹⁶¹ It was a substantial building with single storey wings facing both roads, linked by a convex curved doorway, and with police housing attached each side.⁹⁶² This too was demolished after the police moved into the new community campus in *Beechfield Road* in 2015. The campus is described in Chapter 6.

Cricklade

In 1840 a police station was created in the house where the superintendent lived, now *No 4, The Priory*.⁹⁶³ This is an early 19th century addition to the larger and earlier building set at right angles to the road and incorporating medieval work. No. 4 is in stone block, three bays and three storeys plus attic; a painted police station sign apparently remained above the round-arched central doorway until the early 20th century.⁹⁶⁴

From c1850 the police were using *76 High Street*, one of a pair of three-storey houses of probably early 19th century date,⁹⁶⁵ and in 1903 they moved to new premises at *91 High Street*.⁹⁶⁶ These replaced ramshackle tenements on the site of the ancient St John's Hospital and comprised a police house with a ground floor office.⁹⁶⁷ Alterations in 1962 converted the whole of the ground floor to police accommodation but the building was closed and sold in 2022. In 2023 it was undergoing conversion in a community project to create commercial units below and flats above. Prior to conversion the building had a ground floor of stone blockwork with a row of five windows in the rendered first floor.

Devizes

The 1835 Municipal Corporations Act gave policing powers to the Devizes corporation and they kept these until amalgamating in 1847 with the county force.⁹⁶⁸ From c1836 the police were based at the old bridewell in *Bridewell Street*, now called The Grange. This is a timber-framed building, probably purpose-built as a prison in 1579, with multiple alterations including re-facing in brick in the 18th century. It was converted into five flats in 1971.⁹⁶⁹

The police were not there long as by 1855 they were based in the *Town Hall*,⁹⁷⁰ described in Chapter 2. They stayed here until a move to the *Assize Courts*, described in Chapter 4, in 1937,⁹⁷¹ using the former caretaker's quarters there.⁹⁷² That was followed by a period in *Barford House, St John's Street**, from 1969.⁹⁷³ This handsome building is grade 2* listed and has rusticated pilasters defining its

Devizes, the old Bridewell, Bridewell Street, used for some years as a police station

Devizes, Barford House

tall three-storey front of patterned brick, with stone cornice, brick parapet and scroll brackets supporting a cornice and broken pediment above the central door. The building, also used for a period as a post office (see Chapter 9) is now in use as offices.

The first purpose-built police station followed not long afterwards, with the construction in 1976 of the two-storey brick divisional headquarters in *New Park Street.*[974] The entrance is set back to the right of the main run of five bays of segmental-arched ground floor windows, themselves slightly inset below plain first floor windows. The façade is completed by an unsightly canted first-floor oriel window at the west end and there is a substantial yard behind, with ancillary buildings.

There was debate in other contexts about where in the county should be the central headquarters point for countywide public services – see Chapter 7 – but a decision in favour of Devizes for the county police HQ was taken at an early date and so the town was long host to two sets of police offices, for the borough and for the county. It seems that there was already a county police presence in *Bridewell Street* in 1855, presumably using the same premises as the borough police had before they

Devizes, County Police Headquarters, London Road

moved to the town hall.[975] They remained there through to 1879, although the force's second chief constable, Captain Robert Sterne, had established his administrative offices in *Northgate House*,[976] which was later used for council offices - see Chapter 7.

In 1879 the county police moved to the county militia stores on the *Bath Road* just east of the canal bridge. Designed by T H Wyatt and built in 1856 as an open quadrangle of buildings,[977] part was converted as a police headquarters and remained in use as such until 1962.[978] It was subsequently demolished and replaced by the houses of High Lawn. The row of brick houses opposite, previously used as military quarters, may also have been taken over by the police.[979]

The move in 1962 was to the premises where the county headquarters remains, on the west side of *London Road* just north of the canal bridge. These were designed in the office of the county architect, F I Bowden,[980] and comprise a substantial front block with a large and growing number of subsidiary buildings behind, containing since 2003 a joint control room for police, ambulance and fire services. The main three-storey block, in brick under a hipped roof, is of 13 bays with the middle three brought forward, and is three bays deep. The proportions are appropriately neo-Georgian but the lack of detailing gives a bland appearance.

Highworth

The first police house was in Lechlade Road near the junction with Station Road and was certainly there by 1842.[981] It seems that a succession of rented houses in Westrop may have been used before, eventually, a new police station was built at the junction of *Lechlade Road with Grove Hill* c1930.[982] This, now a care home, is in plain two-storey brick but much altered in recent years. A replacement police station was built in *Newburgh Place* in the late 1960s. Small and single-storey, of brick under a pitched roof, it closed in 2018[983] and was empty in 2022.

Malmesbury

Officers were stationed at Malmesbury within a year of the establishment of the county force in 1839 and a police station at an unknown location was in use by 1844.[984] This was replaced in 1855[985] by a new station in *Burnham Road*, designed by J M Peniston, the county surveyor. Of stone block with ashlar dressings under a hipped slate roof, this has the typical appearance for that date of a semi-detached pair of double-fronted villas. Of the four bays, three contain living accommodation for the superintendent and constables and only the second from the right-hand end contains a police office. A corridor behind the right-hand door led through to a block of two cells in a rear extension and there was a stable block at the rear corner of the substantial yard behind.[986] A small extension was added later to the left hand end and the cell block and stables were demolished after the police moved out, though the mark of the roof angle of the cell block can still be seen on the rear of the building, now split into three houses.

The Burnham Road police station stayed in use for 100 years until the eventual opening of a replacement in *Burton Hill* in 1955, just south of the A429 roundabout.[987] This, in stone block under a tiled roof, has a single-storey wing to the left and a two-storey wing at right angles to the right. It shares a small campus with

Malmesbury, Burnham Rd police station

police housing in similar style. The station closed as part of plans announced in 2017 to close and sell off a number of police stations in the county.

Marlborough

A police station, probably improvised, was provided at an unknown location in **St Margaret's**, south east of the town centre, by c1850. In 1854 the former bridewell in **Bridewell Street**, which had been judged to be no longer adequate for that role, was taken over and converted into a police station; the bridewell itself is attributed to John Hammond, who later designed the third version of the town hall (Chapter 2). The conversion was to provide a superintendent's office, accommodation for two constables and stabling as well as cells.[988] This was used until 1899 after which it was sold to Marlborough College,

Marlborough, the former police superintendent's house at the Old Bridewell

the purchase money being used to fund the new police station at Cricklade.⁹⁸⁹ In 1908 much of it was rebuilt by C S Ponting as a gymnasium for the college, incorporating barred windows from the bridewell on the front.⁹⁹⁰ The former police superintendent's house at the north west corner was retained in altered form, now called *Southfield* and in use by the College, as are other buildings from the original bridewell behind it, mostly in brick but with some use of render and of flint.⁹⁹¹

The borough police became part of the county force in 1875 and in 1899 a new police station was opened.⁹⁹² This was designed by the county surveyor C S Adye and was south of the road at the east end of *George Lane*. It was a long block, from the outside a terrace of four houses but with a pediment over the central two bays carrying a scroll, 'Wilts Constabulary', and the monarch's initials below a crown. The three right-hand doors led to constables' living accommodation and that on the left to the charge room and superintendent's office, with three cells in a rear extension; the upper floor was given over entirely to sleeping accommodation.⁹⁹³

This was replaced on the same site in *George Lane* in c1996⁹⁹⁴ by the building still standing in 2023, with the insignia from the gable of the previous station incorporated into the low wall adjacent to the pavement. The new station is of two-storey brick under a hipped roof with large amounts of metal-framed glazing. It closed in 2019 and in 2022 planning permission was given for its replacement by a development of 24 houses.⁹⁹⁵

Melksham

The town's first police station was that built in 1847 concurrently with the town hall in the *Market Place** and linked to it by an archway; it may well have been designed by the same builders, Daniel and Charles Jones of Bradford on Avon.⁹⁹⁶ It is symmetrical in three bays of ashlar with paired round-headed windows separated by pilasters under a cornice, the whole a smaller version of the town hall next door.

Melksham, the Town Hall police station a smaller version of the town hall itself.

Melksham, Semington Road police station. (Melksham and District Historical Association)

By 1925 the lease had run out and the police station was anyway seen as inadequate The search for another site eventually led to one some way out on *Semington Road*, though against considerable opposition from the local magistrates and others who thought this was too far from the centre.[997] The new station, east of the road about 100 metres from what is now the bypass, opened in 1929. The premises were of conventional appearance, with two pairs of hipped-roofed semi-detached brick villas providing living accommodation, the windows paired and a string course at first floor level; these were linked by a single-storey central block with similarly paired windows either side of the central door to the police station itself. After the station closed in 2002 the site was redeveloped and the central block removed to provide access to a small close of houses to the rear, named appropriately enough Peel Court. Additional houses were added, for some reason asymmetrically, to each end of the original block.

Melksham, County Division police operational headquarters, Hampton Park

The operational headquarters for the county division of the police was in 2024 at *Hampton Park*, just west of the A350 south of the town. It had been intended to site a new operational headquarters in Trowbridge but, a suitable site not being found, this was chosen instead and the county operations added to those of the local force.[998] Designed by Bruges Tozer,[999] it opened in 2002 and is a substantial two-storey block, brick below and with continuous glazing in the rendered first floor below a low-pitched and partly flat roof.

Mere

There was a police station in Mere from at least 1855[1000] and by 1896 the police were using a small house attached to an adjoining cottage: in that year it was decided to lease both buildings so that a constable and an inspector could both be accommodated.[1001] It is not certain where any of the early police houses were but a house in *North Street*, double-fronted in stone under a tiled roof and now called The Old Police House, was taken over as a police station between 1900 and 1907.[1002] This was in use until at least 1942 and probably until the construction of the new police station for which tenders were invited in 1956.[1003] The new police station was on *White Road*,[1004] the size of a large house with a central part gable-on to the road and adjoining sections at right angles, a bay at the south end canted a further 45 degrees. The building, rendered with brick dressings, is hard to read but it may be that the police station proper occupied the southern part and the rest was domestic. Each part is now a separate house and the whole called The Copse, a choice of name perhaps even improving on 'Peel Court' at Melksham. It was closed and sold in 2001 and the police moved to a single storey brick block attached to the rear of the *fire station* almost opposite.[1005]

Salisbury

Salisbury had had some policing before the 19th century but in no sense adequate to the need. Thus, when the Municipal Corporations Act of 1835 produced a remodelled corporation with a new power to establish a police force, they took advantage of this power immediately. Uniquely in the county, the city retained a separate force until 1946 when the Police Act of that year made the county the authority for this service: the forces had been temporarily combined during the war years also.[1006] Thus for a period of around 100 years separate police stations for both city and county forces were provided within the Salisbury urban area.

Salisbury, the 1858 police station as built, warehouse buildings alongside underlining the utilitarian nature of New Canal at that date. (Salisbury Museum)

Salisbury, the same building now, the inevitable parked cars emphasising its assimilation into the modern street

The city at first struggled to provide premises for its new force, initially using the guildhall council chamber as a police office,[1007] but in 1838 they took over what had been a house occupied by the weighbridge attendant in **Butcher Row**. This was replaced in 1858 by a new station on the same site, this time fronting onto **New Canal***, (now No.20), designed by Henry Peniston.[1008] The new station, in 2024 the rear entrance to 'White Stuff', has the door surround and window above slightly brought forward beneath a small pediment with a string course and inset windows, all beneath a hipped roof. The ground floor windows were originally double sashes to either side, there were steps up to the door and basement windows below. It was a handsome building before the brickwork was painted and shop bay windows were added to obliterate most of the lower detail.

By the 1880s improved premises were thought to be 'much needed'.[1009] They were provided in 1883 at the **Endless Street/Salt Lane** junction, in a former bank building altered to suit by J C Bothams.[1010] This was also of modest size, of two storeys with a gable to Endless Street, a window and door to Salt Lane and a plaque to Endless Street carrying the city's coat of arms; the cell block was of a single storey on the Salt Lane side. It was substantially altered in 1935 on conversion to municipal offices (see Chapter 7): the cell block was extended upwards, the whole provided with more windows and the main entrance moved to a canted corner where the door stands beneath a segmental pediment containing the city arms and the date. In the meanwhile, in 1930 the police had moved across the street to **13/13a Endless Street**, previously used by the city council, and occupied this building until their eventual incorporation with the county police and move to the new building in Wilton Road in 1955.[1011] The second Endless Street premises are of five bays and three storeys in brick, plain Classical but for a stuccoed ground floor and a central door with a curved hood supported by semi-engaged columns.

The county police may have had earlier premises but the first recorded are those built in 1859, in Fisherton Anger and hence outside the city boundary, at the junction of **Devizes Road and Gas Lane**, on a corner of the land belonging to the soon-to-be-closed county gaol. The architect was again Henry Peniston, appointed county surveyor the previous year.[1012] The main building is said to have been very similar in appearance to that of 1857 at Warminster, though in brick. With a similar frontal appearance of semi-detached double-fronted villas, it served as police offices and living accommodation for the superintendent. The modest block of cells to the rear was replaced later in the century by a much larger one, with 10 cells on each of two floors.[1013]

This police station was closed and sold in 1930[1014] and it seems likely that the county and city police shared the second Endless Street premises thereafter.[1015] The two

Salisbury, former police station at Endless St/Salt Lane junction. Compare with image in Chapter 7. (Salisbury Museum)

forces combined formally in 1946 but by 1952 the Endless Street station was seriously dilapidated and authority was given to design the new headquarters on **Wilton Road** which opened in 1955.[1016] This is a substantial neo-Georgian building in brick, of three storeys and 13 bays under a hipped roof, designed by the office of the county architect F I Bowden.[1017] It has short wings at right angles at each end and the attic floor is stepped in above a stone string course. A concrete and glass extension, also by the county architects, was added in 1971.[1018] In 2014 the police moved out to share premises at **Bourne Hill** with the Wiltshire Council (see Chapter 7) and the former police station was taken over by the short-lived 'University Technical College' which had failed by 2019.

It soon appeared that the accommodation at Bourne Hill was insufficient and in 2023 it was suggested that the police might be moving to a new development at High Post, north of the city on the A345.[1019]

Swindon

There was a superintendent of police in Swindon by 1842, based in High Street in what may have been rented premises.[1020] A police station was to have been built on a vacant plot at the junction of Devizes Road with Britannia Place[1021] but this proposal seems to have been abandoned and instead, in 1854,[1022] they adapted Canford House at what is now ***13 Devizes Road***, just to the south on the same side of the road.[1023] This is a modest double-fronted terraced house, probably of the 1830s,[1024] in stone blockwork now painted. It seems small for the purpose, even at that date,

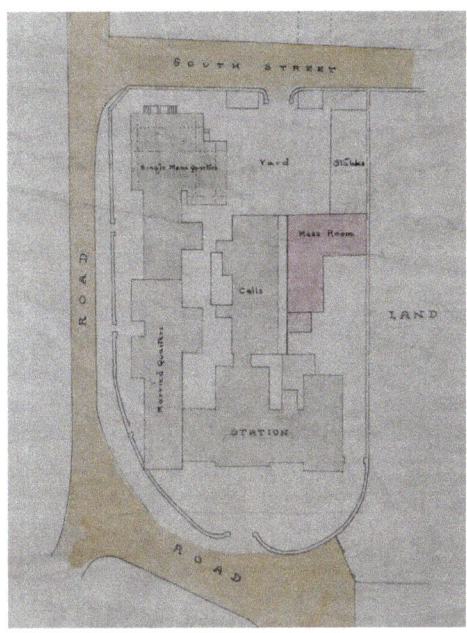

Swindon Eastcott Hill police station, underlining how much space was given over to domestic accommodation even in a large urban station. (WSA)

but it probably incorporated attached cottages to the south and so may have been larger than might appear. By the early 1870s the station was being criticized as inadequate and the three cells to the rear as unhealthy – one prisoner had died of scarlet fever.[1025] A new site was therefore obtained and this one sold when the new premises were opened in 1873.[1026] At this date there appears still to have been no police station in the New Town.

The new premises were on the east side of **Eastcott Hill**, just south of the junction with South Street, and were a much more ambitious affair. Designed by the county surveyor, Henry Weaver, and built at a cost of £4400, they contained substantial offices, a row of police cottages and a petty sessions hall.[1027] There was a long façade containing the main offices and the superintendent's house to the

Swindon Eastcott Hill police station in its final years. (Local Studies (Swindon Library & Information Service)

right, the central bays brought forward with a first floor Venetian window under a pediment.[1028] The cells were in a wing at right angles behind this and the policemen's cottages in a separate wing stretching up Eastcott Hill. A further building was added to the north west corner, beyond the cottages, in 1891,[1029] and by 1915 there were 36 constables as well as seven sergeants, two inspectors and a deputy chief constable based here.[1030]

This site was half-way between the Old and New Towns and it was followed in 1883/4 by the construction of a police station in the New Town proper, on **Station Road** on the east side of the junction with what was then Cheltenham Street and is now Beales Close.[1031] It was a smaller affair on a modest plot and must have remained subsidiary to that on Eastcott Hill. Early in the new century a second police station opened in the New Town, a conversion of **Gorsehill House** on Cricklade Road, about 200 metres north of the railway bridge. The conversion was designed in 1905 by Charles Adye, the county surveyor, and it probably opened that year. In a minimal alteration of the existing house it provided one small charge room and two cells, the remainder being living accommodation for a superintendent and constables.[1032]

Swindon, former Gorsehill police station

This was a very small police station for such a rapidly expanding area, and presumably intended only as a stop-gap. Indeed it was followed in 1928 by the **Gorse Hill** station which still stands, on the same site and designed by the county architect, T Walker.[1033] This one, with its 15-bay stone front, is much larger. It follows to some extent the semi-domestic pattern of earlier stations with their multiple doors, but its bulk and the projecting end pairs of bays make clear that this is indeed a public building. Almost equally remarkable are the long rows of constables' cottages erected at the rear, probably very shortly afterwards, in a line at right angles to the main building and taking advantage of the long rear garden of the former Gorsehill House. They are in brick, in a pair and two terraces of six. The outer bays of the main block also contained accommodation for officers.

The Station Road police station may have closed on the opening of this one and was certainly closed by 1942:[1034] it has subsequently been replaced by a large modern office block. Gorse Hill remained in use until c1966 and was then converted into the flats of Mervyn Webb Place. In the Old Town the Eastcott Hill station remained in use until it was finally deemed to be too small and was demolished in 1973, to be replaced by small blocks of flats.[1035]

Of modern stations, that in *Princes Street* at the corner of Fleming Way was constructed in 1968 to designs by Wiltshire county architects, a ten-storey tower with a first floor circular control room on the corner and a longer frontage of two to three storeys on Princes Street.[1036] This was the main replacement for the Gorse Hill and Eastcott Hill stations; it closed in 2005 and was demolished in 2006 and replaced by another building.[1037] Its replacement as a police station is at *Gablecross*, the operational headquarters for the Swindon division, on the Oxford road not far east of the A419 bypass. This was built in 2004-5, a substantial three-storey block with long brick wings at angles to a central block in white render, the whole with curved metal roofs.[1038]

Swindon, Gablecross divisional police headquarters

A number of suburban police stations were built, amongst which a plain building in white brick was constructed on *Link Avenue* as part of the West Swindon district centre.

Trowbridge

There was a police station of some sort in Fore Street in 1842, perhaps in rented premises. There seems to have been no proper station here until the decision by a committee of the county quarter sessions in 1853 - that there should be a lock-up together with accommodation for a superintendent and two constables in each petty sessional division - produced action.[1039] As a consequence land was bought on *Stallard Street* immediately north of the railway bridge and the first police station was built in 1854, to designs by J M Peniston, the county surveyor.[1040] It contained a court room for the petty sessions as well as rooms for the magistrates and the usual police accommodation, but despite that managed to retain the domestic appearance of so many police stations of the period. Of seven bays, with police living accommodation

Trowbridge, the former Stallard Street police station. (Trowbridge Museum).

at each end, it was built of stone, had a hipped roof, four prominent chimney stacks and a broad string course at first floor level. As well as the court room there were two cells, and immediately to the south was a separate house containing more living accommodation, bringing provision in total for a superintendent, two sergeants and seven constables.[1041]

In 1874, following criticism of the accommodation, the county surveyor Henry Weaver drew up plans for small extensions comprising a waiting room for witnesses and an extra cell. The police station then remained in this form until the move to larger premises in Polebarn Road in 1926, prompted partly, no doubt, by the poor condition of the Stallard Street station: the constables' houses were said in 1923 to be no longer fit for habitation.[1042] The station was sold to the Wiltshire Holloway Benefit Society who rebuilt it as Holloway House, opening in 1929, and it survives in this form though under different ownership.[1043]

The new station in **Polebarn Road** was built on part of the gardens of Polebarn House, to plans by the county architect T Walker. The design was conventional, a long two-storey block in brick under a hipped roof, two bays at the south and two near the north end projected forward, the

Trowbridge, Polebarn Road, the 2004 police station

usual mixture of living accommodation and offices, and five cells in a rear extension. There was a substantial yard behind and at the rear of that was a block of six houses for married constables.[1044]

This in turn was replaced in 2004 on the same site in *Polebarn Road* by the present building. Designed by Aaron Evans of Bath,[1045] it is of brick, the first floor mainly rendered, with the long sides at right angles to the road. Its most conspicuous feature is the curved metal roof on thin legs projecting forward as a canopy over the entrance.

Warminster

A police office was established in 1840 in the *London Inn*, subsequently demolished to make way for the Athenaeum, but it was here only until 1842 before a move to an unknown location in *Weymouth Street*.[1046] There was a further move, to a yard adjoining 6 Market Place,[1047] but in 1857 the police obtained more permanent quarters in a new station built at the south end of *Ash Walk** on land acquired from the Marquess of Bath. This is amongst the most attractive of all the county's police stations and was probably designed by J M Peniston, the county surveyor, although assisted by his son Henry who took over as county surveyor the following year on his father's death.[1048] In ashlar under a hipped roof, it is of typical form, appearing as a semi-detached pair of houses, symmetrical except that the right-hand doorway, projected slightly forward as is that to the left, is slightly wider. This door would have led to the police office and the cells, of which originally there was only one, but both doors would have given onto the accommodation provided for three officers.[1049] A separate stable block was built at the rear of the yard. By 1932 the station was seen as old and expensive to maintain[1050] and it closed that year on the move to new premises in Station Road, becoming a Christian Science church until at least 1963 before conversion to offices.[1051]

The *Station Road* premises opened in 1932 and are a larger and neo-Georgian version of those on Ash Walk, designed by the department of T Walker, the county architect. The police station is of 11 bays, in brick under a tiled roof with three symmetrically placed doors dressed in stone, the central one with pilasters and an architrave, frieze and cornice. The two bays at each end project forwards and a central extension to the rear contained two cells and various service rooms. All this was typical of police station design, as was the placing of accommodation at the two ends, accessed through the doors here and with bedrooms above, and the superintendent's office and charge room accessed through the main door with a corridor leading through to the cells.[1052]

A terrace of four police houses, in identical style, was built adjacent to the north; these are of relatively generous size and were presumably intended for married officers.

The Station Road station closed in 2020 as part of the countywide programme of closures and it was then planned to sell it and the police houses, against considerable local opposition. In 2023 they were undergoing redevelopment as housing. The police meanwhile had moved into a new 'community policing hub' created by refurbishment of the former Wiltshire College premises in *The Avenue*.[1053] This is L-shaped in brick, single-storey and of modest dimensions.

Warminster, Station Road police station, replacing the Ash Walk station illustrated in chapter introduction.

A police station was open in Warminster Common, at that date a largely separate community, by 1871.[1054] A two-storey rubblestone cottage at **32 Bread Street,** side-on to the street, was used for the purpose. The cottage carries a date-stone for 1858 so the police could possibly have used it from then. It was no longer marked on the Ordnance Survey as a police station in 1899 so may have lost its public function by that date, although a police constable and family were noted as living there through to 1911.[1055]

Westbury

There were no police here in 1835 but it is not clear when the town first acquired a police presence.[1056] The first identified police station was that which still stands towards the north end of **Edward Street***. This is in brick, constructed in the 1860s probably to the design of Henry Peniston the county surveyor,[1057] and distinctive

Westbury, curved front of the Edward Street police station

both for its curved front following the curve of the street and for the way the brickwork is formed with inset panels. The words 'Police Station' are still just visible on a panel at first floor level. The accommodation would have followed the usual pattern with just a single room for the police office; a rear extension, since demolished, provided space for perhaps a single cell.

This closed in the 1930s and was sold off for housing in 1940.[1058] Its larger replacement in *Station Road* was probably built in 1935/6[1059] and is of typical form, symmetrical in brick under a hipped roof with the ends projecting and the central three bays likewise but to a lesser extent; raised brick string courses provide a faint echo of the panelling in the Edward Street building. It was closed in early 2020 in the countywide programme of closures and was being sold off for housing in 2022.[1060]

Wilton

Wilton had nominal control of its own borough police force, although it is perhaps doubtful whether the town ever employed officers, and formal consolidation with the county force came in 1887.[1061] A 'superintendent of rural police' was stationed here by 1841 and there was a police station by 1848 but it is not known where the early premises were.[1062] In c1890 the police moved to the *Town Hall*: the offices were located behind the left hand door, which was subsequently replaced by a window.[1063]

In about 1926 the police moved to a new building on the *Salisbury Road* in Fugglestone St Peter, about 250 metres east of the present A36 roundabout. This was designed by the office of T Walker, county architect, and looked much like others by this office of the same period, being a linked pair of L-shaped brick villas under hipped roofs with brick string courses. The linking section here was of only one storey, with a central door, a plaque reading 'County Police' above and a cornice above that dipped to the centre.[1064] Immediately to the west is an identical pair of police houses, these joined directly without the linking section. After the police moved out the linking section in the police station proper was removed, leaving two detached houses, and all four were sold for housing as part of a small development on the site.

The police moved from here in around 1991[1065] to *45 Russell Street*, a pair of brick cottages of perhaps the 1860s, with an arch between them leading through to a rear yard. An unusual choice of building for such a late date, this was closed in 2020 as part of the countywide programme of closure.[1066]

Royal Wootton Bassett

Wootton Bassett has one of the most distinctive police stations in the county, but in a sorry state in 2023. Early police presence here appears not to be documented but a police station was built on the west side of *Station Road* in 1875, paid for by Sir Henry Meux.[1067] This was of five bays parallel to the road, in two storeys of brick; the right-hand two bays had 'County Police Station' on a wide wooden board at first

Wootton Bassett, the first police station on Station Road. (Wiltshire Museum, Devizes)

Wootton Bassett, plans & elevations for the 1912 police station, Station Road. (WSA).

floor level, with a separate door, and a central door with porch led to the three bays of domestic accommodation.[1068] In 1912, having been judged to be in poor condition, it was replaced by the present **Station Road*** building.[1069] Designed in the office of the county surveyor, J George Powell, this is a double-fronted villa in brick with emphatic stone dressings and a gable over the central bay with 'County Police Station' on a stone scroll. Inside was the usual mix of the domestic with a single police office and two cells in an extension to the rear.[1070] The stables from the earlier building at the back of the yard were retained as was a section of that building, since replaced, containing living accommodation and two more cells. Alongside at right angles a police court was built, described in Chapter 4. After closure the police station was converted into a pub, 'The Old Nick', but in 2023 this attractive building had been closed for around 10 years and was boarded up and vandalized.

Plans in 1973 for a replacement station in Wood Street[1071] came to nothing but in 1984 a new station opened adjacent to the Manor House towards the north end of **High Street**. This was designed in the office of the county architect, R I E Haynes, is of brick under a hipped roof, and consists of a main two-storey block facing the road

Wootton Bassett, the 1912 police station in use as a public house. (Royal Wootton Bassett Town Hall Museum).

and single-storey wings off to the rear, one containing the cell block. It had a major refurbishment in 2020 and was still operational in 2023, though without a public office.[1072]

9
Post Offices

Introduction

A POSTAL SERVICE became available to the public for the first time in the early 17th century when Charles the First's royal domestic mail service was opened up so as to generate revenue. The service, initially centred on London, gradually expanded during the 18th century, by the end of which there was a nationwide network of post offices operated by self-employed postmasters who were paid according to the quantity of mail handled. The small volumes then dealt with required little in the way of facilities and most post offices were located in inns, the obvious link being with the requirement to service the mail coaches.[1073] Marlborough, on the main mail route from London to Bristol, provides an early example of this.[1074]

The industrial revolution and the growth in population through the early 19th century saw a steady rise in mail volumes, which were increased dramatically further

The Mail Coach. (Author's collection)

by the introduction of the penny post in 1840. Before then, postage was paid on receipt, based on the distance carried and tracked through a complicated system, all this resulting in high charges. The gamble with the penny post was that the simpler system of payment by the sender would greatly reduce costs and so allow a profit to be made despite the much-reduced charge. It worked spectacularly well: the increase in volume – from 76 million letters nationally in 1839 to 168 million in 1840 after the introduction of the penny post and 347 million ten years later – produced extra revenue far outweighing the loss from the reduced charge per letter.

This increase meant that more space was needed at post offices, for dealing with the public, for sorting both incoming and outgoing mail, and for managing delivery rounds. The response was the gradual movement of post offices from inns into separate shop premises, and the introduction by the General Post Office from 1854 of the first 'crown' post offices run by salaried employees.

The growth continued, reaching 877 million letters a year by 1870, 3.7 billion by the turn of the century, 8.5 billion by 1950 and peaking at nearly 20 billion by 2000.[1075] To this vast increase in trade were added other responsibilities, including the hugely popular Post Office Savings Bank in 1861, the telegram service, nationalized in 1870 after two decades of private development, the parcel post in 1883, the new telephone exchanges from around the turn of the century, and a steadily increasing number of licences and other forms all administered by post office staff.

This growth meant that post offices often had to move premises at relatively frequent intervals in pursuit of more space. A second notable aspect was the way in which, with this wide range of services used by almost every person in the community, the post office came to be seen as being at the centre of the town's life. As just one example, when there was a threat in 1919 that Malmesbury's post office would be downgraded to sub post office status, the town council protested that 'this would lower the dignity of the ancient borough.'[1076]

Each town had a central post office, not always a crown office, and the larger towns had a number of sub offices in the outer areas: these were almost always in shop premises, of limited interest and so not described in this analysis, though for most places those listed in a 1931 directory are noted. Business in the smaller post offices was usually combined with other retail trades in the same premises, typically booksellers, stationers and the like but covering a wide range.

The space requirements were straightforward, at least initially, and explain the ease with which they were moved between different shop premises. Westbury's post office, for example, in the early 20th century had the public office to one side of the central doorway, with a counter, one or more desks for writing telegrams at and, in later years, a soundproof kiosk containing a telephone. The 'instrument room' was placed to the right of the doorway and contained the telegraph instruments: even a modest office like Westbury allocated a room to them and in a large office like the 1907 one in Chipper Lane, Salisbury, space was allocated for 30 telegraph operators, showing just how important the telegram was as a means of communication before the widespread use of telephones.

At Westbury the full-width room at the rear of the building was used as the sorting office. Sorting, along with the provision of a yard for the loading and unloading of mail carts and subsequently motor vehicles, provided the most strain on capacity:

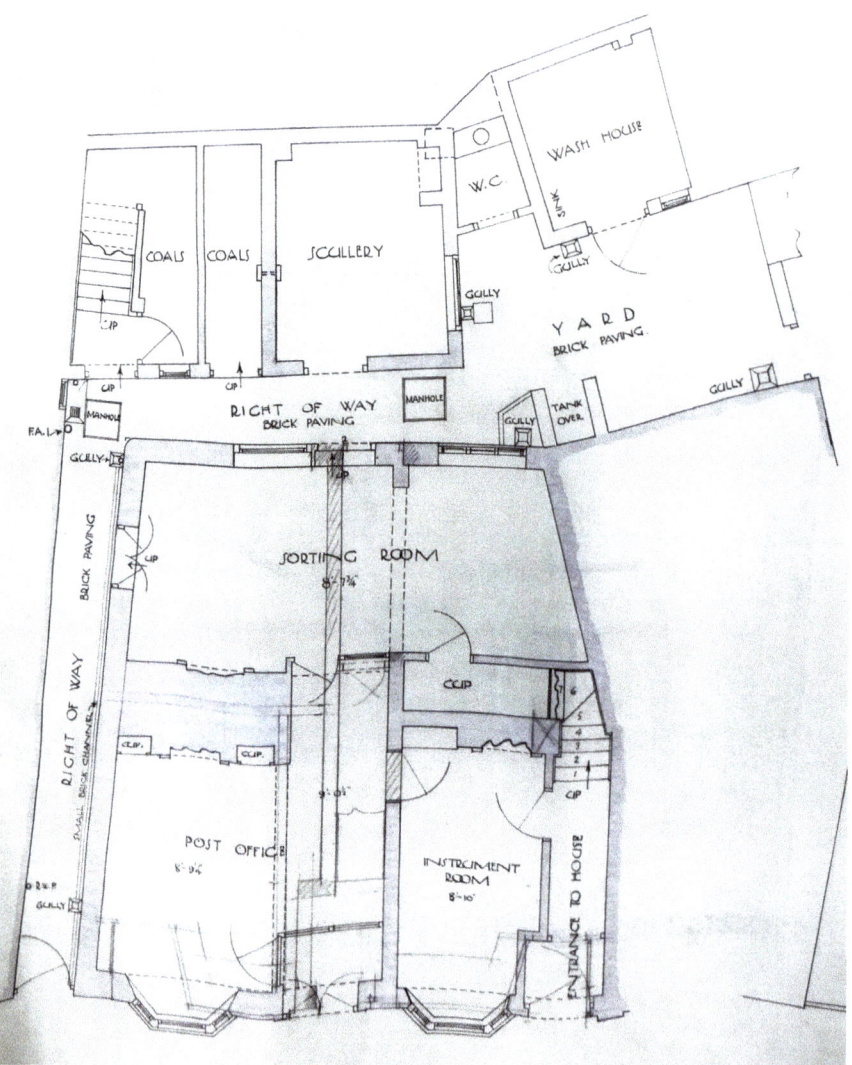

The three main rooms of an early 20th century post office are shown in this ground plan of the Edward Street office in Westbury: public office, instrument room for telegraphs and sorting room for mail. (WSA)

it was common for the sorting office in later years to be separated from the post office itself and contained in a different building where land was more readily available. Sometimes this was a source of conflict, as when the Swindon sorting office was moved to the GWR railway station in the 1870s against the protests of people in the Old Town, who thought this would lead to earlier last postal collections.[1077]

At Barford House in Devizes, converted for post office use in 1920, there was substantial space for the main offices as well as ancillary rooms for staff, and by the time the larger post-war post offices in Chippenham and elsewhere were built the move away from shop-based premises allowed provision for accounting, engineering and other functions absent from the earlier buildings. Telephone exchanges, added to some post offices in the early years of the 20th century, were before long separated and moved elsewhere, though in a process of reverse integration some of the new purpose-built post offices also made provision for offices for other government departments, notably the inland revenue.

The ready adaptability of shops to post office use helps to explain why there are so few purpose-built ones and indeed only 11 survive: there were never many more. Most were designed by the Office of Works and its successor government departments and often the name of the individual architect is not recorded, though it is given here where known. A group from around the turn of the century includes Cricklade (1896), Malmesbury (1902) and Marlborough (1909) – all built by others and then used by the GPO – along with the appealing Arts and Crafts building of 1901 at Bradford and the grandest of them all, the 1907 post office at Salisbury. The austere Victoria Road office at Swindon, of 1935, is the only one of the inter-war period, and last are a batch from after the Second World War, many planned much earlier but delayed because of a lack of resources. Of these, Calne (1953) and Chippenham (1959) have some interest, Melksham (1969) has considerable integrity in its design, while Devizes (1969) and Trowbridge (1966) must be considered victims of the period at which they were built.

The number of post offices nationwide rose from approximately 10,000 in 1850 to 22,000 by the turn of the century, and remained at similar levels thereafter, still standing at about 25,000 in 1970. Changes in the competitive environment and the introduction of electronic communication from around the turn of the new century produced a rapid decline such that by 2010 there were only 12,000. The number has since stabilised but the type of facility has changed greatly, 99% now being franchised outlets in other stores. In 2023 there were only 117 crown post offices across the country, of which Wiltshire possessed just one, at Melksham.[1078]

The Buildings

Amesbury

Amesbury had a post office by 1842.[1079] Its early location is uncertain although it is suggested that it was at various times in premises on both High Street and Salisbury Street.[1080] By 1877 it was located in a small thatched house on the east side of the junction of Salisbury Street with **Salisbury Road**.[1081] This burnt down, along with the adjacent houses, in 1911[1082] and the post office moved, although where to is uncertain: it may have been for a time in the small hipped-roofed building immediately west of the Wesleyan chapel on Church Street, and also at the east end of the same street opposite the former Lloyds bank.[1083] Its penultimate move, perhaps c1960, was to the building at the corner of High Street and Countess Road, part of ***Comilla House****.[1084] This is mostly of the 18th century, the main part on Countess Road in brick but the former post office in flint with Chilmark stone chequer-work, the shop windows a mid-20th century insertion and perhaps contemporary with the post office's move here. The final move was to ***16 Salisbury Street***, one of an unexceptional early 20th century terrace of shops.

Amesbury, Comilla house, former Post Office

By the mid-1950s the town had ambitions to have a crown post office, and it seems the GPO were actively considering a site at the junction of Salisbury Street with Flower Lane by the late 1960s. But a prospective date of 1970 was put back to 1974 and in the end no crown post office was built.[1085]

Bradford on Avon

Bradford had a postmaster by 1769 and by 1822 the post office was at a location near the town bridge, probably in **St Margaret's Street**.[1086] It stayed there until 1844 when it was taken over by Joseph Rawling, a printer and nonconformist minister, who relocated it next door to his printing business in *Market Street*. The printing business was in the building, later the Bradford on Avon Club, fronting the old Methodist Chapel there and the post office was in what was in 2024 a hairdresser's immediately to the north. This is small, of stone with a mansard roof, two windows per floor above and a 19th century inserted shopfront below, again perhaps contemporary with the conversion.[1087]

Joseph Rawlings died in 1866 and his son Charles took over, retiring in 1898. At that time there was no longer a building for the post office and a private company undertook to build one and lease it to the GPO, which they did in 1899; the GPO bought it outright in 1923. The new post office opened in the *Shambles** in 1901, another building nearby having served temporarily.[1088] The 1901 building is in coursed stone blockwork with mullioned and transomed windows, the side to the Shambles restrained but that to Market Street bursting out into a mass of Arts and Crafts detail, splendid but hard to see now in the narrow and congested streets of the town centre. At the corner is a projecting turret and beyond that two half-timbered gables, the further one with a round-arched head.

This was designed by William Henry Stanley of Trowbridge; the 1936 addition to the east was by the Office of Works and perhaps by Henry Seccombe, who designed a number of post offices in the West of England.[1089] This, of two bays, is generally compatible in appearance with the 1899 original but the addition of a hoist, high up at the east end and used to raise sacks of mail for sorting, caused some outcry because of its effect on the appearance of the street.[1090] The door was moved to the east end at this time and other internal changes included the installation of a lift for mail. The post office carries the highly unusual cipher of Edward VIII, though strangely attached to the old part of the building rather than the new. In 1931 there were also sub post offices at 116 Trowbridge Road and 28 Huntingdon Street.[1091]

Bradford on Avon, the 1901 Post Office

The Shambles post office closed in 2013 and the service has since been part of a grocery store just north of the town bridge in **Bridge Yard**.

Calne

A post office was recorded at the Catherine Wheel, later the Lansdowne Arms, in the 1790s.[1092] By 1822 it was in the High Street but it seems also to have been in Church Street in the early 19th century.[1093] By 1855 it was established in the Market Place and by 1885 it was in a building opposite to the Lansdowne Arms, immediately south of the then position of the river.[1094] This proved too small for the increasing volume of mail and in 1890 a **New Post Office** was opened a few doors to the north in an adapted former jeweller's: at the time of opening, trade was said to have increased by over 50% in the last seven years.[1095] The new library now occupies the sites of both these but the 1890 post office was a building of some pretensions, in ashlar with raised quoins, the second floor window heads cutting through the entablature. It lasted until 1968 when it was demolished as part of the A4 widening scheme.[1096]

The 1890 post office was altered to increase its capacity in 1905[1097] and was in use until replaced by the new post office and sorting office in 1953.[1098] This is at the junction of **High Street and Curzon Street**, built after many years of planning.[1099] The two-storey building in stone block, by C J Woodbridge, shows some imagination in following the curve of the corner but the simple framing of the repetitive windows makes little impact. The post office is to the High Street end, the main double doors the most impressive part of the building in their rigidly rectangular framing with the

Calne, the 1953 Post Office

royal cipher for 1953, apparently the first of Queen Elizabeth's reign.[1100] The sorting office is at the Curzon Street end.

The sorting office was still used in 2022 but the post office closed in 2000[1101] and postal business was in 2024 carried out in a newsagent's almost opposite this building.

Chippenham

In 1792 there was a post office in the *White Hart* inn, associated with the London to Bristol mail.[1102] This is almost opposite the Yelde Hall and retains a fine mid-18th century façade, almost symmetrical, with two sets of two-storey canted bays either side of a pedimented centre, the archway below now filled in, with a first floor Venetian window and a Diocletian window above that. The White Hart, long the town's principal inn, closed c1850.[1103] After a century of commercial use it was converted into a supermarket in 1970-72 by the Percy Thomas Partnership, with all but the façade destroyed in the process.[1104]

By 1822 the post office was probably at *12 High Street*, which is a 5 bay 19th century re-fronting in ashlar of an earlier house, with an inserted shopfront.[1105] By the 1870s, and possibly as early as 1853, it had moved to *50 Market Place* where it remained until replaced by the new post office in 1959.[1106] The Market Place building, also a re-facing in ashlar of an earlier building, is a narrow three storeys with a modern shopfront at the ground floor. The shopfront replaces that from its time as a post office which was of much more attractive appearance, having a segmental arch with 'Post Office' inscribed above over a mullioned and transomed window, an ornate columned doorway and a string course at first floor level decorated with scrolls.[1107] In 2022 the building was occupied by a building society.

In 1931 there were sub post offices at 24 New Road and in Lowden.[1108]

The new post office, long delayed by the second world war, finally arrived in 1959.[1109] This is by Cyril George Pinfold of the Ministry of Works and, like its near-contemporary in Calne, it follows the curve of a street corner, this time from *St Mary Street* into Market Place.[1110] The whole is in ashlar below a tiled roof, the public office on the Market Place side, with five tall windows and the royal cipher dated 1959 etched on glass above the doors at the south-east end. The sorting office is on the St Mary Street side and above is a substantial suite of offices behind a long line of anonymous small windows whose styling shows similarities to those in Calne.

The post office closed in 2012 and the service moved to *28-29 Market Place*, a convenience store near the start of The Causeway. The former premises were used by a firm of chartered accountants in 2024.

Chippenham, the 1959 Post Office.

Corsham

The town had a post office from at least the 1760s and it seems likely that not long after that date this was located in the Red Lion Inn which, after alteration in the early 19th century, became the *Methuen Arms**.[1111] The front range of the Inn, in coursed rubblestone, is of three storeys and three bays with a large Roman Doric porch. The long side range of inn buildings to Lacock Road starts with one of perhaps 18th century date, of two storeys and three bays with a central door in round-arched surround and the words 'Post Office' still faintly visible above a ground floor window. This has chequer markings on the door pilasters indicating that it may have been the original main building of the Red Lion.

By 1855 the post office had moved from the Methuen Arms to the premises of John Scott, a bookseller, at an unidentified location in the High Street,[1112] and by 1859 it had moved again to those of James Bromley, an ironmonger, also in the High Street.[1113] This was almost certainly *23 High Street*, at the south west corner of the junction with Post Office Lane, a two-storey building of probably early 19th century date, four windows to each aspect, the visible sides rendered over rubblestone and the roof hipped.[1114] It was still at this location in 1875 and 1884.[1115] By 1899, and perhaps as early as 1885,[1116] it had moved again to *15 High Street* where, at least up until 1919, it appears to have shared the premises with a bank. This three-storey building is

Corsham, Methuen Arms front to Lacock Road, perhaps the original front of the inn as indicated by the chequer markings. Post Office wording still faintly visible above window to left of door

in rubblestone with ashlar dressings and mullioned windows. It was built in the 17th century, altered in the 18th, and during its life had been a house, a shop and an inn before its later use as a bank and post office.[1117]

The final move came in 1938, to **84 High Street**, opposite the town hall, where the post office remains.[1118] This four-bay, three-storey building is of the 17th century but re-fronted in ashlar in the 18th. There was originally a symmetrical disposition of 12-pane windows on the front, below a stone-tiled valley roof, hipped to the front, but in the 20th century a neo-Georgian shop front was inserted at the right-hand side of the ground floor.[1119]

Corsham, the Post Office at 84 High Street.

Cricklade

Cricklade had a postmaster from 1781 or earlier and a post office from at least 1830.[1120] The location of early post offices is not known but by the end of the 19th century it was at *Garfield House, 29 High Street**, the 1896 rebuilding by the postmaster of an earlier house destroyed by fire.[1121] This is of brick under a tiled roof, the first floor conventional with paired sash windows either side, a single one to the centre and the year and house name inset to either side of that. Below is altogether more exuberant: three decorated pilasters space out the shopfront and the central house door, their tops corbelled out to support stone balls; the house window to the right, another pair, also has decorated pilasters. The postmaster conducted a bakery business from the same premises.[1122]

In 1929 the post office was moved north to *39 High Street*, incorporating the town's first telephone exchange, where it remains in what is now a small supermarket.[1123] This is of late 19th century date, of brick with ashlar dressings, four bays of sash windows above an inserted modern shop front below.

Cricklade, turn of the century flamboyance at Garfield House, formerly the Post Office.

Devizes

Devizes had a postmaster by 1675 and a post office in the Market Place by at least 1822.[1124] The post office has moved repeatedly over the two centuries since then, but never far from the Market Place. By 1847 it was at *44 Market Place* in half of a now much-altered 18th century building of three storeys under a hipped roof, in stucco with stone quoins and a plate glass shop-front.[1125] This is adjacent to the Shambles and now houses a bakery.

In 1880 the post office moved to larger premises nearby at *39 Market Place,* in a building formerly the *Wiltshire Times* office and subsequently replaced by Lloyds Bank.[1126] In 1887 it moved again, to *24 Market Place*, this one the former premises of the Wiltshire Friendly Society. It is of three storeys in ashlar stone, dated to around 1840 with four windows to each floor above and a shop window below.[1127]

The post office stayed there until 1920 when it moved into *Barford House* on St John's Street, described in Chapter 8. This building was large enough to provide a substantial sorting office behind the main block, together with other offices and a flat on the top floor.[1128] In 1931 there were sub post offices at 27 Bath Road and at Estcourt Street.[1129]

The first purpose-built post office arrived finally in 1969 when that in *Sheep Street*, designed by E W Judd, opened.[1130] This two-storey building, which formed part of a block of public offices, is of brick below with aggregate panels above, flat-roofed and with large oblong aluminium-framed windows and doors. It fits uncomfortably with the character and scale of the surrounding streets.

This closed c2007[1131] and the post office was in 2024 in *Sainsbury's*, diagonally opposite across the street.

Highworth

The town's post office moved in typical fashion from location to location over the years. By 1811 it was in the High Street and by 1855 at *1 Vicarage Lane*.[1132] This is late 18th century, rendered with brick quoins, rubblestone sides and two hipped dormers. The post office was still there in 1859 but by 1875 had moved to *18 High Street*, on the south side, an 18th century building of rubblestone with tall fifteen-pane first floor windows and arcaded Victorian shop windows either side of a central doorway. The post office seems to have occupied only the right-hand half of this building.[1133]

At that date the building opposite at *35 High Street** was the Cross Keys inn, but by 1898 this had closed and the post office had moved across the street to occupy the premises. The building is perhaps of late 17th century date, in painted rubblestone of basically conventional three-bay appearance with inserted shop windows either side of a central door. Its most conspicuous feature is a projecting gabled tower porch, the arched entrance below and above that a room with windows on three sides.[1134]

Highworth, former Post Office at 23 High Street.

By 1922 there had been a further move, to *23 High Street*. This, formerly the Greyhound Inn, has a roughcast front of c1800, of two storeys with a parapet hiding the roof; the door is asymmetrically placed and originally the post office counter was to the left and the sorting office to the right. It is grade 2* listed, perhaps partly because of the original angled bow windows above and multi-paned bow windows below but perhaps also because of its role in the Second World War when, under the management of postmistress Mrs Mabel Shranks, it was used to screen people going to the military general headquarters at nearby Coleshill House. To maintain security, visitors were not sent directly to Coleshill but instead to the Highworth post office where Mrs Shranks made phone calls to check their credentials before they were collected in a blacked-out truck and driven to Coleshill.[1135]

The post office, now under the management of Mrs Shranks' son, moved to *5 Sheep Street* at the north side of the Market Place in the 1950s. This is of three bays with a plastered front, two small hipped bays below and the door to the right hand side.[1136] The final move was to the new Co-operative food store in *Brewery Street*.

Malmesbury

The town had mail from London three times a week as early as 1689 and the first identified postmaster, in the mid-19th century, was a watchmaker occupying premises at *31 High Street*, a small two-storey building with inserted shop-front immediately to the south of the King's Arms.[1137] A new post office was built in 1902 at *41 High*

Malmesbury, the 1902 Post Office

Street* and originally leased to the GPO, though it was bought by them much later. It is an imposing brick building of three storeys with ashlar dressings, segmental-arched windows with prominent keystones, rusticated quoins and string courses between the floors. The door is to the left of the ground floor with two post office windows to the right and beyond that an archway to the rear sorting office which was increased in size in 1960 to accommodate motor vans. The telephone exchange occupied the first floor from 1907 to 1946 after which it moved elsewhere.[1138] In 1931 there was a sub post office in Westport.[1139]

The post office stayed here until 1990, at which date it moved to become part of the co-operative supermarket at *8 High Street*.

Marlborough

Marlborough stood on the main postal route from London to Bristol and so had a postmaster from an early date, certainly by 1610.[1140] The first recorded post office was in 1822, in the **High Street**, probably a building on the south side which was burned down in 1879.[1141] This belonged to the Lucy family from at least 1827 to 1853 and was a substantial three-storey five-bay building with raised quoins, segmental arched windows with prominent keystones, a central porch on two pillars and a protruding shopfront inserted to the left-hand two bays on the ground floor.[1142]

After the fire the post office was moved north of the High Street, perhaps to No.133 before a move next door in 1883 to the larger premises at **No.131 High Street**, now part of the **Merchant's House** museum.[1143] This had been a cabinet maker's and is described in Chapter 5.

From there in 1909 it moved along to **No.101 High Street**, a large part-timbered building inserted into two of what had been a row of four terraced brick houses dating from 1748.[1144] The post office, insensitively out of scale, has a broad central gable above pairs of bay windows on two upper floors. The ground floor has three shop windows and a door to the left and was a restaurant in 2024. In 1931 there was also a sub post office at 8/9 London Road.[1145]

Marlborough, elevation drawing of the Post Office at 101 High St, the front now coarsened by changes to the fenestration. (WSA)

The post office moved to a 'one-stop' shop at **33 High Street** in 1994/5.[1146]

Melksham

There was a post office in Melksham by 1782[1147] and in 1817 it was said to be in the Market Place almost opposite the King's Arms.[1148] It was still there in 1855 but by 1867 had moved north, probably into what is now **29 Bank Street**.[1149] This is early 19th century in ashlar of three storeys and four bays with paired windows to the first floor, single to the second and a 20th century shop front.

In 1901 the post office moved to a more central position at **14 High Street***, opposite the entrance to Church Street.[1150] This is in ashlar, of the early 19th century, three bays by three storeys with four pilasters, plat bands between each floor and a cornice in front of a hipped roof. Despite the depredations of 20th century shop windows the façade remains handsome.

Melksham, the Church Street Post Office

It was substantially altered in both 1909 and 1931, the post office for some years occupying the left-hand half of the ground floor with a stationery shop to the left, and eventually the post office expanded to occupy the whole building. It moved in 1969 to the new building at *31 Church Street*.[1151] This, designed by P G Smith, is described as 'a conscientious effort' by the Buildings of England. It is of re-used stone block, the main building of two storeys and four bays, the first floor jettied out on a band of white concrete over the row of shop windows below and the whole further enlivened by a bay window in the first floor at the east end, creating an appearance which is decidedly harmonious, particularly bearing in mind the date at which it was built. To the rear is a substantial sorting office and yard.

In 1931 there was a sub post office in Bath Road.[1152]

Mere

There was a post office in the town by 1817.[1153] It was in Castle Street by 1848 and by 1871 it was said to have been in a house opposite Barton Lane.[1154] The post office had moved to the Square by 1880 and by 1895 was in the ownership of the Walton family, the town's major retailers.[1155] It may have moved to several locations in *The Square* over the next 100 years but probably the major part of that time was spent at the building on the north side known as the Walton's building and in 2023 a charity shop.[1156] This used to be the home of John Walton the ironmonger and originally had sash windows to domestic scale on the ground floor, with three similar above, the central door having the columned doorway which it retains. The shop windows were enlarged and the first floor ones altered sometime after 1928.[1157]

In 1985 the link with the Walton family was broken, though the name was retained, when the post office moved into the newly-built small single-storey shop at the top end of *Boar Street*, where it remains.

Salisbury

Salisbury had a post office by 1645. An office is again recorded in 1807 and by 1822 it was located in **New Canal**, though the exact location is not known.[1158] By 1844 it had moved to **Blue Boar Row**, on the north side of the market place, again in an unknown location, but c1855 it moved back to New Canal, almost certainly to the premises at **23 New Canal** where it remained for the next 50 years.[1159] This building was of three storeys, the ground floor a broad shop front below rendered upper storeys with five windows to the first floor and three, broadly spaced, to the second.[1160] It has since been replaced by what was in 2023 Marks and Spencers.

By late in the century this was becoming too small and in 1899 the GPO surveyor advertised for a new site in the city centre.[1161] The site chosen was at the corner of ***Castle Street and Chipper Lane*****, where previously there were shops and houses, and the new post office opened in March 1907. Inside, the public office, 40ft long, was accessed from Castle Street and contained, in addition to a counter, desks for writing telegrams and a telephone cabinet. The telegram dispatch office on a higher floor had space for up to 30 telegraph instruments and a third of the building, on the north side, was allocated for use by other civil service departments.[1162]

The architect was H N Hawks of the Office of Works, and the building he created is in neo-Tudor style in Chilmark stone ashlar, tall with mullioned and transomed windows and multiple small gables above dormer windows. The public door on the Castle Street side of the corner has a four-centred arch with carved spandrels and 'Post Office' inscribed above, and the royal insignia are displayed on the corner angle; at the

Salisbury, Chipper Lane Post Office when newly built. (Salisbury Museum)

roof level two substantial chimney blocks are joined by a small domed bell-cote.[1163] Adjacent on Chipper Lane is the 1936 telephone exchange by D N Dyke, of six bays in ashlar, again three storeys, with pedimented dormers breaking through the roofline, the whole handsome in what the listing describes as a 17th century French style.

In 1931 there were 10 sub post offices at locations around the city.[1164]

The Castle Street post office closed in 2016 and in 2023 a planning application had been made for conversion to into flats and shops.[1165] The city's main post office thereafter was that which had opened in 1960 in a small shop at *56 High Street*, a grade 2* listed 18th century refacing of a 14th or 15th century timber framed building.[1166]

Swindon

By 1830 there was a post office in the *Bell Hotel* in the High Street.[1167] In the early 1840s it moved to Wood Street, to a room off a passage two doors east of the King's Arms where business was transacted through a narrow window.[1168] One directory indicates a move by 1853 to Bath Road but this may be just confusion between adjacent street names and the post office was in any case in Wood Street from 1859 to at least 1867, at some point moving to premises on the south side of the street next to Deacon's the jewellers.[1169] By 1875 it had moved to *11 Bath Road*, almost opposite what is now Victoria Road.[1170] This is one of a three-storey terrace, each unit of two bays, with shop fronts at the ground floor level, first floor windows with continuous string courses linking above through the bases of blind recessed semicircular arches, and attic windows above that. Alterations to the post office were made in 1901 by William Drew.[1171]

The New Town probably had its own sub post office by the 1840s and certainly by the early 1850s, in the unidentified premises of a druggist.[1172] It was initially in *Emlyn Square*, then called High Street, and it seems likely that this was followed sometime after 1864 by an office at *58 Bridge Street*, at the junction with Fleet Street.[1173] By the 1880s there was a further post office, perhaps a sub office, at the northeast corner of *Read Street* and Westcott Place.[1174] That on Bridge Street closed by 1899 and that on Read Street closed between 1899 and 1922.[1175] The most long-lasting New Town post office of this era was that erected at the northeast corner of *Faringdon Road* and *Milton Road* at a date between 1885 and 1899, which remained there until at least the 1940s.[1176] All three of the early New Town post offices whose locations have been identified have been either substantially altered or demolished.

Until the turn of the century the Bath Road and Milton Road offices acted for Old and New Towns respectively, though the tensions between the two led to complaints from the Old Town when the mail sorting activity was moved from there to premises at the GWR station in the mid-1870s.[1177] By this date there were six sub post offices in the town.[1178] With the continued growth of the New Town it became apparent that the head post office in Bath Road was too far from the centre of the urban area and in 1900 an auctioneer's premises in *Regent Circus* was taken over and adapted as a new head post office. At this date the Bath Road premises became a 'branch office' with a status above that of a sub office, which is what that in Milton Road remained.[1179]

The new head office was at the north end of the circus, stretching into Princes Street on a site now occupied by a nondescript office block just north of the new

Swindon, Regent Circus Post Office before 1911. The building to the right was later enlarged. (Local Studies (Swindon Library & Information Service)).

library. It was of brick with stone dressings to mullioned ground floor windows and a door on the corner angle. Above were six four-light windows, that on the corner angle blocked in with the royal arms attached, and over that three dormer windows broke through the roofline. The weaknesses of the conversion soon became apparent and in 1911 the building was enlarged, with a substantial new two-storey four-bay block stretching up Princes Street, the ground floor windows round-arched and those above mullioned and transomed. The original conversion may have been by Henry Tanner; the 1911 extension was by Edward Cropper.[1180] In 1935 the town's sorting office was moved back from the GWR station to here.[1181]

The Bath Road premises remained until 1935 when they were replaced by the new branch post office at **119 Victoria Road**, not far north of the Bath Road junction. This is a severe affair of three storeys and seven bays in brick, attributed to Henry Seccombe.[1182] The ground floor is composed of arched openings, with doors either end and the central five recessed for windows though one of these has now also been converted to a door. Above are two tiers of sash windows; prominent drain pipes at either end emerge from a parapet concealing the hipped roof. The upper floors were used by the Inland Revenue; the public office, with its counter, writing tables and two telephone boxes, was praised as overshadowing the facilities at Regent Circus.[1183]

The Regent Circus post office was demolished in the early 1970s. In 1969-70 a new head post office had opened on **Fleming Way**, a substantial three-storey block, the ground floor anonymous but those above in pale ribbed panels.[1184] But perhaps more useful for the public was the new building on the west side of **Theatre Square**, largely glass below, divided by concrete uprights and the first floor of dark brick broken by a horizontal line of narrow windows. A redevelopment of the Fleming Way building to replace this was planned c2000 but did not go ahead.[1185] In any event the Fleming Way building closed and was demolished c2005 and the Theatre Square post office was subsequently converted into artists' studios and shop units.[1186]

The Victoria Road office remains in use, albeit now taking up only half of the ground floor of the building, and the main outlet post office is in *W H Smith's* on Regent Street, in a building of apparently 1930s date with a two-storey pilastered front above the shop windows. There is also a branch at *58 Commercial Road*, in a small brick terraced building with spectacularly large round-arched first floor windows. In 1931, as well as Regent Circus and the branch at Bath Road, there were 15 sub post offices at locations around the town.[1187]

Swindon Victoria Road Post Office. The Post Office formerly occupied the whole frontage.

Trowbridge

There was a postal service to Trowbridge from at least 1672 and by 1822 the post office was in an unidentified location in Fore Street where it remained in 1844.[1188] By 1855 it was said to be in Back Street, although it is possible that this actually refers to its place in *Fernleigh House* in Church Street, where it was from at least 1857 until 1870.[1189] Fernleigh House, 18th century and immediately next to the entrance to the Tabernacle church, is brick-built, two storeys plus basement, with a pedimented door case, sash windows either side and three above.

The move in 1870 was to *The Limes*, the predecessor building to the town hall, where the postmaster rented the house and the grounds behind,[1190] but by 1886 it had moved again, to premises on the south side of *Wicker Hill* at No. 5.[1191] When occupied as a post office the ground floor had a series of segmentally arched openings

Trowbridge, Fernleigh House, surprisingly domestic for an urban post office.

but this building appears to have been demolished, perhaps as late as the 1950s, and replaced by the strange-looking edifice now occupying the space.[1192]

From there it moved in 1911 up the hill to *4 Fore Street*,[1193] a five bay, three storey building in ashlar with pilasters either end, a cornice, and string courses between the floors. The ground floor has two central shop windows, replacing the four there when the post office occupied it, with a tall doorway to the right and a broad rusticated segmental arch to the left leading through to the rear.[1194] It was considerably larger than its Wicker Hill predecessor and had a substantial sorting office, concrete roofed, through the passage to the rear, the Inland Revenue having offices at the first floor front.[1195] It was substantially rebuilt in 1936.[1196]

In 1931 there were four sub post offices in the town.[1197]

The town's first and only purpose-built post office followed in 1966, at *1a Roundstone Street* by the junction with Church Street. This was designed by R I Greatrex of the Ministry of Public Building and Works[1198] and has a ground floor mixing shop windows and concrete blockwork, a middle floor of stone panelling with five inset windows and a top floor of continuous window, the whole making few concessions to the surrounding streetscape. This closed in the late 2010s, though the rear yard was still in use in 2023, and the post office is now located in *W H Smith's in Fore Street*, the former White Hart public house, of the 18th century though now much altered.

Warminster

In the 1790s the town's post office was in the *Angel Inn*, which by 2023 had been converted to two shops at 9 High Street.[1199] This is of three storeys and five bays, in coursed rubblestone with ashlar dressings, plain other than for the pedimented doorway. By the early 19th century the post office had moved to an unknown location in George Street where it remained until c1854 before moving into the market place.[1200] Here it occupied what is now *70 Market Place*. This is on the south side, almost opposite the entrance to Station Road, and is in painted brick, dated 1810 on a rainwater head There are flush stone quoins, three first floor sash windows, a parapet above, a curved corner into the side street and two modern shop windows below.[1201] The post office was run in conjunction with a stationer and tobacconist's business.[1202]

In time this became too small, in May 1903 it was announced that the post office was looking for larger premises and by late that year they had taken over part of the savings bank on the opposite side of the road, on the corner of *Station Road and East Street**.[1203] This is a building of much greater pretension on an important corner site. It was built as a savings bank in 1852 in 17th century style, in coursed and dressed rubblestone with ashlar dressings. On the Station Road side are a Dutch gable and mullioned and transomed windows, the central one of the three at first floor level carrying a rather out of place pediment to provide a suitable complement to the doorway below with its pilasters and Tudor strapwork. On the corner angle is a two-storey curved bay and the East Street façade, while more subdued, has two Dutch gables and an equally ornamented doorway with the monogram of Queen Victoria above it.

Warminster, Station Road Post Office. (Warminster Historical Society).

Initially the savings bank retained the southern part of the building but by the mid-1930s the post office had taken over the whole.[1204] In the late 1960s there were plans to replace it in conjunction with a road widening scheme[1205] but these came to nothing and in 1984 it was renovated with the entrance moved to the East Street side.¹²⁰⁶ In 1995 the service was put out to tender and the post office moved to Martin's in *Three Horseshoes Walk*;¹²⁰⁷ the Station Road/East Street premises were largely empty in 2023 though the adjoining post office yard was still in use.

In 1931 there were sub post offices at 16 Silver Street and at Warminster Common.¹²⁰⁸

Westbury

The first mention of a postal service in Westbury was in 1783 although it was no doubt in place earlier than that.¹²⁰⁹ By 1844, and quite possibly by 1822, the post office was established in Maristow Street at what is now *14/16 Edward Street**, where it remained until 1923.¹²¹⁰ This is opposite the former police station at the junction of the two streets, dated to 1774, in brick with two storeys plus attic windows behind a parapet and a mansard roof to the left. Two canted first floor bays remain, originally carried down to ground level either side of a substantial door with fanlight but sliced off and replaced by plate glass windows for two shops in alterations carried out in the mid-1920s, a considerable desecration not helped by the state of the building in 2023.¹²¹¹ In post office guise, the public office was to the left of the central doorway, an instrument room for telegraph instruments to the right and the sorting office to the rear.

Westbury, Edward Street Post Office at centre, before later depredations. (Westbury Heritage Society).

In 1923 the post office moved to *26 Edward Street*, opposite Westbury House, early 19th century in brick under a hipped slate roof and previously a bank.¹²¹² This has an asymmetrical façade of five bays with sash windows above and, below, two broad windows to the left of a door with semi-circular fanlight, a further window and one more now bricked in. Inside, the new larger premises incorporated the telephone exchange, a public office to the right of the doorway, a 'spacious and airy' sorting office and a telephone cabinet.¹²¹³ In 1931 there was also a sub post office in Westbury Leigh.¹²¹⁴

The Edward Street office closed in 1991 and the post office moved to Cooper's supermarket at *42 Edward Street*. In 2009, when that was taken over by Morrison's, it moved again, to McColl's in *High Street*. This closed in 2023, leaving the town's only post office in a convenience store at The Ham, northwest of the railway station.¹²¹⁵

Wilton

There were no doubt earlier post offices here but the first noted is in 1855 at an unknown location in The Square.¹²¹⁶ This probably remained until c1879 when it was to be found at *11 Kingsbury Square*, in a small red-brick terraced house with a hipped slate roof, of early 19th century date, which still has the words 'Post Office' painted above a ground floor window.¹²¹⁷ From there it moved for a period to an unknown location in West Street before relocating to the house at the corner of *South Street* and West Street around 1895.¹²¹⁸ This is of two storeys with three bays facing South Street and one to West Street. Of painted brick, it has sash windows, raised quoins, a moulded string course at first floor level, a pilastered doorcase, dentil moulding at the cornice and a tiled roof hipped at the north end.

The post office was here until at least 1939¹²¹⁹ and was at *4 West Street* in the 1950s and 60s, this a nearly square three-storey brick building of perhaps the mid-19th century with a pyramidal roof, the windows segmentally arched but the appearance undermined by the inserted shopfront and central first floor window.¹²²⁰ It had moved to *North Street* by 2008,¹²²¹ where in 2023 it was within the Co-operative store.

Royal Wootton Bassett

There was a post office here by 1838 and by 1859 if not earlier it was in the High Street, probably already at *21 High Street* which was to be its base until at least 1936 and probably until its final post-war move.¹²²² This is a narrow two-storey house of perhaps late 18th century date, a restaurant in 2023, with bay windows at ground and first floor level either side of a central door, the glazing modern.

The post office moved, probably soon after the Second World War, to *33 High Street*, where it remains.¹²²³ This has broad bay shop windows either side of a central door, in render with raised quoins, three sash windows above and two dormers in a hipped roof of graduated stone slates. Originally of c1735, it became in the 1930s a branch of Barclays Bank, was requisitioned in 1939 and thereafter became the post office.¹²²⁴

10
Swimming Baths

Introduction

WE NOW THINK of swimming baths as just that, large pools for people to swim in. But their history takes us in a different and perhaps unexpected direction.

People had swum in rivers and lakes since ancient times and one might expect the development of more formalized bathing facilities to be just a progression from this, but in fact two other considerations played a substantial part. The first was the rapid 19th century development of working class housing in urban areas, much of it with no washing facilities whatsoever. Such unsanitary conditions were the inevitable breeding ground of disease, and concern about this led to the wish to provide communal facilities for both washing clothing and washing oneself.

Calne, cleaning out the old bathing shed by the River Marden. (Calne Heritage Centre)

Trowbridge, the Brown Street pool in typical 1930s lido style. (WBR)

The second was a concern that very few people in the growing population could swim, with the result that the number of deaths by drowning was going up rapidly. This fed a growing belief that there should be places where the population, and particularly children, could be taught this skill.

Some larger cities were already active in providing baths and wash-houses in the early part of the 19th century and in 1846 the Public Baths and Wash-houses Act was passed, giving local authorities powers for the first time to build baths for washing the person and wash-houses for washing clothing and bedding, together with powers to borrow money to that end. These facilities appeared at an accelerating rate following the Act, both local authority funded and privately owned, one notable local example being the individual 'slipper'[1225] baths provided by the Great Western Railway from early in the life of its Swindon works. Many of the private baths survived well into the 20th century[1226] only to reduce in number thereafter as more houses acquired bathrooms.[1227]

River bathing was being improved, with formalised bathing places, changing huts, sometimes diving boards and often some supervision. People used such places for washing as well as swimming – there was a report in 1884 that men had been forbidden from using soap at the bathing station in Devizes, this one in a canal[1228] - and the inadequacy of these facilities became increasingly recognized, alongside growing concern about the safety and hygiene of river bathing. This was reflected in the 1878 amendment to the 1846 Act which gave local authorities powers to erect covered swimming pools also. It opened the door to the late-Victorian baths of which Wiltshire still retains two notable examples, in Swindon and Westbury. These combined a swimming pool with a series of individual baths for washing, and in Swindon's case much else besides under the paternalistic ownership of the Great Western Railway.

The slipper baths originally built with the Swindon and Westbury pools were removed in the new century as the availability of bathrooms in homes improved, but in the meantime many towns had still not moved on from the river-bathing stage. The typical pattern was of repeated calls for a public swimming pool in the town, recognizing the benefits it would bring, countered by an unwillingness to commit the funds necessary for building and running it. The comment of Melksham's borough surveyor to his council as late as 1935 is indicative: 'When you are prepared to put a nice slice on your rates you can have your scheme.'[1229] Melksham finally acquired a pool in 1957 and Chippenham only in 1960, and that was open-air not enclosed.

Bathing in both rivers and swimming baths was typically segregated between women and men, often by having swimming available to women during the day when men were supposed to be at work and women not: an advertisement of 1890, for example, states that the canal bathing place in Devizes was then available for the use of women at certain times, with a female attendant present.[1230] Some, like Swindon, imposed segregation a different way by having a separate, smaller, pool for women.

Early baths were often put to other uses in the winter. Here the Bradford baths host a Liberal dinner in 1910. (Bradford on Avon Museum).

Enclosed pools had the potential to be used year-round but in practice were for long open only in summer, the pool often boarded over in winter and made available as a hall for a range of other activities. In earlier days the water was untreated and soon became unpleasant – at Bradford on Avon's first enclosed pool, for example, the charges for swimming were reduced as the water became progressively more dirty prior to changing.[1231] Filtering and chlorination were introduced after the turn of the century to overcome this problem.

By the mid-20th century many towns had open-air pools of the 'lido' type with ranges of single-storey changing rooms, often in white render: they developed much nostalgia at their passing but the brevity of the summer season severely limited their usefulness. Their modern replacements, enclosed and providing a much more comfortable swimming experience, seldom offer any particular interest in their design.

'Taking the waters' at spa towns - notably of course Bath in this part of the country but also for a short and unsuccessful period at Melksham - became a popular activity for the gentry from the mid 18th century. Spa waters are not discussed further in this chapter, and nor are those modern swimming baths provided by private sports clubs.

The Buildings

Amesbury

There was a swimming club in Amesbury in the early 20th century using a bathing place in the River Avon. A bathing shed was provided, perhaps at the South Mill where river bathing took place until at least the 1950s, but alternatively perhaps at Ham Hatches in West Amesbury, or Countess: bathing took place at both these locations also.[1232] There has never been a public baths there.[1233]

Bradford on Avon

A swimming club was formed in 1881 and erected a bathing place on the north bank of the Avon, just east of Greenland Mills and wisely upstream of all the town's mills.[1234] Its use probably reduced rapidly once the new pool opened and it was gone before 1922.[1235]

The town's first indoor baths were built in 1898 as a commemoration of Victoria's diamond jubilee, funded largely by John Moulton and Lord Edward Fitzmaurice.[1236] They were in Bridge Street, immediately south of the town bridge where the library now stands, and replaced a run-down industrial area. They were sideways on to the river, the long façade in vaguely Tudor style with gabled bays at either end linked by a

Bradford on Avon, the old baths. (Bradford on Avon Museum)

five-bay arcade, with a skylit roof ridge; the architect was the town's surveyor, Sydney Howard. The interior was conspicuously narrow, with no walkway at all down one long side, though it was still floored over and used for other events in the winter.

This pool was demolished c1965 and the library and museum eventually built on the site; the original railings with Moulton's initials remain. The new swimming pool, similarly adjacent to the river but 100m downstream off *St Margaret's Street*, opened in 1971. It is inconspicuous in pale brick and glass.

Calne

A bathing place was provided on the west bank of the River Marden south east of the town, on land given by the Marquis of Lansdowne behind what is now Churchill Close. It was in place from at least 1885 and perhaps as early as 1866. A **bathing shed** was added here in 1896, the walls of timber and the pool brick-lined, and lasted until 1939.[1237] By 1955 the town was considering the provision of a swimming pool[1238] and in 1964 the council built a pool off the A4 to the south east. This was later taken over by the North Wiltshire district council and then Wiltshire Council and, after a major refurbishment, was reopened as the *Calne Community Campus*.[1239] The building's exterior, in brick and corrugated sheeting, has nothing to commend it but amongst its facilities is a 25 metre pool.

Chippenham

Chippenham's first bathing place was established alongside the Avon south of the town in 1878, on the bend of the river by what was in 2024 the Sea Cadets' headquarters off Long Close.[1240] There was discussion of a covered baths around the turn of the century but no progress was made and the next initiative seems to have been in 1931 when approval to borrow money for a new baths was sought, without success.[1241]

Concerns about river pollution led to the bathing place by the river being closed in 1948.[1242] The town then had no baths until the open-air pool in **Monkton**

Chippenham, Olympiad Sports Centre.

Park was opened in 1960; this had a single-storey range of service buildings at one of the narrow ends and a diving platform at the other. It was closed in the late 1980s, despite protest, and replaced by a new indoor pool at the *Olympiad sports centre*.[1243] The new centre opened in 1989, built alongside the site of the open air pool and set into the hillside above the river and behind the police and council offices on Monkton Hill. It is almost square in plan but with six separate hipped roofs over the different elements of the building, the walls of coursed stone block and windows framed in red metal.

Corsham

There appears to have been no formal bathing place here, though informal swimming took place in the Weavern pool in the valley some way north of the town, and perhaps elsewhere also.[1244] The parish council considered a suggestion for swimming baths in 1934, as a memorial to the late Lord Methuen,[1245] but no baths were built until the erection of the modern pool at what is now the *Springfield Campus* in 1974.[1246] The initiative to create a 'community campus' here in 2014 led to the refurbishment of the pool along with the introduction of a library, police offices and other functions in a new building described in Chapter 6. The swimming pool occupies the south east wing of this substantial set, the white-rendered walls comprising a series of broad columns with inset space between, the windows at right angles to the main alignment.

Cricklade

There is no evidence of public baths having been provided in Cricklade. There is said to have been informal swimming in the Thames at Hatchetts Ford, at the end of Abingdon Court Lane in the north east of the town, and also in the 'lido' established in the 1930s and 1940s in a water-filled gravel pit in the nearby village of Latton.[1247]

Devizes

The first bathing place was that established on the Kennet and Avon canal on the western outskirts of the town behind St Peter's church. It was in place in 1884 and may well have been there for some years already at that date.[1248] Part of the canal was cordoned off for the pool at a wide point and was lined by sheets of corrugated iron. At one time it had two diving boards and about a dozen changing rooms on the north side. In the late 19th century there was an attendant on duty, with men and women required to bathe at different times.[1249]

The conditions were not hygienic – bathers were advised to keep moving to avoid leeches and slugs attaching themselves – and there was soon agitation for the provision of a proper swimming baths.[1250] For a long time the usual problem of a perceived lack of affordability persisted but the difficulty was overcome by Lord Roundway who offered land in 1934, the baths following in 1936.[1251] They were built where the houses of **Sheppard Close** now stand, between Waiblingen Way and Rotherstone, and followed the pattern of a 1930s lido with a broad single-storey white-rendered building at the south end in front of the pool, a smaller pool and a stand to one side and a row of changing cubicles to the other. The front block had pavilions either end and a low-angled pediment over the centre.

The canal bathing place fell out of use after the new pool opened, and that itself lasted until 1989, after which it was replaced in 1990 by the indoor pool at the *Devizes Leisure Centre*. This is of modest size, in pale brick with red-brick bands and grey cladding to a partial first floor.

Highworth

There is no evidence of public baths in Highworth before an open air swimming pool opened as part of the *Recreation Centre* in The Elms in 1968. After a fund-raising effort this was roofed and reopened in 2008. The front building is in pale brick, the pool to the rear with a semi-circular cover.

Malmesbury

It is likely that there was always informal swimming in the Avon but no specific bathing place has been identified. As in most other towns in the county, people in Malmesbury felt the need for public baths at an early date – a resident complained in 1891 that they 'should have been provided years ago'[1252] – but in fact the town had to wait until 1961 before the first ones appeared, albeit delayed by the Second World War as fundraising had started in the 1930s.[1253] They were open air and seasonal with only basic facilities, built at the rear of *Alexander Road*. These had to do until the replacement pool was opened as part of the *Activity Zone* in 2004.[1254] This is in brick with a red steel frame and a curved roof of laminated timber covering a substantial pool.

Marlborough

In 1878 the Marquess of Ailesbury gave land for a bathing place on the river Kennet at Granham Hill, a little way south of the Pewsey Road bridge. Part of a former mill leat was adapted and the alterations, which included filling in the former mill pond, cost £230.[1255] The bathing place was in use into the 20th century and may have survived until the town's first swimming pool opened. At around the same time Marlborough College created a bathing place just to the north west of this and south of the castle mount, also fed from the Kennet.[1256] This lasted until after the Second World War.

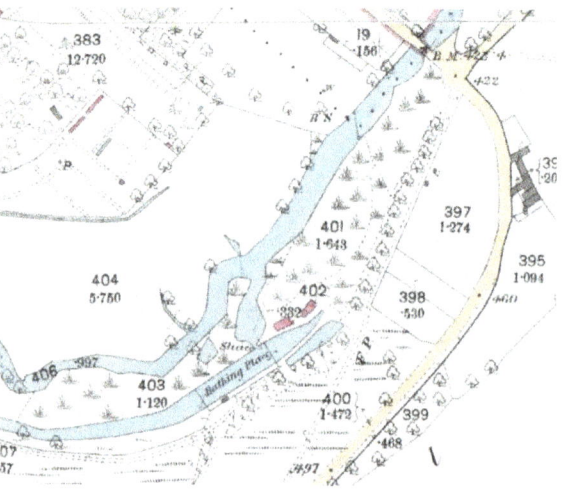

Marlborough, bathing place by the Kennet off the Pewsey Road. (Mapping from Ordnance Survey 25" 1st edition, 1886).

An open-air swimming pool was built on the island of the town mill, south of *Kennet Place*, and opened in 1928; initially privately sponsored, it was bought by the town council in 1937.[1257] It had only basic facilities but in 1968 a heating plant for the water was added and in 1971 a clubhouse.[1258]

In 1984 this was replaced by the *Barton Dene* Leisure Centre pool off College Fields, in anonymous brick and corrugated panelling. The Kennet Place pool was replaced by houses forming part of the new development on the town mill site.

Melksham

A swimming club was formed in the town in 1895 and created a bathing station on the Avon adjacent to Scotland Road, with bathing sheds.[1259] The site was criticized as being unsuitable for learner swimmers and was soon in trouble for pollution, being condemned on these grounds on more than one occasion up to 1949.[1260] There was agitation for a public baths from the 1930s but, with the intervention of the Second World War, no baths appeared until 1957. These were what were later called the *Blue Pool*, open air and on land given by Avon Rubber behind the Assembly Hall. It was roofed over in anonymous style in 1987/8 to provide for all-year-round use and closed eventually in 2022.[1261] Its future in 2023 was undecided.

The Blue Pool was replaced in August 2022 by the pool forming part of the new Melksham Campus, further west on the same site and described in Chapter 6.

Mere

There appears to be no evidence of public baths having been provided in Mere.

Salisbury

Salisbury was always plentifully supplied with water and there are likely to have been various informal swimming places in and around the city. Discussions on the provision of a more formal bathing place started in 1868 if not before and one was created c1874. This was a short way north of the town mill, where a channel joined the mill stream to the main course of the Avon just south of the market house. Public baths – presumably individual – and perhaps 20 dressing boxes were supplied and the fulling mill was adapted to this purpose, but a total expenditure of £41 does not imply any substantial works.[1262]

These baths, which were leased out by the season,[1263] seemed to suffer from the sorts of cleanliness problems one might expect in such a location[1264] but nevertheless were still in use through to the 1920s despite the appearance in 1892 of new baths in **Rollestone Street**.[1265] The company set up to establish these latter built not only the baths but also, at the east side facing St Edmund's Church Street, a steam laundry. The baths were accessed via an archway through what is now called Victoria Hall, the 2* listed 18th century pair of houses fronting Rollestone Street, and comprised six private slipper baths, a swimming bath 80ft x 34 ft with a diving stage, walls of red and yellow bricks, a gallery holding 220 and 41 dressing boxes around the edges.[1266]

The baths lasted until the early 1930s, opening only for the summer months with the pool boarded over and used for other purposes in the winter.[1267] They were later demolished and the buildings replaced by the Church Gate development: 12 and 14 Rollestone Street were converted into flats. The earlier open-air swimming baths behind the town mill had disappeared before then, the channel culverted beneath new building.

Salisbury, Rollestone Street baths dressed for a special occasion in the early 20th century. (Salisbury Museum).

The next swimming pool to appear was in 1932, on what was in 2023 a small area of car parking just to the north of the city's coach park west of **Castle Street**. The pool was open-air but there is no longer any evidence of it and indeed part is now under the river following a change in the Avon's course to accommodate a new road layout.[1268]

The Castle Street baths were in turn replaced in 1976 by an indoor pool at **Wyndham Park**, where College Street bends north-west. This was in dull brick, almost windowless, but with arcading in white render over the entrance.[1269] The corner of a public park in a historic corner of the city was a surprising choice for a large new building and after the pool closed in 2001 there was debate as to what should replace it.[1270] As of 2022 the ground had been cleared and the site reintegrated into the park.

The final stage in the development of the city's facilities for swimming has been the opening in 2002 of the *Five Rivers* leisure centre, north of the ring road off Hulse Road. This is a large group of buildings in banded brick and render, characterised by shallow-sloping metal roofs and window glass concentrated into vertical columns and the ridges of roofs.[1271]

Swindon

The Great Western Medical Fund Society was formed in 1847 in an initiative to improve the health of the GWR workforce and so benefit the company. Through its many initiatives it produced what has been claimed to be a blueprint for the NHS, founded 100 years later, and in the buildings of 1892 on Faringdon Road it has left a remarkable monument.[1272] The definition of these as public buildings might be questioned as they were built for GWR employees, but in the early days most of

SWIMMING BATHS

Swindon, the new town at least, was employed by the railway and by 1888 GWR facilities were open to all on payment of a fee.[1273]

There were individual baths in the GWR works from c1845 and the newly constructed *Mechanics' Institute* (see Chapter 6) offered individual baths from when it was opened in 1855 until 1864.[1274] The Medical Fund Society itself soon expanded into the provision of baths. A first set was built in 1868 on land immediately north of the railway **west of the canal** where the Gloucester railway line branches off.[1275] These were followed in 1869 by 32 washing baths, together with Turkish and shower baths, in a long single-storey building on the narrow triangle of land between **Taunton Street** and Faringdon Road at the east end. These survived, albeit with different functions, until 1970 when they were demolished and the space left to grass.

Swindon, Faringdon Road baths, showing the considerable size of the building in its final form.

The ever-growing railway works swallowed up the 1868 baths before the end of the century and they were replaced by the 1892 building on **Faringdon Road***, designed by the Swindon architect J J Smith in brick in Queen Anne style. The main two-storey façade is to Faringdon Road with the original entrance at the centre, stepped forward in a taller section with a grandly pedimented door originally covered by a glass awning stretching far out over the pavement. There are subsidiary pediments along the facade and a strong string course between the floors; the original seven-bay front down Milton Road is similar but more subdued. The medical dispensary and consulting rooms were behind this side and a small pool, 60ft long and originally for women and children, behind the

Swindon, Faringdon Road baths, the Milton Road entrance

Swindon, Faringdon Road baths under construction, men's bath to the left and women's to the right, the earlier washing and Turkish baths seen in the background on the other side of Faringdon Road. (Swindon Health Hydro)

Faringdon Road baths, Swindon – the men's pool

Faringdon Road baths, Swindon, the men's pool boarded over and prodigiously filled for a public event. (Local Studies (Swindon Library & Information Service))

main entrance. The large pool for men, 110ft long, lies behind the western end, its front onto Chester Street with plain brick below and a long dormer clerestory in the roof betraying the interior roof trusses, manufactured in the GWR works and allegedly to the same profile as standard railway lines. This pool, which originally had changing cubicles round it, was designed to have an inserted floor in winter months and was much used for meetings, concerts and the like as well as serving as a temporary hospital ward during the First World War.

Between 1898 and 1905 successive additions added washing baths, changing rooms and a Turkish bath, such that the building now occupies the whole block. The medical facilities are long gone following the formation of the NHS, and questions have been raised from time to time over the future of the baths,[1276] but both they and the Turkish baths are still in use, well maintained, and much of the decoration of tiles and window glass remains to be seen.

Coate Water, south east of the town, was built in the 1820s as a feeder reservoir for the Wilts and Berks canal. It was purchased by the borough council in the 1930s, a diving platform built in the reservoir and an **Art Deco swimming pool** built alongside at the north end.[1277] The swimming pool has since been demolished but the diving platform, also Art Deco and designed by the borough surveyor J B L Thompson in 1935, remains and was restored in 2022, though swimming in the reservoir has not been permitted since 1958 because of fears of pollution.[1278]

The *Oasis leisure centre*, off North Star Avenue, was built in 1976 with a Perspex dome of 45m diameter over the swimming pool, the largest in Europe. Designed by

Gillinson Barnett & Partners, it was much praised but closed in 2020 and its future appeared uncertain in 2023.[1279] There are also modern swimming pools in the **Link Centre** in West Swindon and the **Dorcan Centre** in the east of the town.

Trowbridge

Walter Long of Rood Ashton gave a site for a bathing place on the Biss in 1877; it opened in 1879, funded by public subscription and was taken over by the local board in 1880. It was situated south of the West Ashton road in what is now **Biss Meadows** country park and had a bathing hut, and an attendant in summer months. As so often, the main motivation for the scheme seems to have been to teach boys and men to swim so as to reduce the number of drownings.[1280]

This stayed in use until abandoned and the remaining huts demolished in 1939.[1281] The town's politicians, meanwhile, had repeatedly debated funding a purpose-built pool but fought shy of the cost: they debated at Queen Victoria's golden and diamond jubilees, for the coronation of Edward VII, in 1932 when they turned down an offer of a site from Salters', and in 1936 when they considered one to commemorate the silver jubilee of George V. At last, in 1939, they opened a new open-air pool not far away from the bathing place, on **Brown Street**. The main pool was 100ft long with the usual limited facilities in single-storey white render and the low stepped gables and windows of the period. It stayed in use until demolished in 1989 to make way for a Tesco's supermarket.[1282]

The proceeds of sale were used to build the pool at the *Trowbridge Sports Centre*, off the Frome road, in banded brick, metal roof and glass ridge-lines.

Warminster

After a number of calls for swimming facilities in the town, a bathing station was opened in 1898 on the River Wylye at **Smallbrook Mill**, south of what is now Willow Crescent.[1283] This had corrugated iron fencing, a pool of 125ft length for swimmers and a separate pool, oak-lined, for non-swimmers. It may not have lasted long and was certainly gone by 1922.

Its replacement formed part of the **Lake Pleasure Grounds** on Weymouth Street, opened in 1924 and including a small open-air pool as well as a boating lake and grounds. Originally planned to commemorate the coronation of George V, it was built by unemployed workers.[1284] The pool was filled in and converted into a rock garden in 1997 although a few remnants remain.[1285] It had been replaced by the pool which was built as part of the new sports centre off **Woodcock Road** in 1973.[1286] This is in a hall set back behind other buildings, in pale brick and largely windowless with the roof supported on laminated wood beams.

Westbury

Two Victorian swimming baths survive in the county, both interesting buildings and both still in use. While neighbouring towns were making do with bathing stations on rivers, Westbury opened its baths on **Church Street*** in 1888, the gift of the town's leading mill owner William H. Laverton to commemorate Victoria's golden jubilee: Swindon followed four years later.[1287] The building, designed by Halliday and

Westbury Baths, original changing cubicles to the left now walled off.

Anderson of Cardiff, had a swimming pool 67ft long by 23ft wide with changing cubicles down one side, and ten individual slipper baths. It was opened with the usual fanfare and a patronising speech from Laverton about its being not only for the health and enjoyment of the townspeople but also for their 'moral welfare.'[1288]

Westbury Baths, women's and men's separate entrances now replaced by single entrance behind this façade

To the street the main gable at the right hand end fronts the pool, in brick with plentiful and fussy Bath stone dressings including multiple pilasters and a roundel of Queen Victoria with the date at the head. To the left are the former women's and men's entrance doors, no longer used, the men's for some reason more substantial than the women's. Further left again, the final single-storey section of the front originally contained four slipper baths for women.

As elsewhere, in its earlier years the pool was boarded over in the winter and used for other activities. Water came originally from the Bitham spring but mains water, heated, was introduced in 1901, the same year as the baths were handed over to the Urban District Council.[1289] The slipper baths have been lost over succeeding years, the poolside changing cubicles removed and both replaced by changing rooms where the slipper baths formerly were. In substantial renovations in 1984 the entrance was moved round to the left hand side. The pool, surprisingly light with the roof timbers now painted, has the former brick arches to the left hand side blocked in but the rear gallery still in place; it retains its original roof trusses carrying the coats of arms of W H Laverton and Westbury Town Council.

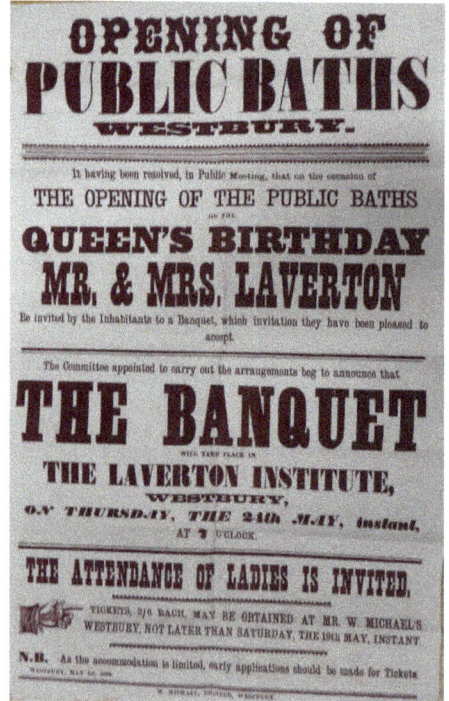

Westbury Baths, advertising poster for opening day. (WSA)

Wilton

Wilton has both the Nadder and the Wylye running through it and it seems that there was informal bathing in the Wylye in **Castle Meadow** from an early date, with some sort of changing hut provided at one stage.[1290] This use was apparently 'abused' and later a local farmer allowed boys to access the river via his land. Calls were made for the establishment of a formal bathing place but it seems nothing was ever done.[1291] An initiative of the Literary and Scientific Institute in 1872 to combine with other groups to create a 'common public hall, baths and wash houses' seems to have come to nothing.[1292]

Royal Wootton Bassett

There is some evidence from the early 20th century of occasional use of the lake at Ballard's Ash, now called Jubilee Lake, for swimming galas.[1293] It seems there was never a formal bathing station or swimming pool in the town.

Notes

2 Town Halls

1. *Our Mutual Friend*, Charles Dickens, Book 2 Chapter 3
2. The earliest British examples are 15th century – source Buildinghistory.org, accessed 8/6/2023
3. *Victorian and Edwardian Town Halls*, Colin Cunningham, Routledge & Kegan Paul, 1981
4. VCH15
5. VCH15
6. See Chapter 3
7. Main sources for the history of the town hall in this and following paragraphs are VCH7; BoE; an account on the Bradford museum website accessed 21/1/2023; WBR B191 and HE. WSA G13/132/51 describes the UDC's consideration in 1910 of whether to buy the town hall.
8. *The year of the map*, Gee Langdon, Compton Russell 1976
9. VCH17
10. VCH17
11. DZSWS1983 7557; VCH17
12. WSA G18/303/1
13. WSA G18/152/4
14. WSA G18/152/4
15. *Devizes & Wiltshire Gazette* 29/7/1886
16. BoE; HE; Cunningham *op. cit.*.
17. *Kelly* 1889; WSA G18/152/4; *Devizes & Wiltshire Gazette* 20/12/1888
18. WSA G18/701/6PC
19. The Yelde Hall has been well studied and only a brief description can be given here. Main sources are the draft text of VCH20; HE; BoE. WBR B1233 includes a report on an archaeological investigation in 2001/2.
20. VCH20 draft text
21. BoE
22. VCH20 draft text; Analysis by Ray Alder for Chippenham Museum published by the museum 2023; *Devizes & Wiltshire Gazette* 27/3/1834.
23. VCH20 draft
24. Alder *op. cit*
25. Alder *op. cit*
26. VCH20 draft; Alder *op. cit*
27. Information from Beth O'Brien of Chippenham town council
28. For example, advertisement in The Era, 5/7/1916
29. For example, *Trowbridge and North Wilts Advertiser* 15/12/1877
30. Information in this paragraph from VCH20 draft

31 Information on this building comes from a sketch plan and elevation from the Methuen archives, courtesy of James Methuen-Campbell, and further information from him and Tom Brakspear
32 Information from James Methuen-Campbell derived from a 1740s plan
33 Information from James Methuen-Campbell
34 H Brakspear in *WAM* 43, 1927
35 1873 photograph in *Around Corsham*, Corsham Civic Society, *Images of England*, History Press 2011; H Brakspear *op. cit.*.
36 *Trowbridge Chronicle* 19/5/1883; H Brakspear *op. cit.*.
37 *Trowbridge Chronicle* 19/5/1883; *Devizes & Wiltshire Gazette* 17/5/1883
38 *Devizes & Wiltshire Gazette* 17/5/1883
39 Orbach BoE notes
40 *Kelly* 1899
41 Plaque in building
42 VCH18
43 VCH18
44 *Devizes and Wiltshire Advertiser* 23/1/1862
45 WBR B1419, containing note of archaeological survey and report by David Faulkner for North Wiltshire District Council, 2000
46 WBR B1419
47 *North Wilts Herald* 3/2/1933 and 21/7/1933
48 BoE; WSA G4/760/467
49 *North Wilts Herald* 21/7/1933
50 Orbach BoE notes.
51 The early history is taken from VCH10
52 VCH10 and WBR B381
53 VCH10 and WSA 241/31
54 BoE; VCH10
55 Description in this paragraph from VCH10
56 VCH14
57 VCH14
58 VCH14
59 HE; BoE
60 WBR B3763; photograph and accompanying text in Historic England archive, accessed 30/9/2023
61 *Malmesbury's Past, People and Places*, Charles Vernon, Malmesbury Civic Trust 2014. This is the source of all information in this paragraph except where otherwise stated.
62 BoE; *Devizes & Wiltshire Gazette* 15/6/1848
63 Described in *Wiltshire Nonconformist Chapels and Meeting Houses*, James Holden, Wiltshire Buildings Record 2022
64 HE listing
65 Information about the history of the various town halls is from VCH12 except where otherwise noted
66 Images are reproduced in, for example, *Marlborough Journal*, magazine of Merchant's House museum Marlborough, September 1993, and Archive Photographs Series, *Marlborough*, Michael Gray, Chalford 1997
67 Images in Gray, *op. cit.*.
68 *Wiltshire Independent* 13/6/1867 and 14/11/1867
69 Images in Gray, *op. cit.*.
70 Gray, *op. cit.*; *Marlborough Journal op. cit.*.

NOTES 245

71   A 1924 aerial photograph in the town hall shows the arches open.
72   Information in this paragraph from *Devizes & Wiltshire Gazette* 24/12/1846 and 16/9/1847
73   Plans in WBR B4115
74   *Devizes & Wiltshire Gazette* 16/9/1847. See also Chapter 6
75   *Devizes & Wiltshire Gazette* 16/9/1847
76   *Around Melksham in Old Photographs*, Kenneth Merritt, Sutton 1989; *Wiltshire Times* 13/3/2015
77   For example *Wiltshire Independent* 14/3/1850 and *Salisbury & Winchester Journal* 8/12/1855
78   WSA G14/150/16; *Devizes and Wiltshire Advertiser* 13/4/1914
79   WBR B2006; *Wiltshire Times* 23/11/1907
80   WBR B2006
81   WBR B2006
82   WBR B3047
83   *Mere Buildings and People*, David Hope, Mere Historical Society 2009
84   *The Book of Mere*, Dr David Longbourne, Halsgrove 2004
85   Hope, *op. cit.*; *Warminster & Westbury Journal* 21/1/1899
86   Hope, *op. cit.*; VCH19 draft text.
87   The history of the Guildhall is well researched and all references in this description rely on one of the following major sources unless otherwise indicated: VCH6; RCHME; *Salisbury Guildhall*, by John Chandler and Adela Goodall, Salisbury & South Wilts Museum 1994; BoE; HE
88   This was nominally the work of JC Bothams, then still the city surveyor, but seems more likely to have been by his son AC Bothams who was assistant surveyor at that date. See *Salisbury & Winchester Journal* 9/5/1896 and Orbach architects notes.
89   Statistics on WCH
90   *Wiltshire Independent* 27/5/1852; but it was described much later as 'old stables and a warehouse' (*Swindon Advertiser* 17/3/1885) and is not referred to in the Victoria County History
91   VCH9
92   VCH9
93   VCH9
94   *Swindon Advertiser* 17/3/1885
95   VCH9; BoE
96   The claim that this was used as a butter market is made in a press article referenced in WBR B5038.
97   Swindon archives 1859 print of the Old Town Hall
98   VCH9
99   *Kelly* 1920
100 WBR B5038
101 VCH9
102 VCH9
103 *Marlborough Times* 24/10/1891
104 W H Read, one of the town's most prolific architects, was apparently an unsuccessful competitor for this work (*Architects and Buildings Craftsmen with work in Wiltshire* part 2, Pamela M Slocombe, Wiltshire Buildings Record 2006)
105 OS 1899 and 1922 revisions; The Work of Brightwen Binyon, Architect, 1846-1905 – unpublished dissertation 2014 by Michael J Gray
106 VCH9

107	Gray, *op. cit.*; *The Builder*, 27/4/1889, illustrates the difference
108	VCH7; WBR B1527; *Devizes and Wiltshire Advertiser* 13/1/1887
109	WBR B1527, Town Hall Centenary 1889 – 1989 Official Souvenir Guide, Trowbridge Town Council 1989
110	*Devizes and Wiltshire Advertiser* 20/6/1889
111	*Devizes and Wiltshire Advertiser* 20/6/1889
112	Town Hall Centenary 1889, *op. cit*
113	Town Hall Centenary 1889, *op. cit*
114	*Devizes and Wiltshire Advertiser* 20/6/1889
115	*Trowbridge Chronicle* 22/6/1889
116	*Wiltshire County Council, The First 100 Years*, Ken Rogers, Wiltshire County Council 1989
117	WSA G15/700/35HC
118	Information from town hall trust website, accessed 2/6/2023
119	VCH8
120	VCH8 for all material in this paragraph except where otherwise noted
121	Reproduced in *Old Pictures of Warminster*, Warminster History Society 1984
122	VCH8
123	*Devizes & Wiltshire Gazette* 31/5/1832
124	*Kelly* 1899
125	*Wiltshire Times* 28/11/1903
126	WBR B14461
127	Warminster Preservation Trust website accessed 4/6/2023
128	VCH8; WSA X3/147/2 (Sketch map of 1762, with burgage plot list)
129	WSA X3/147/2
130	"Westbury". In Thorne, R. G. (ed.). *The House of Commons 1790-1820*. The History of Parliament Trust, 1986
131	VCH8
132	BoE
133	BoE
134	VCH8
135	VCH8; 1904 plan in WSA G17/701/1PC
136	Information from Steve Hobbs
137	VCH8; *Wiltshire Times* 26/10/1929
138	WSA G17/701/1PC (1904 plan)
139	VCH8; see also Chapter 4
140	*Wiltshire Times* 15/8/1925 and 5/9/1925; WSA G17/701/1PC (plan dated 22/9/1925)
141	WBR B850
142	*White Horse News 20/10/2015;* Western Daily Press 9/11/2013
143	VCH6
144	VCH6
145	VCH6
146	Photograph in *Images of England – Around Wilton*, Chris Rousell, Tempus Publishing 2001; at time of listing in 1978 it still had two doors to the front
147	HE; information from Yvonne Crossley
148	HE; information from Yvonne Crossley
149	*Salisbury & Winchester Journal* 4/8/1888; *Devizes and Wiltshire Advertiser* 31/1/1889
150	Rousell *op. cit*
151	WSA G29/7/8/1/453
152	VCH9

NOTES 247

153 VCH9; photograph on town hall museum website accessed 5/6/2023
154 BoE
155 HE listing; WBR B338
156 *North Wilts Herald* 18/7/1890
157 WSA 1208/33; VCH9; Walter Ineson in Wiltshire Local History Forum newsletter January 2002
158 WSA 1208/33

3 Market Halls

159 Analysis of the development of markets is given in the volumes of the Victoria County History. These were available in 2024, published or in draft, for all Wiltshire towns except Corsham and Highworth.
160 *The British Market Hall, A Social and Architectural History*, James Schmeichen and Kenneth Carls, Yale University Press 1999, gives an extensive analysis of this subject.
161 Except where otherwise noted, sources for this entry are VCH15 and *Amesbury, History and description of a south Wiltshire town* – John Chandler and Peter Goodhugh, Amesbury Society 2012
162 *Post Office Directory* 1855
163 VCH7; *Trowbridge Chronicle* 22/4/1882
164 *Kelly* 1903 and 1911
165 Description of the old market house taken from VCH7
166 *The year of the map*, Gee Langdon, Compton Russell 1976
167 Website of Bradford on Avon Museum, accessed 11/6/2023; *Bradford on Avon: the Medieval Town*, Ivor and Pamela Slocombe, Bradford on Avon Museum 2015
168 Renamed as such at this time from its previous name of Pippet Street
169 Plan from *Civil Engineer and Architect's Journal* 1854, copy in WBR B191
170 That to the east appears in the 1884 revision to the OS 25" map; that to the north appears in the 1899 revision but not that of 1922.
171 It is shown on the 1922 revision
172 Description of the market hall from VCH17
173 VCH17
174 VCH17
175 The market history of the town is derived from VCH20 draft text except where noted
176 Information on the Butter Cross from the website of Chippenham Town Council, accessed 7/7/2023
177 *Devizes and Wilts. Gazette*, 15/9/1836
178 Analysis by Ray Alder for Chippenham Museum, published by the museum in 2023, provides much of the information for this description
179 c1888 Town plan
180 Information in this paragraph, except where otherwise noted, from VCH20 draft text
181 *Wiltshire Times* 3/4/1954
182 Information in this paragraph from Gil and Ray Alder
183 WCH
184 *Salisbury & Winchester Journal* 5/6/1815
185 *Wiltshire Independent* 7/9/1843
186 *North Wilts Herald* 2/3/1872
187 Description of Cricklade markets is from VCH18 except where otherwise noted
188 *Salisbury & Winchester Journal* 30/1/1837; *Wiltshire Independent* 25/1/1838; *Post Office Directory* 1855

189	VCH10 gives a full description of the markets and their locations through time
190	VCH10 is the source for all further description of the market house except where otherwise noted
191	VCH10, though there appears to be no record of a builder or architect of that name in Frome
192	VCH10; Dore's 1759 map of Devizes
193	VCH10
194	*Wiltshire Independent* 7/12/1837
195	Devizes Heritage website, accessed 12/6/2023, gives a detailed history of the building and later life of the corn exchange
196	VCH10; BoE
197	Description in this paragraph from Devizes Heritage website, accessed 12/6/2023
198	Description of Highworth market is from 'Highworth Markets and Fairs' on the website of Highworth Historical Society, accessed 15/6/2023
199	Information from Christine Suter
200	A solicitor's account book for the Faringdon Turnpike Trust records an attempt to buy it for demolition in 1810, an attempt which may have been successful (information from Christine Suter)
201	Information from Christine Suter
202	The description of Malmesbury's markets is taken from VCH14 except where otherwise indicated
203	*Kelly* 1931; information from Charles Vernon
204	*Builder* 29/7/1848
205	Information from Charles Vernon
206	VCH12
207	VCH12
208	VCH12
209	*Salisbury & Winchester Journal* 5/4/1862
210	*Devizes & Wiltshire Gazette* 24/3/1864
211	*Devizes and Wiltshire Advertiser* 16/6/1864
212	For example *Salisbury & Winchester Journal* 4/5/1872; *Devizes & Wiltshire Gazette* 4/10/1883
213	*Warminster & Westbury Journal* 29/12/1900
214	Notes to HE online; *Kelly* 1920
215	VCH7
216	VCH19 draft text
217	*The Book of Mere*, Dr David Longbourne, Halsgrove 2004
218	*Kelly* 1889
219	VCH6 for information on early markets
220	*Endless Street – A History of Salisbury and its People*, John Chandler, Hobnob Press 1983
221	Information on the market house is taken from VCH6; Chandler *op. cit.*; RCHME; BoE; WSA1220/15: *The first 100 years, a short survey of the work of the Salisbury Railway and Market House Company*, Charles J Lee 1956; *Salisbury Library - a brief historical account*, B M Little, Salisbury City Council 1975; WSA1220/40
222	OS 1923 revision
223	BoE
224	VCH9
225	VCH9
226	VCH9; *Central Swindon Through Time*, Mark Child, Amberley Publishing 2013
227	WBR B540 - P Sheldon collection photograph; OS 1899 revision

NOTES 249

228 *Kelly* 1920
229 Photographs in Swindon Libraries collection
230 Orbach BoE notes
231 *Swindon Advertiser* 2/5/2023
232 *Marlborough Times* 23/4/1887
233 OS, various, and information from Tom Smith
234 VCH7 for entries in this paragraph, but *Images of England, Trowbridge*, Michael Marshman and Ken Rogers, Tempus Publishing 1997, for information on initial location of market
235 *Wiltshire Times* 4/10/1862
236 VCH7
237 Description of the building when new from *Wiltshire Times* 4/10/1862
238 BoE
239 *Trowbridge Chronicle* 26/11/1892
240 *Trowbridge Through Time,* Kevin J Hartley & Andrew D Jones, Amberley 2009
241 BoE
242 Description of early markets from VCH8
243 VCH8; OS 1886 revision
244 Photograph in *Warminster in the Twentieth Century*, Celia Lane and Pauline White, Warminster History Society 1999
245 VCH8
246 VCH8
247 *Wiltshire Times* 8/1/1921
248 Lane and White, *op. cit*
249 Lane and White, *op. cit.*; *Wiltshire Times* 8/1/1921 and 4/2/1928
250 VCH8
251 VCH8; OS 1886 revision
252 VCH8
253 VCH8; OS 1922 revision; Lane and White, *op. cit*
254 Lane and White *op. cit..*
255 Market history is taken from VCH8
256 *Wiltshire Times* 23/2/1889; *Warminster & Westbury Journal* 6/12/1890; no references to the market found in newspaper archives after 1893
257 Description of market history is from VCH6
258 Description of market history is from VCH9

4 Law Courts

259 See town entries below for details of this and the following paragraph
260 VCH5
261 The Petty Sessional Divisions (Wiltshire) Order 1991
262 *Salisbury & Winchester Journal* 20/5/1848; *Swindon Advertiser* 24/12/1866; *Swindon Advertiser* 30/4/1892; *Devizes and Wiltshire Advertiser* 11/5/1893; *Wiltshire Times* 17/6/1939
263 See Chapter 3
264 VCH15
265 For example *Kelly* 1889; negative search in British Newspaper Archives
266 *Salisbury & Winchester Journal* 13/3/1847
267 *Kelly* 1875
268 *Kelly* 1903, 1915, 1920 and 1923; *Wiltshire Times* 19/10/1918

269 VCH7; *The year of the map*, Gee Langdon, Compton Russell 1976
270 *Kelly*, various; Langdon *op. cit.*; VCH7 for use of Pippet Street Methodist; building described in *Wiltshire Nonconformist Chapels and Meeting Houses*, James Holden, Wiltshire Buildings Record 2022
271 *Wiltshire Times* 22/10/1910
272 *Wiltshire Times* 18/12/1954
273 The Petty Sessional Divisions (Wiltshire) Order 1991
274 Information on early history of courts in Calne from VCH17
275 VCH17; *Pigot's Directory* 1822
276 VCH17
277 For example *Kelly* 1895; *Devizes & Wiltshire Advertiser* 23/4/1863
278 *Kelly* 1895 and 1915; negative search in British Newspaper Archive
279 *Salisbury & Winchester Journal* 13/3/1847; *Wiltshire Independent* 14/4/1864; *Post Office Directory* 1855; *Kelly* 1889, 1915 and 1939; *Wiltshire Times* 19/5/1956; information from Edward Spearey
280 *Wiltshire Times* 25/11/1956
281 The Petty Sessional Divisions (Wiltshire) Order 1991; information from Edward Spearey
282 Information on early history of courts in Chippenham from VCH20 draft text
283 *Devizes & Wiltshire Gazette* 23/2/1854
284 *Chippenham, Francis Frith's Town and City Memories*, Mike Stone, The Francis Frith Collection, 2002; *Wiltshire Independent* 1/4/1847; *Devizes & Wiltshire Gazette* 23/2/1854; information from Mike Stone and Ray Alder
285 Information from Ray Alder
286 VCH20 draft text; information from Gil and Ray Alder
287 WSA F2/2335/1 and F10/100/65/17HC
288 *Devizes & Wiltshire Gazette* 19/11/1846
289 *Wiltshire County Mirror* 12/1/1859; *Kelly* 1875 and 1889
290 *Wiltshire Times* 21/12/1956; *Bristol Evening Post* 8/10/1969
291 Information on early courts in Cricklade from VCH18
292 *Wiltshire Independent* 16/5/1839
293 VCH18
294 *Swindon Advertiser* 3/10/1896; *Kelly* 1899
295 *North Wilts Herald* 6/1/1933
296 VCH18
297 VCH10
298 VCH10; *Kelly* various and *Gillman's Devizes Directories* for 1859 and 1861
299 *Kelly* various; information from Colin Johns, architect to Wiltshire Historic Buildings Trust, on website of assize court trust accessed 1/8/2023; *Wiltshire Independent* 7/11/1839
300 VCH10
301 For example *Gillman's Devizes Directory* for 1916
302 VCH10; *Wiltshire Independent* 1/4/1847
303 *Gillman's Devizes Directories* 1859 and 1916; *Kelly* 1889
304 *Kelly* various; OS 1885 to 1922 revisions
305 *Wiltshire Times* 2/3/1895
306 *Kelly* 1931 and 1939; Colin Johns *op. cit.*
307 VCH10; WSA 946/34
308 *Salisbury & Winchester Journal* 24/8/1835
309 VCH10

NOTES

310 VCH10
311 Additional information in this description from Colin Johns *op. cit*
312 VCH10
313 *Wiltshire Gazette* 12/7/1984
314 Colin Johns, *op. cit.*, and *Voices from the assize courts,* Padmini Broomfield and Jane Schon, Wiltshire Museum 2023, contain useful information on this period.
315 *Gazette & Herald* 1/7/2009
316 *Kelly*, various
317 *Kelly*, various; negative searches in British Newspaper Archive for the period
318 VCH14 for information on early courts
319 *Salisbury & Winchester Journal* 28/1/1822
320 *Post Office Directory* 1855
321 *Wiltshire Independent* 10/10/1839; *Devizes & Wiltshire Gazette* 3/7/1851
322 *Devizes & Wiltshire Gazette* 3/7/1851
323 *Kelly* various
324 VCH14; HE listing; Orbach BoE notes
325 Full history and description of the courthouse is available on the website of the Warden and Freemen of Malmesbury, accessed 10/11/2023
326 VCH14; The Petty Sessional Divisions (Wiltshire) Order 1991; *Malmesbury's Past, People and Places*, Charles Vernon, Malmesbury Civic Trust 2014
327 Information on the early history of courts in the town is taken from VCH12
328 *Wiltshire Independent* 1/4/1847
329 VCH12; *Kelly* various 1867 to 1939; *Wiltshire County Mirror* 12/1/1859. The police station was also occasionally used as a court (for example *North Wilts Herald* 17/1/1880)
330 *Wiltshire Times* 31/5/1952
331 The Petty Sessional Divisions (Wiltshire) Order 1991
332 VCH7
333 Photograph in the possession of Melksham and District Historical Association
334 *Salisbury & Winchester Journal* 31/7/1820
335 *Wiltshire Independent* 1/4/1847; *Post Office Directory* 1855
336 *Wiltshire Times* 15/9/1956 and 21/12/1956
337 The Petty Sessional Divisions (Wiltshire) Order 1991
338 VCH19 draft text
339 *The Book of Mere: Portrait of a Wiltshire Town*, David Longbourne, Halsgrove, 2004
340 *Post Office Directory* 1859; *Kelly* 1867 and 1889
341 *Salisbury Times* 8/1/1887 and 9/8/1895; *Swindon Advertiser* 30/11/1895; *Kelly* 1898
342 *Salisbury & Winchester Journal* 29/2/1896; *Warminster & Westbury Journal* 14/8/1897
343 *Wiltshire Times* 5/10/1935
344 *Wiltshire Times* 20/9/1941
345 *Kelly* various
346 *Endless Street – A History of Salisbury and its People*, John Chandler, Hobnob Press 1983
347 VCH6
348 *Kelly* various; Chandler *op. cit*
349 WSA G29/7/8/1/624; Orbach BoE notes
350 SBYWM:2012.50.1; WSA G29/7/8/1/624
351 BoE
352 *Salisbury Journal* 20/4/2011
353 *Salisbury & Winchester Journal* 2/3/1829
354 *Salisbury & Winchester Journal* 25/3/1833
355 Article in Wiltshire Family History Society, Swindon branch, February 2024 newsletter

356 *Wiltshire County Mirror* 12/1/1859
357 *Wiltshire Independent* 1/4/1847; for example *Kelly* 1867
358 *Devizes & Wiltshire Gazette* 2/7/1857
359 *Kelly* 1867; *Swindon Advertiser* 29/9/1873 and 17/3/1885
360 *Kelly* 1867, 1889 and 1899
361 *Devizes and Wiltshire Advertiser* 2/2/1899; VCH9; *Kelly* 1920 and 1939
362 BoE
363 OS 1942/3 revision
364 WSA G24/718/32PC; *Swindon in old photographs, a second selection*, The Swindon Society, Alan Sutton 1989. The building was imposing, quite narrow but with three tiers of round-arched windows below an ornamental gable head
365 BoE; WSA F2/2335/2
366 *The Swindon Book Companion*, Mark Child, Hobnob Press 2015
367 BoE; information from Clive Carter
368 VCH7
369 OS 1886, 1899 and 1922 revisions.
370 *Post Office Directory* 1855; *Kelly* 1875, 1920 and 1939
371 *Wiltshire Independent* 1/4/1847
372 *Salisbury & Winchester Journal* 10/4/1847
373 BoE
374 Court Hall owner's website, accessed 19/8/2023
375 *Wiltshire County Mirror* 17/5/1853
376 *Trowbridge Then & Now*, Michael Marshman & Ken Rogers, History Press, 2012
377 *Kelly* 1875
378 *Kelly* 1889
379 WBR B567
380 WSA F10/100/271/11HC; *Wiltshire Times* 28/11/1997; *Gazette & Herald* 9/11/2001; BBC News online 10/6/2003
381 HM Courts and Tribunals Service Direction, March 2013.
382 VCH7; WBR B389; OS 1886 revision
383 VCH5
384 *Salisbury & Winchester Journal* 14/8/1815
385 *Salisbury & Winchester Journal* 27/3/1847
386 *Kelly*, various
387 VCH8; *Pigot's Directory* for 1822
388 *Warminster in the Twentieth Century*, Celia Lane and Pauline White, Warminster History Society 1999; The Petty Sessional Divisions (Wiltshire) Order 1991
389 *WAM* 25, p49; VCH8
390 Analysis from Steve Hobbs
391 Information from Steve Hobbs: Leighton estate 1911 particulars and OS 1941 revision
392 *Devizes & Wiltshire Gazette* 2/1/1840 and 1/10/1840; *Salisbury & Winchester Journal* 13/3/1847; information from Steve Hobbs
393 *Kelly*, various
394 *Wiltshire County Mirror* 12/1/1859
395 *Wiltshire Times* 8/1/1938; *Kelly* 1939
396 VCH8; *Wiltshire Times* 18/11/1944
397 *Wiltshire Times* 16/11/1956
398 *Kelly*, various 1867 to 1915
399 *Salisbury Times* 21/7/1877 and 1/2/1879; *North Wilts Herald* 2/9/1882
400 VCH9

NOTES 253

401 *Kelly* 1899
402 WSA F10/100/299/2HC
403 *Kelly*, various from 1915; *Wiltshire Telegraph* 20/4/1912
404 *Wiltshire Telegraph* 20/4/1912

5 Museums and Art Galleries

405 'Britannica' website accessed 29/3/2023
406 *Salisbury & Winchester Journal* 25/8/1823
407 Information from the website of the Ashmolean museum, Oxford, accessed 19/4/2023; *Wiltshire Independent* 25/4/1839
408 *Salisbury Times* 16/6/1899; *Swindon Advertiser* 16/6/1911; information from Peter Goodhugh
409 VCH15; information from Barbara Fisher, Antrobus House trustee
410 *Salisbury Journal* 17/8/2019; Orbach BoE notes; Amesbury History Centre website accessed 23/8/2023
411 For example *Wiltshire Times* 7/3/1936
412 *North Wilts Herald* 24/4/1936 and 24/12/1936; 1997 paper by Paul Robinson, WANHS curator.
413 Robinson, *op. cit*
414 Information from Pamela Slocombe
415 *Wiltshire Times* 5/5/1956 and 15/9/1956
416 Bradford on Avon museum website, accessed 22/3/2023.
417 Information from Calne Heritage Centre website, accessed 23/3/2023.
418 VCH20 draft
419 *Wiltshire Times* 12/5/1951
420 *Wiltshire Times* 19/6/1954
421 VCH20 draft
422 VCH20 draft
423 BoE; HE
424 BoE
425 *WAM* 53; *Wiltshire Times* 20/5/1950.
426 OS 1875, 1898 and 1920 revisions.
427 *Wiltshire Nonconformist Chapels and Meeting Houses*, James Holden, Wiltshire Buildings Record 2022; Museum website accessed 24/3/2023.
428 WANHS centenary history 1953: the chief promoter lived in Devizes (VCH10)
429 *WAM* 13, 1872
430 *Salisbury & Winchester Journal* 3/2/1872; *Swindon Advertiser* 14/9/1874
431 19th century census returns
432 WBR B763; HE listings; BoE
433 *Devizes & Wiltshire Gazette* 9/5/1872
434 *Salisbury & Winchester Journal* 17/8/1872; *Swindon Advertiser* 14/9/1874 (the curator of the Blackmore museum seconded a motion of congratulation at the opening)
435 DZSWS MSS362
436 *Times & News* 29/1/1982
437 Wiltshire Museum website accessed 29/3/2023.
438 Information from Christine Suter
439 *Wiltshire Times* 16/6/1923; *North Wilts Herald* 17/10/1930
440 1931 is usually quoted but a press cutting from the latter year - *North Wilts Herald* 9/9/1932 – suggests it was then.

441 Athelstan Museum website accessed 24/3/2023
442 Athelstan Museum website as above
443 Holden, *Wiltshire Nonconformist Chapels*, op. cit
444 *North Wilts Herald* 9/9/1867; *Salisbury & Winchester Journal* 9/8/1879
445 *North Wilts Herald* 11/3/1938
446 Information in this paragraph drawn mostly from the website of the Merchant's House Museum, accessed 25/3/2023.
447 BoE
448 *Wiltshire Times* 3/3/1956
449 Website of Mere Historical Society, accessed 25/3/2023
450 *Salisbury & Winchester Journal* 26/1/1861 and other press coverage of this date
451 VCH6; BoE; *Salisbury & Winchester Journal* 28/4/1860 and 23/1/1864; *Devizes & Wiltshire Gazette* 28/1/1864
452 HE
453 *Salisbury & Winchester Journal* 7/9/1867
454 Salisbury museum website accessed 28/3/2023; DZSWS MSS362; WSA G29/7/8/1/252
455 Information from Pamela Slocombe
456 WSA G29/7/8/1/369
457 BoE. For a more complete description of this important building see BoE, RCHME and HE
458 WBR B569; BoE.
459 Article by Sue Johnson on Young Gallery website accessed 28/3/2023; *Salisbury & Winchester Journal* 28/6/1913, 5/7/1913 and 6/9/1913; WSA G23/132/20; Orbach architects notes
460 WBR B3427
461 *Wiltshire Independent* 20/7/1848
462 For example *North Wilts Herald* 9/6/1905 which records the town council adopting the Museums and Gymnasiums Act 1891, giving them powers to support a museum financially.
463 *North Wilts Herald* 5/8/1938 provides a biography.
464 Holden, *Wiltshire Nonconformist Chapels*, op. cit
465 Photograph in *Swindon in Old Photographs: A Second Collection*, Swindon Society, Sutton Publishing 1989
466 *North Wilts Herald* 5/1/1912
467 *Central Swindon Through Time*, Mark Child, Amberley Publishing 2013
468 WBR B4968; HE
469 Orbach BoE notes.
470 *North Wilts Herald* 5/8/1938 and 19/12/1941
471 There are numerous press references to support from the people of the town, for example *North Wilts Herald* 25/5/1934 recording bank holiday crowds.
472 A sale for conversion to commercial premises was agreed in early 2023
473 *Swindon Advertiser* 11/10/2022; conversion work was reported as 'well under way' in late 2023
474 *Devizes & Wiltshire Gazette* 8/8/1872
475 *Wiltshire Times* 28/5/1880, 5/3/1938 and 11/2/1939
476 WSA2751/29
477 BoE
478 Information in this paragraph from *Wiltshire County Council, The First 100 Years*, Ken Rogers, Wiltshire County Council 1989
479 Website of the Warminster History Society, accessed 27/3/2023; *Wiltshire Times*

29/12/1951.
480 Information from Yvonne Crossley
481 For example *North Wilts Herald* 25/11/1887; *Devizes & Wiltshire Gazette* 24/7/1890; *Swindon Advertiser* 21/2/1891 and *Kelly* 1895.
482 WSA1208/33; website of Royal Wootton Bassett Town Hall Museum accessed 27/3/2023.

6 Libraries and Reading Rooms

483 *Salisbury Library, a Brief Historical Account*, B M Little, Wiltshire Library and Museum Service, c1975; *Pigot Directory* 1822
484 'British Circulating Libraries' website, accessed 23/5/2023
485 'British Circulating Libraries' *op. cit.*.
486 Historic England Introductions to Heritage Assets – Mechanics' Institutes gives general background. *Wiltshire Wiltshire Village Reading Rooms*, Ivor Slocombe, Wiltshire Buildings Record 2012, gives background and describes several of those in Wiltshire towns.
487 *Learning and Living 1790-1960: A Study in the History of the English Adult Education Movement*, J F C Harrison, *Routledge 1961*
488 Good sources for general information on the history of public libraries are Historic England Introduction to Heritage Assets – The English Public Library 1850-1939 and analysis of public libraries on politics.co.uk website.
489 *Wiltshire County Council, The First 100 Years*, Ken Rogers, Wiltshire County Council 1989
490 WSA F1/100/17/68; see also for example *Wiltshire Times* 29/11/1924 and 24/8/1935
491 WSA F1/250/47
492 Rogers *op. cit*
493 VCH15; *Salisbury Times* 1/1/1904, 30/9/1904 and 2/11/1906
494 *Salisbury Times* 30/9/1904 describes the parish room as 'adjoining'
495 Information on Antrobus from VCH15 and from Barbara Fisher, Antrobus House trustee
496 VCH15; BoE; HE listing
497 WSA F1/100/17/68
498 *Salisbury Journal* 6/1/1961
499 VCH15; *Amesbury, History and description of a south Wiltshire town* – John Chandler and Peter Goodhugh, Amesbury Society 2012
500 VCH7
501 Information from Pamela Slocombe.
502 Information in this and succeeding sentences from article on Bradford on Avon museum website by Ivor Slocombe, accessed 19/4/2023
503 *Rawling's Directory* 1869; *Bristol Mercury* 4/4/1863 quoted in Ivor Slocombe, *Wiltshire Wiltshire Village Reading Rooms, op. cit.*.
504 *Trowbridge Chronicle* 3/4/1875
505 Information in this paragraph from *Trowbridge Chronicle* 18/8/1879 and website of Bradford on Avon museum accessed 30/5/2023.
506 VCH7; WSA F1/250/47
507 WSA F1/100/17/68
508 Information from Wiltshire Buildings Record
509 VCH7; WSA F1/100/17/68; *Wiltshire Times* 23/10/1926 and 18/5/1929; information from Pamela Slocombe

510 Information from Bradford on Avon museum website, accessed 19/4/2023; information from Pamela Slocombe
511 BoE
512 VCH17; *Wiltshire Independent* 14/1/1841
513 *Devizes & Wiltshire Gazette* 27/10/1870 and 5/1/1871
514 *Wiltshire Independent* 5/2/1874; *Devizes & Wiltshire Gazette* 16/2/1888; *A Source of Pride, a brief history of Calne Library*, Sue Boddington, Wiltshire County Council Library and Museums Service 1993
515 See introduction to this chapter. Most information in this paragraph is from Boddington *op. cit.*.
516 Archaeological Appraisal and conservation plan, November 2003, by D P Faulkner, Historic buildings officer for North Wilts DC., in WBR B6514.
517 WSA F1/100/17/68; Boddington *op. cit*
518 BoE
519 VCH20 draft text
520 *Devizes & Wiltshire Gazette* 11/6/1857; *Devizes & Wiltshire Gazette* 4/2/1886 refers to Goldney closing his reading room 'at the other end of town' to the Temperance Hall in Foghamshire
521 *Wiltshire Independent* 13/8/1863
522 *Wiltshire Independent* 19/11/1863
523 *Devizes & Wiltshire Gazette* 4/2/1886
524 *Devizes & Wiltshire Gazette* 1/12/1887
525 *Wiltshire Independent* 13/8/1863; BoE
526 *Devizes & Wiltshire Gazette* 31/5/1888
527 HE
528 *Devizes & Wiltshire Gazette* 31/5/1888
529 *A Chippenham Collection* – Sally Jefferies, Chippenham Civic Society 1987; *Wiltshire Times* 11/4/1925
530 WSA F1/250/47; *Wiltshire Times* 11/4/1925, 11/7/1925, 25/7/1925, 17/7/1926 and 7/7/1928
531 WSA F1/100/17/68; *Wiltshire Times* 17/2/1934 and 6/10/1934; Jefferies *op. cit.*.
532 BoE
533 *Corsham Revealed*, Giuliano (Julian) Carosi, privately published, 2nd edition 2019; *Wiltshire Independent* 11/7/1839; *Salisbury & Winchester Journal* 12/11/1853; *Devizes & Wiltshire Gazette* 17/3/1887
534 *North Wilts Herald* 19/3/1877 and 7/12/1878; *Wiltshire Times* 8/2/1897
535 Carosi *op. cit.*; *Devizes & Wiltshire Gazette* 17/5/1883
536 WSA F1/250/47; Carosi *op. cit*
537 WSA F1/100/17/68; Carosi *op. cit.*; information from Corsham Civic Society website accessed 22/2/2023.
538 WBR B6517; Orbach BoE notes; Carosi *op. cit*
539 BoE
540 *Wiltshire Independent* 9/11/1865; *Swindon Advertiser* 10/4/1908; *Wiltshire Independent* 26/11/1863
541 VCH18; information from Pam Debenham
542 VCH18; HE
543 VCH18
544 VCH18
545 VCH10; HE; *Salisbury & Winchester Journal* 28/10/1833; *Salisbury & Winchester Journal* 22/7/1833; *Devizes & Wiltshire Gazette* 14/11/1867

546 VCH10; *Wiltshire Independent* 11/5/1848; *Wiltshire Independent* 3/11/1842
547 VCH10; *Wiltshire Times* 5/1/1907
548 *Warminster & Westbury Journal* 26/9/1903
549 *Trowbridge Chronicle* 2/4/1904
550 *Wiltshire Times* 13/8/1927
551 VCH10; information from David Buxton
552 VCH10; WSA F2/2284/4; WSA F1/100/17/68
553 VCH10
554 BoE
555 WBR B640
556 *Pigot* 1830 and 1842 in WRS47
557 *Post Office Directory* 1855; *Wiltshire Independent* 26/3/1863
558 *Swindon Advertiser* 20/12/1890; *Swindon Advertiser* 22/12/1905
559 *North Wilts Herald* 23/11/1874; Ivor Slocombe, *Wiltshire Wiltshire Village Reading Rooms*, op. cit
560 *Kelly* 1927
561 *Swindon Advertiser* 25/1/1901; *North Wilts Herald* 24/4/1936; information from Christine Suter
562 *Kelly* 1939
563 *A Study of the Library Services of Highworth*, by W.G. Raschen, privately published 1983
564 Raschen *op. cit.*; information from Christine Suter
565 WBR B10586; Raschen *op. cit*
566 WBR B11369
567 *Pigot* 1830 and 1842 in WRS47
568 *Wiltshire Independent* 5/4/1838
569 VCH14
570 *Wiltshire Independent* 5/4/1855 and 21/1/1864
571 *Swindon Advertiser* 31/3/1883
572 *Devizes & Wiltshire Gazette* 26/4/1888; *North Wilts Herald* 10/1/1936; *Malmesbury's Past, People and Places*, Charles Vernon, Malmesbury Civic Trust 2014; Slocombe *Wiltshire Village Reading Rooms*, op. cit
573 VCH14; local information.
574 Vernon, *Malmesbury's Past, People and Places*, op. cit
575 *Wiltshire Times* 10/7/1897
576 *Wiltshire Times* 20/3/1926
577 VCH14; WSA F1/250/47
578 *Malmesbury Reflections*, Charles Vernon, Malmesbury Civic Trust 2020.
579 *Malmesbury Reflections*, op. cit.; VCH14
580 BoE
581 *Pigot* 1830 in WRS47
582 *Devizes & Wiltshire Gazette* 17/10/1844
583 *Wiltshire Independent* 9/2/1854; VCH12.
584 *Devizes & Wiltshire Gazette* 16/3/1905
585 *Wiltshire Independent* 12/1/1865
586 *Swindon Advertiser* 16/3/1906
587 WSA F1/250/47; *North Wilts Herald* 7/8/1925, 11/1/1929 and 11/1/1935
588 VCH12; WSA F1/100/17/68
589 *Wiltshire Times* 14/12/1946; VCH12; information from David Chandler
590 BoE
591 VCH7

592 *Pigot* 1830 in WRS47
593 *Wiltshire Independent* 23/11/1837 and 11/1/1838
594 *Devizes & Wiltshire Gazette* 28/10/1852
595 *Devizes & Wiltshire Gazette* 28/10/1852
596 *Wiltshire Times* 17/12/1949
597 WSA F1/250/47; *Wiltshire Times* 13/12/1924
598 Full description in *Wiltshire Nonconformist Chapels and Meeting Houses*, James Holden, Wiltshire Buildings Record 2022
599 *Wiltshire Times* 13/2/1954 and 27/3/1954
600 *Wiltshire Times* 27/3/1954
601 Orbach BoE notes
602 *The Book of Mere*, Dr David Longbourne, Halsgrove 2004; *Salisbury & Winchester Journal* 26/1/1862
603 Longbourne, *op. cit*
604 Ivor Slocombe, *Wiltshire Village Reading Rooms, op. cit*
605 Longbourne, *op. cit*
606 Full description in Holden, *Nonconformist Chapels, op. cit*
607 WSA F1/100/17/68; Longbourne, *op. cit*
608 BoE
609 *Salisbury Library, a Brief Historical Account*, B M Little, Wiltshire Library and Museum Service, c1975
610 Little, *op. cit.; Salisbury Mechanics Institution 1833-41*, Wiltshire Monographs No 2, Monte Little, Wiltshire Library and Museum Service 1982
611 Information in this paragraph from VCH6; *Salisbury & Winchester Journal* 17/1/1820, 2/1/1847, 19/1/1861 and 19/7/1862; WSA 451/376; further information from Monte Little; *Post Office Directory* 1855; *Kelly* 1867 and 1915
612 Most information in this paragraph is from Little, *Salisbury Mechanics Institution op. cit*
613 Holden, *Nonconformist Chapels, op. cit.*, has a full description.
614 Little, *Salisbury Mechanics' Institution, op. cit*
615 Orbach BoE notes; WSA 776/213
616 *Salisbury & Winchester Journal* 25/2/1911
617 *Salisbury & Winchester Journal* 22/12/1849
618 *Salisbury & Winchester Journal* 30/9/1871
619 *Salisbury & Winchester Journal* 30/9/1871; BoE
620 BoE; VCH6
621 Ivor Slocombe – *Wiltshire Village Reading Rooms, op. cit.*; HE; 1900 and 1923 OS revisions.
622 VCH6; BM Little, *A brief historical account…, op. cit.*; WSA G23/132/20
623 BM Little *op. cit.*; Holden, *Nonconformist Chapels, op. cit*
624 VCH6
625 BoE
626 BM Little, *A brief historical account…, op. cit*
627 Information from Monte Little
628 *Pigot* 1830 and 1842 in WRS47
629 *Devizes & Wiltshire Gazette* 15/1/1852
630 *Salisbury & Winchester Journal* 26/11/1859
631 *Swindon Advertiser* 1/7/1861
632 *North Wilts Herald* 22/1/1872 and 15/4/1872
633 *Swindon Advertiser* 23/12/1882
634 *Swindon Advertiser* 14/11/1885; information from Tom Smith and Clive Carter

NOTES 259

635 1881 census returns
636 VCH9
637 There are numerous sources for the history of the Mechanics' Institute, including VCH9; *Swindon: The legacy of a railway town*, RCHME, John Cattell and Keith Falconer, HMSO 1995; BoE; and HE. All the information in this description, unless otherwise noted, comes from one of these or from the detailed history in his unpublished 2014 MSc dissertation for the University of Bath by Michael Gray.
638 Information in this and the following paragraph from Clive Carter in *Swindon Heritage* Winter 2016 edition.
639 For more detail on the chapel see Holden, *Nonconformist Chapels, op. cit.*.
640 VCH9; *Wiltshire within living memory*, Wiltshire Federation of Women's Institutes, Countryside Books Newbury, 1993
641 *North Wilts Herald* 8.11.1935; information from Tom Smith
642 *Central Swindon Through Time*, Mark Child, Amberley Publishing 2013; 1948 plans at WSA G24/717/2PC
643 Information from Tom Smith
644 BoE
645 WSA G24/717/17PC
646 Swindon Borough Council website, accessed 1/5/2023; BoE; Orbach BoE notes
647 BoE; information from Tom Smith and Clive Carter
648 VCH7
649 *Pigot* 1842 in WRS47
650 *Wiltshire Independent* 21/3/1839; *Devizes & Wiltshire Gazette* 24/6/1841
651 *Wiltshire Independent* 7/4/1842; *Devizes & Wiltshire Gazette* 30/7/1846
652 *Devizes & Wiltshire Gazette* 22/10/1846; WSA 927/94.
653 *Trowbridge Then & Now*, Michael Marshman & Ken Rogers, History Press, 2012
654 *Devizes & Wiltshire Gazette* 10/1/1867
655 Welsh School of Architecture, University of Cardiff, project 'Shelf Life' accessed online 23/5/2023; *Devizes and Wiltshire Advertiser* 19/11/1903; *Trowbridge Chronicle* 12/3/1904
656 WSA F1/250/47; *Wiltshire Times* 17/1/1920
657 WBR B567; WSA G15/132/73; *Wiltshire Times* 26/12/1925 and 7/8/1926.
658 WSA F1/250/47
659 Description of building from WBR B567; WSA F1/100/17/68
660 Orbach architects notes
661 *Trowbridge Then & Now*, Michael Marshman & Ken Rogers, op. cit
662 WILBR B567; Holden, *Nonconformist Chapels, op. cit.*
663 WSA F10/100/271/35HC; WSA F10/100/271/36HC; *Wiltshire Times* 31/12/1955; *Wiltshire County Council, The First 100 Years*, Ken Rogers, Wiltshire County Council 1989
664 WBR B567; WBR B8642; information from Kenneth Rogers
665 Rogers, *op. cit*
666 BoE; *Wiltshire Times* 12/9/2012.
667 *Wiltshire Times* 5/7/1919 and 17/1/1920; WSA F10/100/271/28HC
668 *Wiltshire Times* 6/6/1925
669 WSA F1/100/17/68
670 WSA F10/100/271/28HC; *Wiltshire Times* 9/6/1934; Rogers, *op. cit*
671 WBR B778 shows staff at Prospect Place in 1968; photograph of former HQ courtesy of Pamela Slocombe; Rogers *op. cit*
672 Information from Nikki Ritson of Trowbridge Museum

673 *Pigot* 1830 in WRS47
674 WSA 540/304; *Devizes & Wiltshire Gazette* 24/4/1834
675 BoE
676 HE
677 WSA 132/37
678 WSA 540/304
679 *Warminster Herald* 24/4/1875
680 *Wiltshire Independent* 27/12/1838 and 23/11/1843
681 *Salisbury & Winchester Journal* 24/1/1842
682 Information about the Athenaeum, except where otherwise referenced, is from *The Athenaeum, A Chronology of the Building*, Andrew Frostick, Warminster 2022, for the Warminster Athenaeum Trust.
683 Ivor Slocombe, *Wiltshire Village Reading Rooms, op. cit*
684 Ordnance Survey 1st and later 25" editions
685 Ivor Slocombe, *Wiltshire Village Reading Rooms, op. cit*
686 WSA F1/250/47; *Wiltshire Times* 10/5/1924 and 6/12/1924
687 *Wiltshire Times* 6/12/1924
688 Frostick *op. cit.*; *Wiltshire Times* 27/6/1953
689 Frostick *op. cit*
690 BoE; *Gazette & Herald* 17/11/2012 records celebration of 30 year anniversary
691 *Pigot* 1842 in WRS47
692 WSA A1/460; *Wiltshire Times* 26/2/1876; information from Steve Hobbs
693 *Wiltshire Times* 26/2/1876
694 OS 1936 revision
695 *Post Office Directory* 1855; *Wiltshire Independent* 13/3/1856
696 WSA F1/250/47; VCH8; *Wiltshire Times* 9/2/1924 and 29/11/1924
697 *Wiltshire Times* 7/11/1925
698 WSA F1/100/17/68; *Wiltshire Times* 10/9/1938 and 8/10/1938.
699 *Wiltshire Times* 1/6/1946 and 10/9/1949; VCH8
700 WSA F10/100/281/6HC
701 WSA F10/100/281/6HC; *Wiltshire Times* 20/3/1970
702 BoE; HE
703 WCH; *Salisbury Times* 18/1/1894
704 For example, *Salisbury & Winchester Journal* 13/11/1858
705 *Kelly* 1867; see evidence which follows on the link with the Talbot and Wyvern hall. *Kelly* describes the building as in Silver Street and the house to the other side of the Talbot and Wyvern is in Kingsbury Square.
706 *Devizes and Wiltshire Advertiser* 12/12/1878
707 *Devizes and Wiltshire Advertiser* 14/10/1880.
708 *Salisbury & Winchester Journal* 18/11/1911; *Kelly* 1920
709 Information from Yvonne Crossley
710 *Warminster Herald* 11/1/1868; *Salisbury & Winchester Journal* 9/11/1872; *The Book of Wilton*, Chris Rousell, Halsgrove 2006, records a programme for an 1888 event.
711 *Devizes & Wiltshire Gazette* 18/10/1855; *Salisbury & Winchester Journal* 1/2/1913
712 WSA F1/250/47
713 WSA G25/760/188; WSA F1/100/17/68
714 Full description in Holden, *Nonconformist Chapels, op. cit.*; WCH
715 *Wiltshire Independent* 18/10/1838 and 28/2/1839.
716 *Swindon Advertiser* 20/12/1858; *Wiltshire Independent* 23/2/1865 and 3/12/1874
717 Ivor Slocombe, *Wiltshire Village Reading Rooms, op. cit.*; *The History of Wootton Bassett*,

NOTES 261

718　P J Gingell, Wootton Bassett Historical Society 1977
　　North Wilts Herald 4/1/1889; Slocombe *op. cit.*.; Gingell *op. cit.*; *North Wilts Herald* 8/1/1897; WCH
719　WCH; *North Wilts Herald* 18/7/1890; Gingell *op. cit.*
720　Gingell, *op. cit.*.
721　WSA G26/112/2; *Wiltshire Times* 29/11/1924; *North Wilts Herald* 12/8/1927
722　Gingell, *op. cit.*
723　WCH; Gingell, *op. cit.*; *North Wilts Herald* 20/12/1935
724　WCH; information from Roger Smith
725　WCH; information from Roger Smith

7 Council Buildings

726　VCH5
727　Information on local government provision in Wiltshire in this introduction is from VCH5
728　VCH8
729　*Trowbridge Chronicle* 3/3/1866
730　See Calne text, below
731　VCH5
732　VCH20 draft text
733　VCH5
734　*Kelly* 1895 and 1920
735　Workhouses.org.uk
736　He normally worked with George Gilbert Scott but this was an example of him working alone.
737　VCH15; workhouses.org.uk
738　*Wiltshire Gazette & Herald* 11/3/2004
739　Information from Peter Goodhugh and the town clerk, Wendy Bown
740　Information on the history of local government in the town up until c1950 is drawn from VCH7
741　See Chapter 2
742　*Post Office Directory* 1875; *Kelly* 1889
743　*Kelly* 1899 and 1907
744　See Chapter 2
745　*Kelly* 1920 1927 and 1931
746　See Chapter 4
747　VCH7
748　VCH7; *Wiltshire Times* 30/5/1953
749　BoE; Bradford on Avon museum website accessed 8/7/2023
750　BoE
751　Information on early local government in the town is drawn from VCH17
752　Information from Calne Heritage Centre; *Wiltshire Times* 13/10/1956
753　*Kelly* 1899
754　Workhouses.org.uk
755　VCH17
756　Information from Cllr Tony Trotman
757　Information on the local government history of the town is taken from VCH20 draft text
758　VCH20 draft text

759 VCH20 draft text; *Wiltshire Times* 9/2/1924; *North Wilts Herald* 10/10/1924; analysis by Ray Alder for Chippenham Museum published by the museum 2023
760 VCH20 draft text; Ray Alder op. cit
761 VCH20 draft text
762 Orbach BoE notes
763 *Kelly* 1939; information from Ray Alder
764 *Chippenham Walkabout*, Cecil Smith, Chippenham Civic Society 1983
765 BoE
766 BoE
767 Orbach architects notes
768 Description of post-1974 town council history is taken from VCH20 draft text.
769 VCH20 draft text
770 VCH5
771 *Wiltshire Times* 30/3/1895
772 *Wiltshire Times* 10/8/1895
773 For example *Wiltshire Times* 10/8/1895 and 18/11/1919
774 WCH
775 VCH18
776 Various *Kelly*'s directories; *Swindon Advertiser* 12/12/1894
777 VCH18; *Trowbridge Chronicle* 23/7/1898, *Marlborough Times* 26/11/1898
778 VCH18
779 Information from Pam Debenham
780 VCH10 for the history of the borough
781 VCH10
782 BoE
783 *Kelly* 1899 and 1920
784 Workhouses.org.uk
785 *Kelly* 1939
786 1960s photograph reproduced in *Gazette & Herald* 24/2/2022
787 Orbach BoE notes
788 For example *Devizes & Wiltshire Advertiser* 18/8/1881
789 *Kelly* 1915 and 1939
790 Information from Christine Suter
791 VCH14
792 VCH14
793 *Malmesbury's Past, People and Places*, Charles Vernon, Malmesbury Civic Trust 2014; *Kelly*, various
794 *Kelly* 1931 and 1939. VCH14; information from Charles Vernon
795 VCH14; website of the warden and freemen of Malmesbury, accessed 8/11/2023
796 *Kelly* 1899
797 Workhouses.org.uk
798 Workhouses.org.uk
799 *Kelly* 1939; Vernon, *op. cit.*
800 *Wiltshire Times* 30/5/1953; information from Charles Vernon
801 VCH14
802 VCH12
803 Workhouses.org.uk; BoE
804 *Kelly* 1931 and 1939
805 *Wiltshire Times* 30/5/1953; information from David Chandler
806 Information on the early history of local government in Melksham is taken from VCH7

NOTES

807 VCH7
808 VCH7; *Kelly* 1889
809 *Kelly*, various from 1889 to 1920; information from Peter Maslen
810 VCH7
811 *Kelly* 1923 and 1927
812 *Kelly*, various
813 Workhouses.org.uk
814 VCH5; *Kelly* 1935
815 Information on local government history in Mere is taken from VCH19 draft text
816 Workhouses.org.uk
817 *Kelly* 1931; information from Mere Historical Society
818 *Kelly* 1939
819 *Wiltshire Nonconformist Chapels and Meeting Houses*, James Holden, Wiltshire Buildings Record 2022
820 *London Gazette*, 18/10/1949
821 For example, *Wiltshire Times* 15/9/1928 and 14/6/1930; information from Mere Town Council
822 Information from Mere Town Council
823 Information on the early history of local government in Salisbury is taken from VCH6
824 It is not shown as such on Ordnance Survey maps until the 1923 revision but nevertheless this seems the most likely location for the building given by J Woodlands
825 Best described in RCHME and BoE. Building description draws from both these sources
826 *Kelly* various 1899 to 1920; workhouses.org.uk
827 *Kelly* 1931 and 1935
828 BoE; blue plaque on building
829 BoE
830 The early history of local government in Swindon is taken from VCH9
831 *Post Office Directory* 1875; *Kelly* 1889
832 *The Buildings of England, Wiltshire*, 1st edition, Nikolaus Pevsner, Penguin 1963
833 *Kelly* 1899
834 VCH9; *Kelly* 1903
835 *Swindon Link* 13/3/2020
836 *Kelly*, various
837 Workhouses.org.uk
838 *North Wilts Herald* 15/2/1924 and 27/2/1925
839 HE
840 Information from Clive Carter
841 BoE
842 Information from Tom Smith and Clive Carter
843 Information on the early years of the county council, unless otherwise noted, is taken from VCH7; Ivor Slocombe in *Trowbridge History* Volume 4, Friends of the Trowbridge Museum, 2009; and *Wiltshire County Council, The First 100 Years*, Ken Rogers, Wiltshire County Council 1989
844 Supplementary information from Ivor Slocombe; Rogers, *op. cit*
845 HE
846 BoE
847 VCH7; Slocombe *op. cit.*; Rogers *op. cit.* for this description
848 BoE; Rogers *op. cit*
849 Rogers *op. cit*

850 VCH7
851 *Trowbridge Then & Now*, Michael Marshman & Ken Rogers, History Press, 2012; *Trowbridge Chronicle* 22/7/1871 and 3/2/1872
852 *Wiltshire Times* 11/11/1876; *Trowbridge Chronicle* 16/8/1879
853 VCH7
854 *Kelly*, various
855 Orbach BoE notes
856 Wiltshire Council planning documents, application 17/05669/FUL
857 BoE
858 Information on early local government in the town is taken from VCH8
859 *PO Directory* 1875; *Kelly* 1889
860 *Kelly* 1899, 1920, 1931 and 1939
861 *Wiltshire Times* 30/5/1953
862 BoE
863 *Warminster in the Twentieth Century*, Celia Lane and Pauline White, Warminster History Society 1999
864 *Kelly* 1899
865 Workhouses.org.uk.
866 *Kelly* 1939; Lane and White *op. cit*
867 Lane and White *op. cit*
868 Lane and White *op. cit*
869 Full description in *Wiltshire Nonconformist Chapels and Meeting Houses*, James Holden, Wiltshire Buildings Record, 2022
870 BoE
871 Information on local government history in Westbury from VCH8
872 *Trowbridge Chronicle* 18/11/1894; *Warminster & Westbury Journal* 22/12/1894.
873 For example *Trowbridge Chronicle* 30/1/1897 and *Warminster & Westbury Journal* 24/4/1897
874 VCH8; *Wiltshire Times* 7/10/1899
875 VCH8; *Warminster & Westbury Journal* 24/4/1897; *Kelly* 1915
876 See for example photographs in Westbury Heritage Centre; Westbury Through Time, Elizabeth Argent, Amberley 2013
877 BoE
878 WSA G31/1/4/4PC; information from Steve Hobbs
879 Workhouses.org.uk
880 OS 1936 revision
881 Westbury town council website accessed 19/7/2023
882 Information from Westbury town council
883 The history of local government in the town is taken from VCH6 except where otherwise noted
884 *Salisbury & Winchester Journal* 14/4/1855 refers to it but no earlier references found
885 *Salisbury Times* 24/10/1885
886 *Salisbury & Winchester Journal* 15/3/1862
887 *Images of England – Around Wilton*, Chris Rousell, Tempus Publishing 2001.
888 Holden, *op. cit.*
889 *Kelly*, various up to 1931 and 1935
890 Workhouses.org.uk
891 VCH9
892 *Kelly* 1920 and 1931
893 Workhouses.org.uk

894 *Kelly* 1935 and 1939
895 BoE
896 *Wiltshire Wiltshire Village Reading Rooms*, Ivor Slocombe, Wiltshire Buildings Record 2012
897 *Swindon Advertiser* 2/3/1906 and 17/11/1911
898 *The History of Wootton Bassett*, P J Gingell, Wootton Bassett Historical Society 1977
899 Gingell, *op. cit.*; *Wiltshire Times* 14/8/1954
900 *Wiltshire Times* 14/8/1954
901 Information from Owen Collier; Gingell *op. cit.*
902 VCH9; *Wiltshire Times* 16/2/1895
903 *Swindon Advertiser* 27/1/1905
904 Information from Owen Collier
905 WCH
906 BoE
907 *Swindon Advertiser* 18/2/2015
908 Town council website, accessed 20/7/2023

8 Police Stations

909 VCH5
910 Ibid
911 *Salisbury & Winchester Journal* 30/1/1832
912 Quarter sessions minutes, Easter 1839
913 *The Oldest and the Best, a History of Wiltshire Police*, Paul Sample, Wiltshire Constabulary 2003
914 *Salisbury & Winchester Journal* 19/2/1887
915 VCH5
916 VCH8
917 Sample, *op. cit*
918 WBR B1561
919 VCH15
920 Postcards in the collection of Peter Goodhugh
921 VCH15
922 *Salisbury Times* 24/7/1903; *Salisbury Times* 16/10/1903
923 *Swindon Advertiser* 16/7/1910
924 WBR B3665
925 WSA, plans in F10/100/6/5HC
926 OS 1899 and 1923 revisions
927 Postcard in the collection of Peter Goodhugh, and information from him
928 VCH7
929 *The year of the map*, Gee Langdon, Compton Russell 1976
930 *Pigot Directory* 1842, in WRS47
931 Early photograph and information from Pamela Slocombe
932 WSA A1/592/1
933 WSA A1/592/1 (architect's plans); see also Chapter 6
934 *Wiltshire Times* 12/10/1929
935 VCH7
936 *Gazette & Herald* 13/6/2003
937 VCH17; HE
938 WSA G18/701/6PC (architect's plans)

939 VCH17
940 *Wiltshire Times* 14/1/1928
941 *Wiltshire Gazette & Herald* 15/7/2010
942 WSA F10/100/48/6 (plans)
943 *Wiltshire Times* 11/3/2023
944 VCH20 draft
945 VCH20 draft
946 Orbach BoE notes
947 41-42 New Road, Chippenham, Heritage Statement, Dorothy Treasure and Alyson Curtis, Wiltshire Buildings Record 2018
948 *Wiltshire Times* 10/10/1953
949 WSA F2/218/14; *Wiltshire Times* 27/9/1952 and 21/12/1956
950 WSA F2/218/14
951 WSA F2/218/14
952 Information from Mike Stone
953 *Gazette & Herald* 15/4/2016
954 *Devizes & Wiltshire Gazette* 18/11/1847
955 *Devizes & Wiltshire Gazette* 8/1/1870
956 *Corsham Revealed*, Giuliano (Julian) Carosi, privately published, 2nd edition 2019; 1881 census return
957 OS 25" 1899 and 1919 revisions; WSA F10/100/83/6HC
958 *Wiltshire Times* 18/9/1943
959 Information from Julian Carosi
960 WSA F10/100/83/6HC; *Wiltshire Times* 3/5/1952
961 Carosi *op. cit*
962 WSA F10/200/83/6
963 VCH18; HE
964 Information from Pam Debenham
965 VCH18
966 *Swindon Advertiser* 18/7/1902 and 26/1/1903; *Devizes & Wiltshire Advertiser* 23/10/1902, though there is a suggestion that the opening may have been delayed; the date of 1922 quoted in VCH18 is incorrect – the new police station is shown on the 1920 OS revision
967 *Materials for a history of Cricklade*, Ed T R Thomson, OUP for Cricklade Historical Society 1958-61
968 VCH10
969 WBR B6413
970 *Post Office Directory* 1855
971 *Kelly* 1939
972 *Wiltshire Times* 18/4/1936
973 *Wiltshire Times* 5/12/1969
974 BoE
975 *Post Office Directory* 1855
976 Sample *op. cit*
977 OS 25" 1st edition; Sample *op. cit*
978 VCH10
979 *Wiltshire Telegraph* 28/9/1895 re whether lodgers were eligible to vote.
980 Orbach BoE notes
981 Information from Christine Suter; *Devizes & Wiltshire Gazette* 30/6/1842
982 *Wiltshire Times* 16/1/1926 and 20/4/1929

983	*Swindon Advertiser* 11/8/2018
984	VCH14
985	*Devizes & Wiltshire Gazette* 19/10/1854
986	WSA A1/592/5
987	*Malmesbury Reflections*, Charles Vernon, Malmesbury Civic Trust 2020
988	VCH12; WSA A1/592/7; *Devizes & Wiltshire Gazette* 19/10/1854
989	*Wiltshire Times* 4/3/1899
990	HE
991	OS 1885 revision; WSA A1/592/7
992	VCH12
993	WSA F10/100/186/6HC
994	DZSWS 2009 7086; Sample, *op. cit*
995	*Gazette & Herald* 1/10/2019; Wiltshire Council planning permission 20/07915/OUT
996	VCH7; BoE; Orbach BoE notes
997	*Wiltshire Times* 25/4/1925, 15/10/1927 and 14/1/1928
998	*Gazette & Herald* 31/5/2002
999	Orbach BoE notes; Bruges Tozer website, accessed 17/11/2023
1000	*Wiltshire County Mirror* 14/3/1855
1001	*Salisbury & Winchester Journal* 29/2/1896
1002	OS 1900 revision; *Kelly* 1907
1003	OS 1942 revision; *Wiltshire Times* 22/9/1956
1004	Information from Cllr George Jeans
1005	*Gazette & Herald* 29/3/2001
1006	VCH6; Sample, *op. cit*
1007	*Salisbury & Winchester Journal* 16/5/1836; Sample, *op. cit*
1008	BoE; WSA G23/152/3; *Salisbury & Winchester Journal* 14/11/1857
1009	VCH6
1010	Orbach BoE notes; HE; WSA G23/152/3; *Salisbury Times* 5/5/1883
1011	VCH6; OS 1936 revision; WSA 2132/153
1012	WSA A1/592/4
1013	RCHME; Orbach BoE notes; WSA G23/150/137; WBR B8648
1014	WSA 776/249; 25" OS revision 1936/7; *Wiltshire Times* 12/4/1930
1015	*Kelly* 1931 and 1935
1016	*Wiltshire Times* 20/9/1952; BoE
1017	WSA F10/100/233/11HC
1018	BoE
1019	*Salisbury Journal* 25/11/2021; *Salisbury & Avon Gazette* 13/9/2023
1020	*Pigot* 1842 in WRS47
1021	WSA A1/592/9; *Devizes & Wiltshire Gazette* 21/10/1852
1022	*Devizes & Wiltshire Gazette* 19/10/1854
1023	*Swindon, an Illustrated History*, Mark Child, Breedon Books, 2002.
1024	Orbach BoE notes
1025	ibid
1026	VCH9 104-119; *North Wilts Herald* 30/6/1873
1027	WSA A1/592/9; Orbach BoE notes; *North Wilts Herald* 19/4/1873
1028	*Swindon in Old Photographs: A Fourth Selection*, The Swindon Society, Sutton Publishing 1993
1029	WSA G24/760/1299; OS 25" 2nd edition
1030	*Kelly* 1915
1031	OS 1st series onwards; WSA A1/592/10

1032　WSA F10/100/263/9HC; OS 1899 and 1922 revisions
1033　WSA F10/100/263/9HC; WSA G24/760/3002; *Wiltshire Times* 16/1/1926
1034　OS 1942 revision
1035　Information from Tom Smith
1036　*Swindon, a sixth selection, Britain in old photographs*, The Swindon Society, Sutton Publishing 1998; information from Tom Smith and Clive Carter
1037　Information from Tom Smith and Clive Carter
1038　BoE
1039　VCH7
1040　*Wiltshire County Mirror* 21/2/1854
1041　WSA A1/592/12; WBR B1561; *Kelly* 1920; *Trowbridge in Pictures 1812-1914*, Michael Lansdown, Michael Marshman, Kenneth Rogers, Wiltshire Library and Museum Service 1989
1042　*Wiltshire Times* 14/7/1923
1043　WSA 1984/120; VCH7; WBR B1561
1044　WBR B12313; WBR B1561
1045　BoE
1046　*Pigot's Directory* 1844; *Kelly* 1855; VCH8
1047　VCH8; 1851 census returns
1048　BoE; WSA A1/592/13; Orbach architects notes
1049　WSA A1/592/13; HE; information from Warminster Civic Trust
1050　*Wiltshire Times* 9/7/1932
1051　VCH8
1052　WSA F10/100/280/6HC
1053　*Wiltshire Times* 10/3/2021
1054　1871 census; OS 1886 revision
1055　OS 1899 revision; census returns 1881 through to 1911
1056　VCH8
1057　BoE
1058　WSA 816/367; *Wiltshire Times* 8/6/1940; *Kelly* 1931
1059　It appears on the 1936 revision to the OS 25" map
1060　*Wiltshire Gazette & Herald* 3/3/2020
1061　*Salisbury & Winchester Journal* 19/2/1887; *Salisbury Times* 19/2/1887
1062　*Wiltshire Independent* 24/6/1841; *Wiltshire Independent* 8/6/1848
1063　Information from Yvonne Crossley; *Kelly* 1889, 1899 and 1920
1064　WSA F10/100/288/1HC
1065　Planning application S1990/1282
1066　*Wiltshire Times* 2/3/2020
1067　*The History of Wootton Bassett*, P J Gingell, Wootton Bassett Historical Society 1977
1068　Orbach BoE notes; OS 1884 and 1899 revisions; DZSWS:2017.7074.5
1069　*Wiltshire Times* 22/10/1910 and 27/1/1912
1070　WSA F10/100/299/2HC
1071　WSA F10/100/299/2HC
1072　*Swindon Advertiser* 30/7/2020

9 Post Offices

1073　Amongst the many sources for early post office history, that on the National Archives website, describing the post office collections held there, provides one of the best concise summaries.

1074	'The urbanity of Marlborough: a Wiltshire town in the seventeenth century', I L Williams in *WAM*94, 2001
1075	Statistics from the website of the Postal Museum, accessed 11/3/23
1076	*Wiltshire Times* 13/12/1919.
1077	*North Wilts Herald* 21/8/1875
1078	Statistics from the postal museum, *op. cit.*.
1079	*Pigot Directory* 1842
1080	*Amesbury, History and description of a south Wiltshire town* – John Chandler and Peter Goodhugh, Amesbury Society 2012
1081	OS 1877 revision edition
1082	Chandler and Goodhugh *op. cit*
1083	Information from Peter Goodhugh
1084	OS 1937 revision; HE
1085	WSA G1/132/98
1086	VCH7; *Pigot Directory* 1822
1087	HE; Bradford on Avon museum website, accessed 27/2/23.
1088	WBR B9989; Bradford on Avon museum website accessed 27/2/23
1089	BoE; British Post Office Architects
1090	*Wiltshire Times* 7/12/1935
1091	*Kelly* 1931
1092	Barfoot and Wilkes, *Universal British Directory* 1793-98, in WRS47
1093	*Pigot Directory* 1822; information from Sue Boddington
1094	*Kelly* 1855; OS 1885 revision.
1095	OS 1899 revision; *Devizes & Wiltshire Gazette* 23/10/1890
1096	Information from Sue Boddington
1097	*Devizes & Wiltshire Gazette* 9/2/1905
1098	*Heath's Calne directories*, various
1099	For example *North Wilts Herald* 13/9/1935; information from Sue Boddington
1100	British Post Office Architects; *Wiltshire Times* 31/1/1953
1101	British Post Office Architects
1102	*Stage Coaches Explained, the Bristol Example*, Dorian Gerhold, Hobnob Press 2012
1103	VCH20 draft text
1104	BoE; HE
1105	*Pigot* 1822; VCH 20 draft text
1106	Orbach BoE notes; OS 1885 revision; *A Chippenham Collection*, Sally Jefferies, Chippenham Civic Society 1987; VCH20 draft text
1107	Photograph reprinted in *Wiltshire Times* 13/12/2019
1108	*Kelly* 1931
1109	*North Wilts Herald* 19/3/1937; *Wiltshire Times* 8/5/1954; BoE
1110	BoE; British Post Office Architects
1111	*Bath Chronicle* 22/2/1798 records the death of the postmaster for 40 years; WRS47 (*Universal British Directory* 1793-8) P19 records the same person as maltster and postmaster; westcountrybottles.co.uk, accessed 14/10/2023, records him as innkeeper of the Red Lion from 1770-98
1112	*Post Office Directory* 1855
1113	*Post Office Directory* 1859
1114	*Corsham Revealed*, Julian Carosi, privately published, Corsham 2019
1115	OS 1884 revision; *Post Office Directory* 1875
1116	Carosi, *op. cit*
1117	WBR B11135; HE; OS 1899 and 1919 revisions

1118 *Wiltshire Times* 19/2/1938
1119 HE
1120 VCH18
1121 *Towns and villages of England – Cricklade*, Diana Holmes, Alan Sutton Publishing 1993.
1122 Holmes *op. cit.*.
1123 VCH18
1124 VCH10; *Pigot Directory* 1822
1125 VCH10
1126 *Trowbridge Chronicle* 29/5/1880
1127 *Devizes & Wiltshire Gazette* 19/5/1887 and 4/8/1887; HE
1128 VCH10; WSA G20/760/264
1129 *Kelly* 1931
1130 VCH10; BoE
1131 Information from David Buxton
1132 *Pigot Directory* 1844 and *Post Office Directory* 1855; information from Christine Suter
1133 OS 1874 revision; *Kelly* 1875; HE
1134 OS 1898 revision; HE; photograph on Highworth Historical Society website accessed 2/3/2023
1135 OS 1922 revision; HE; Staybehinds.com British Resistance website accessed 3/3/2023
1136 Staybehinds.com *op. cit.*; HE
1137 *Malmesbury's Past, People and Places*, Charles Vernon, Malmesbury Civic Trust 2014; OS 1899 revision
1138 Vernon *op. cit*
1139 *Kelly* 1931
1140 VCH12
1141 *Pigot Directory* 1822; VCH12
1142 *Devizes & Wiltshire Gazette* 20/12/1827 and 22/12/1853; WSA G22/295/1
1143 *Devizes & Wiltshire Gazette* 23/2/1883; OS 1885 revision; Orbach BoE notes
1144 BoE
1145 *Kelly* 1931
1146 Information from Nick Baxter
1147 VCH7
1148 Orbach BoE notes
1149 *Post Office Directory* 1855; *Kelly* 1867; OS 1885 and 1899 revisions; *Wiltshire Times* 24/11/1900 quotes move 'across the road' to new position.
1150 *Wiltshire Times* 19/4/1901; British Post Office Architects; OS 1922 revision; *Kelly* 1907
1151 VCH7; *Around Melksham in Old Photographs*, collected by The Melksham and District Historical Association, Alan Sutton 1989
1152 *Kelly* 1931
1153 *Salisbury & Winchester Journal* 25/5/1818
1154 VCH19 draft; *The Book of Mere*, Dr David Longbourne, Halsgrove 2004
1155 *Kelly* 1880 and 1895
1156 VCH19 draft; OS revisions 1886, 1900, 1923 and 1942; Longbourne *op. cit.*; 'Mere Buildings and People' on Mere Historical Society website, accessed 7/3/2023.
1157 Longbourne *op. cit*
1158 VCH6; *Salisbury & Winchester Journal* 5/10/1807; *Pigot Directory* 1822.
1159 *Pigot Directory* 1844; *Post Office Directory* 1855; *Salisbury & Winchester Journal* 21/4/1855; OS 1879 and 1900 revisions
1160 *The Archives Photographs Series, Salisbury*, Peter Daniels, Chalford Publishing Co 1995
1161 *Salisbury Times* 16/6/1899

NOTES

1162 *Salisbury & Winchester Journal* 23/3/1907
1163 BoE; HE
1164 *Kelly* 1931
1165 *Salisbury Journal* 11/9/2023
1166 HE; *Sarum Chronicle* 20 (2020), 177-84
1167 *Last Orders*, John Stooke, Nice Age Ltd 2019; *Pigot* 1844
1168 *The Swindon Book*, Mark Child, Hobnob Press 2013
1169 *Slater's Directory's Directory* 1852/3 and later directories including *Post Office Directory* 1859 and *Kelly* 1867; Child, *op. cit.*; article in Wiltshire Family History Society, Swindon branch newsletter February 2024
1170 *Post Office Directory* 1875; OS 1885 and subsequent revisions
1171 Orbach BoE notes
1172 Orbach BoE notes; *Slater's Directory's Directory* 1852/3
1173 Information from Tom Smith and Clive Carter; *Post Office directories* 1855, 1859 and 1864; OS 1885 revision
1174 Orbach BoE notes; OS 1884 revision
1175 OS 1899 and 1922 revisions
1176 Orbach BoE notes; OS revisions up to 1942
1177 *North Wilts Herald* 21/8/1875
1178 Child, *op. cit.*
1179 British Post Office Architects; *Kelly* 1907; *Swindon Advertiser* 23/6/1911.
1180 British Post Office Architects; *Swindon Advertiser* 23/6/1911.
1181 Child, *op. cit.*
1182 British Post Office Architects; Orbach BoE notes
1183 *North Wilts Herald* 22/11/1935
1184 Orbach BoE notes; photograph in Swindon Libraries collection
1185 *Gazette & Herald* 15/9/2000; information from Tom Smith
1186 WBR B17795; *Swindon Advertiser* 28/10/2008
1187 *Kelly* 1931
1188 VCH7; *Pigot* 1822 and 1844
1189 *Post Office Directory* 1855; *Town Hall Centenary 1889 – 1989 Official Souvenir Guide*, Trowbridge town council 1989
1190 Trowbridge Town Council *op. cit.*; *Kelly* 1875; *Wiltshire Times* 8/9/1917
1191 *Wiltshire Times* 6/2/1886; OS 1886 revision
1192 *Trowbridge in Pictures 1812-1914*, Michael Lansdown, Michael Marshman, Kenneth Rogers, Wiltshire Library and Museum Service 1989
1193 VCH7; directories before and after this date
1194 WSA G15/770/246
1195 *Wiltshire Times* 8/4/1911
1196 VCH7
1197 *Kelly* 1931
1198 BoE
1199 Barfoot and Wilkes, *Universal British Directory* 1793-98, in WRS47; identified as this building in closedpubs.co.uk, accessed 22/11/2023
1200 VCH8; *Pigot Directory* 1844; *Slater's Directory* 18
1201 OS 1886 and 1899 revisions; VCH8
1202 *Warminster in the Twentieth Century*, Celia Lane and Pauline White, Warminster History Society 1999
1203 VCH8; WBR B11941; *Salisbury Times* 8/5/1903; *Warminster & Westbury Journal* 12/9/1903

1204 OS 1922 and 1936/7 revisions
1205 WSA G16/770/209
1206 Lane & White *op. cit*
1207 Lane & White *op. cit.*; *Wiltshire Times* 9/2/1995
1208 *Kelly* 1931
1209 VCH8
1210 VCH8; *Pigot* directories 1822 and 1844; OS revisions 1886 to 1922
1211 HE; WSA 1451/36HC
1212 *Wiltshire Times* 28/7/1923; OS 1936 revision; WBR B3231
1213 *Wiltshire Times* 28/7/1923
1214 *Kelly* 1931
1215 *Wiltshire Times* 24/9/2009
1216 *Post Office Directory* 1855 and 1859
1217 OS 1879 revision; HE
1218 OS 1900 revision; *Kelly* 1889
1219 OS 1939 revision
1220 Information from Yvonne Crossley
1221 Information from Yvonne Crossley
1222 *Robson's Wiltshire Directory* 1838; *Post Office Directory* 1859; OS revisions 1884 to 1936; *The History of Wootton Bassett*, P J Gingell, Wootton Bassett Historical Society 1977
1223 Gingell, *op. cit.*
1224 Gingell, *op. cit.*

10 Swimming Baths

1225 Called such because the taller sides to the rear of the bath gave it the shape of a slipper
1226 For example in Warminster in 1906 - *Warminster & Westbury Journal* 31/3/1906
1227 The online Baths and Wash Houses Historical Archive is a useful general source for this history, as is *Great Lengths, The historic indoor swimming pools of Britain*, Dr Ian Gordon and Simon Inglis, English Heritage 2009
1228 *Devizes & Wiltshire Gazette* 7/8/1884
1229 *Wiltshire Times* 14/9/1935
1230 *Devizes & Wiltshire Gazette* 17/7/1890
1231 Bradford on Avon museum website accessed 21/3/2023
1232 Information from Peter Goodhugh; letter dated 9/5/1915 in the possession of Amesbury history society.
1233 *Salisbury Times* 3/5/1907 and similar in 1909 and 1913
1234 *Trowbridge Chronicle* 23/4/1881; OS 1884 revision.
1235 OS 1899 and 1922 revisions.
1236 Most information on these baths comes from the website of Bradford on Avon museum, accessed 19/3/2023.
1237 OS 1885, 1899, 1922 and 1936 revisions; *Devizes & Wiltshire Gazette* 24/5/1866; *Kelly* 1899; information from Sue Boddington
1238 WSA G15/132/53
1239 Information from Sue Boddington
1240 VCH 20 draft text; OS revisions 1885 to 1937
1241 For example *Wiltshire Times* 11/12/1897, 19/6/1898, 5/5/1900, 8/2/1902 and 30/5/1931.
1242 VCH 20 draft text
1243 VCH 20 draft text

1244 Information from Julian Carosi
1245 *Wiltshire Times* 5/5/1934
1246 Information from Pat Whalley
1247 VCH18; information from Pam Debenham
1248 *Devizes & Wiltshire Gazette* 7/8/1884; OS 1885 revision.
1249 See for example *Devizes & Wiltshire Gazette* 17/7/1890
1250 See for example *Wiltshire Times* 25/6/1932; the website of the Devizes Amateur Swimming Club, accessed 15/3/2023, gives a concise description of the general history here
1251 WBR B3848; Devizes DZSWS2014 7052 152
1252 *North Wilts Herald* 15/5/1891
1253 *Gazette & Herald* 28/8/2003
1254 *Gazette & Herald*, 8/4/2004
1255 *Warminster Herald* 28/6/1879; *Devizes & Wiltshire Gazette* 15/2/1883; OS 1883 and 1899 revisions; 1840s tithe map
1256 OS 25" maps, various
1257 *Wiltshire Times* 4/8/1928; *North Wilts Herald* 12/11/1937; *Around Marlborough – Francis Frith's Photographic Memories*, Dorothy Treasure, Frith Book Co, 2001
1258 Website of Marlborough amateur swimming club, accessed 17/3/2023
1259 *Wiltshire Times* 1/6/1895. The club soon came under the control of the Avon Rubber works adjacent
1260 *Wiltshire Times* 9/7/1949; *Wiltshire Times* 4/1/1919
1261 *Melksham Independent News* 2/8/2022
1262 *Salisbury & Winchester Journal* 8/8/1868, 6/8/1870 and 6/6/1874
1263 *Salisbury Times* 7/4/1899
1264 For example *Salisbury Times* 9/6/1877 and 7/6/1879
1265 OS 1923 revision; *Salisbury & Winchester Journal* 28/5/1892; *Kelly* 1899
1266 *Salisbury Times* 18/3/1892
1267 *Kelly* 1931
1268 *Wiltshire Times* 25/6/1932; OS 1937 revision
1269 Wiltshire Council (Salisbury District Council) development brief for old swimming pool November 2006; website of Salisbury Stingrays swimming club accessed 18/3/2023
1270 *Salisbury Journal* 16/6/2009
1271 *Gazette & Herald* 11/3/2004
1272 Perhaps the best general descriptions of the Swindon baths and their history are to be found in *Swindon: The legacy of a railway town*, RCHME, John Cattell and Keith Falconer, HMSO 1995, and in the HE listing. These are the sources for information in this section not otherwise referenced.
1273 WSA4337/3
1274 VCH9; Cattell and Falconer *op. cit*
1275 *North Wilts Herald* 10/2/1868
1276 WSA G24/132/715; WSA4337/3
1277 OS 1922 and 1943 revisions
1278 HE listing; restoration information on 'Visit Swindon' website accessed 28/4/2023
1279 Orbach BoE notes; press coverage early 2023
1280 OS 1886, 1899 and 1922 revisions; *Salisbury & Winchester Journal* 18/8/1877; *Trowbridge Chronicle* 31/5/1879; *Wiltshire Times* 15/5/1880
1281 *The History of the Trowbridge Bathing Place*, David Mattock, privately published 2001
1282 *Trowbridge Through Time*, Kevin J Hartley & Andrew D Jones, Amberley 2009; WSA G15/132/53; Mattock *op. cit.*.

1283 *Warminster & Westbury Journal* 25/5/1889 announces a public meeting about a proposed public baths; *Trowbridge Chronicle* 11/6/1898 describes the opening; OS 1899 and 1922 revisions
1284 *Wiltshire Times* 2/8/1924
1285 *Warminster in the Twentieth Century*, Celia Lane and Pauline White, Warminster History Society 1999
1286 *Wiltshire Times* anniversary commemoration 2/1/2013
1287 *Devizes & Wiltshire Gazette* 31/5/1888
1288 BoE; WSA G17/701/2PC
1289 WSA G17/710/2
1290 *Salisbury Times* 4/9/1869; *Salisbury & Winchester Journal* 22/12/1900
1291 *Salisbury & Winchester Journal* 30/3/1901; *Salisbury Times* 31/7/1903; OS revisions 1879, 1900, 1923 and 1936
1292 *Salisbury & Winchester Journal* 9/11/1872
1293 *North Wilts Herald* 8/8/1913

Note on Sources

Frequently used sources are referred to in the footnotes by abbreviation, as follows:

BoE – *The Buildings of England, Wiltshire,* Julian Orbach, Nikolaus Pevsner and Bridget Cherry, Yale University Press 2021.

British Post Office Architects – (britishpostofficearchitects.weebly.com) Details many of those involved in designing post offices.

Builder, The – published from 1843 to 1966 and contains articles outlining the design and construction of many prominent buildings. Volumes from 1843 to 1906 available online at onlinebooks.library.upenn.edu

Census (with year) – extracted information from the national census for that year.

Dictionary of Scottish Architects – (scottisharchitects.org.uk) Includes many who were not Scots but worked there.

DZSWS (with document reference) – document in the collection of the Wiltshire Museum, Devizes

FreeBMD – (freebmd.org.uk) Online transcription of General Registry Office records of birth, marriage and death, 1837-1997.

HE – listing by Historic England. Available online at historicengland.org.uk/listing

Kelly (with year of issue) – county directories issued by Kelly & Co, London. They were the main company involved but directories were also issued by, amongst others, Gilman, Pigot and the Post Office. Some available online at specialcollections.le.ac.uk/digital/collection/p16445coll4.

Newspapers – given under the name of the journal and the date. Britishnewspaperarchive.co.uk provides a searchable database and most extracts before c1960 are taken from there.

Orbach architects notes – dictionary of Wiltshire architects compiled by Julian Orbach and available online in 2023 at julianorbach.weebly.com

Orbach BoE notes – research notes compiled by Julian Orbach for the Wiltshire 'Buildings of England', by kind permission of the author.

OS (with revision year) – Ordnance Survey 25" scale maps, with year in which the mapping was revised. Available online at maps.bristol.gov.uk/kyp and maps.nls.uk.

RCHME – *Ancient and Historical Monuments in the City of Salisbury,* Royal

Commission on the Historical Monuments of England, HMSO 1977. Available online at British-history.ac.uk/rchme/Salisbury

SBYWM (with document reference) – document from the Salisbury Museum

VCH (with volume number) – Wiltshire volumes of the Victoria County History of England. Available in printed form at public libraries and the Wiltshire and Swindon History Centre but volumes 4 to 18 are online at British-history.ac.uk. Page numbers are not given in the online volumes but individual references can be easily found by online search for terms within the relevant volume. Volumes 19 and 20 were in course of preparation in 2023 and draft text could be seen via history.ac.uk.

WAM (with volume number) – *Wiltshire Archaeological and Natural History Magazine*, published annually by the Wiltshire Archaeological and Natural History Society based at the Wiltshire Museum. Volumes from 1854 to 2013 are available online via the Wiltshire Museum's website.

WBR (with document reference) – document from the collection of the Wiltshire Buildings Record at the History Centre, Chippenham. Also used to indicate the source of a photograph.

WCH – (apps.wiltshire.gov.uk/community history) Wiltshire Council database giving a wide range of historical information for each of Wiltshire's (but not Swindon Borough's) communities.

WRS (with volume number) – publication by the Wiltshire Record Society. Volumes 1-69 (2016) can be viewed online at wiltshirerecordsociety.org.uk

WSA (with document reference) – document from the Wiltshire and Swindon Archives at the History Centre, Chippenham. Also used to indicate the source of a photograph.

Workhouses.org.uk – website devoted to detailing workhouses and their history across Great Britain and Ireland.

Index of Buildings

The index lists the buildings described in the text and which are still standing. The numbers refer to the pages on which the main entry for the particular building appears. Subsidiary entries are cross-referenced in the text.

Amesbury
Antrobus House library 112–13
Bowman Centre, council office 148
History Centre 92
Library in former Fire Station 113
New library 113
Police Station, Back Lane 180–2
Police Station, Salisbury Road 182
Post Office, Comilla House 209–10
Post Office, 16 Salisbury Street 209–10

Bradford on Avon
Abbey House council office 150
Church Street library 113
Kingston House council office 150
Museum in new library 93
New library, Bridge Street 114
Police Station, Market Street 183
Police Station, Avonfield Avenue 183
Police Station, Station Approach 184
Post Office, Market Street 210
Post Office, The Shambles 210–11
Post Office, Bridge Yard 211
St Margaret's Hall council office 150
Swimming baths, St Margaret's Street 231–2
Timbrell's Yard library 114
Tolsey, The Shambles 51
Town Hall 7–9
Westbury House council office 148–9

Calne
Bank House council office 150
Carnegie Library 115–17
New Library 116–17
Police Station, 12 High Street 184
Police Station, Town Hall 184–5
Police Station, Silver Street 185
Post Office, 1953 211–12
Reading Rooms, Church Street 115
Swimming baths, community campus 232
Town Hall 9–11

Chippenham
Bewley House council office 151
Butter Cross 51–2
Causeway council office 1527
Constitutional Club, reading room 117
County Court 72–3
High Street council office 151
Jubilee Building, reading room 117–18
Market Place museum 93–4
Monkton Park council office 151
Olympiad Sports Centre 232–3
Police Station, New Road 185–6
Post Office, White Hart 212
Post Office, High Street 212
Post Office, Market Place 213
Post Office, St Mary Street 212–13
Temperance Hall, reading room 117
Timber Street library 118–19
Town Hall 14–16
Wiltshire & Swindon History Centre 94
Workhouse, Rowden Hill 151
Yelde Hall 11–13

Corsham
Police Station, Pickwick Road 186
Post Office in Methuen Arms 213–14
Post Office, 15 High Street 213
Post Office, 84 High Street 214
Springfield Campus library 119
Springfield Campus swimming baths 233
Town Hall 16–18

Cricklade
Bath Road library 120
High Street library 119–20

Museum in former weighbridge 95
Museum, Calcutt Street 95
Police Station, The Priory 188
Police Station, 76 High Street 188
Police Station, 91 High Street 188
Post Office, Garfield House 215
Post Office, 39 High Street 215
Town Hall 1862) 18
Town Hall 1933) 18–19

Devizes
Assize Courts 73–6
Corn Exchange 56–7
Devizes Leisure Centre swimming baths 234
Market House 55–6
Museum at 15 High Street 95
New Hall 20–3
Northgate House council office 153–4
Police Station, Bridewell Street 188–9
Police Station, Barford House 188–9
Police Station, New Parks Street 189
Police Station, London Road 190
Post Office, 44 Market Place 215
Post Office, 24 Market Place 215
Post Office, Barford House 215
Post Office, Sheep Street 215–16
Reading Rooms, 6 High Street 120
Reading Rooms, Former British School, Northgate Street 120
Sheep Street library 121
St John's Street law courts 76
Town Hall 22–3
Wiltshire Museum 95–6

Highworth
Brewery Street library 122
Inigo House, 24 High Street, library 121
Museum in former Lloyds Bank 97
Police Station, Grove Hill 190
Police Station, Newburgh Place 190
Post Office, 1 Vicarage Lane 216
Post Office, 18 High Street 216
Post Office, 35 High Street 216
Post Office, 23 High Street 216
Post Office, 5 Sheep Street 216
Recreation Centre swimming baths 234

Malmesbury
Activity Zone swimming baths 234
Court House 77–8
High Street council office 155
High Street library 123
Library in former primary school, Cross Hayes 123

Museum in Town Hall 97
Museum, 20 Gloucester Street 97
Museum, Moravian church 97
Oxford Street council meeting place 23
Police Station, Burnham Road 190–1
Police Station, Burton Hill 190
Post Office, 31 High Street 217
Post Office, 41 High Street 217
Reading Rooms, 4 Silver Street 122
Town Hall 24–5

Marlborough
Barton Dene leisure centre swimming baths 235
Corn Market 593
High Street council office 156
Library in former St Peter's school 124–5
London Road council office) 156
Merchant's House Museum 98
Police Station, Bridewell Street 191–2
Police Station, George Lane 192
Post Office, 131 High Street 218
Post Office, 101 High Street 218
The Green, council office 155
Town Hall 25–8
Workhouse 156

Melksham
Assembly Hall 29
Blue Pool swimming baths 235
Church Room, Canon Square council office 156
Community Campus swimming baths 235
Library in former Quaker meeting house 126
Library, Lowbourne 126
Library, Community Campus 126
Police Station, Market Place 192–3
Police Station, Semington Road 193
Police Station, Hampton Park 193
Post Office, 29 Bank Street 218
Post Office, 14 High Street 218–19
Post Office, 31 Church Street 219
Reading Rooms, Prospect House, Bank Street 125
Town Hall 28–9
Workhouse 156–7

Mere
Library in former chapel, Boar Street 127
Library in former National school 127
Police Station, North Street 194
Police Station, White Road 194
Police Station, behind Fire Station 194
Post Office, The Square 219

Temperance Hall, reading room 127
The Lecture Hall, council building 157
Victoria Hall 30
Workhouse 157

Salisbury

Alexandra House law courts 81–2
Assembly Rooms, High Street, reading rooms 128–9
Blackmore museum 100–2
Coroner's court, Castle Street 82
Council House new building 158–60
Endless Street council office 158
Five Rivers leisure centre swimming baths 236
Guildhall 30–4
Hamilton Hall, New Street, reading rooms 129–30
Library, Endless Street 130
Library, Chipper Lane 130–16
Market House 60–2
Police Station, New Canal 194–5
Police Station, Endless Street/Salt Lane 195–6
Police Station, 13 Endless Street 195
Police Station, Wilton Road 196
Post Office, Castle Street/Chipper Lane 220–1
Post Office, 56 High Street 221
Salisbury & South Wiltshire museum, King's House 102–3
Salisbury Law Courts 82
St Ann Street museum 99–100
St Ann Street reading room 130
St Edmund's College/The Council House 158–60
Young Art Gallery 103–4

Swindon

Apsley House art gallery 105
Apsley House museum 104–5
Bath Road council offices 162–3
Beckhampton Street council offices 163
Combined Courts, Islington Street 85
Corn Exchange, Old Town 35–6
Council offices in former Clarence Street schools 163
County Court, Clarence Street 83
Cricklade Road/Ferndale Road reading room 134
Cricklade Street council offices 161
Dorcan Centre swimming baths 240
Euclid Street council offices 162–3
Faringdon Road swimming baths 237–9
Libraries, various in outer Swindon 136
Library in Even Swindon Community Centre 136
Library in Swindon Arts Centre, Devizes Road 136
Library in McIlroy's Department Store, Regent Street 135
Link Centre swimming baths 240
Magistrates' Courts, Gordon Road 83–5
Market Hall 62–4
Mechanics' Institute, Emlyn Square 132–4
New library 135–6
New Town Hall 36–7
Oasis leisure centre swimming baths 239–40
Old Town Hall 34–5
Police Station, 13 Devizes Road 196
Police Station, Eastcott Hill 197–8
Police Station, Gorse Hill 198–9
Police Station, Gablecross 199
Police Station, Link Avenue 199
Post Office, 11 Bath Road 221
Post Office, 119 Victoria Road 222–3
Post Office, Regent Street 221–2
Post Office, 58 Commercial Road 223
Rodbourne Road/Morris Street reading room 135
Wat Tyler House, Princes Street council offices 163

Trowbridge

Arlington House council offices 165
Civic Centre, St Stephen's Place 168
County Hall 166–8
Court Hall 86–7
Hill's Public Hall, council building 168
Hill Street council offices and library 165–6
Library Headquarters, Prospect Place 138
Market House 64–5
Museum in former Home mills 106
Polebarn House council offices 166
Police Station, Polebarn Road 200–1
Post Office, Fernleigh House, Church Street 223–4
Post Office, 4 Fore Street 224
Post Office, 1a Roundstone Street 224
Post Office, Fore Street 224
Stallard Street council offices 165
Town Hall 37–40
Trowbridge Sports Centre, swimming baths 240
Wicker Hill council offices 165

Warminster

Athenaeum, reading rooms 140
Civic Centre 170
Craven House, Silver Street, council office 170

Dewey House, North Row, council offices 170
Literary & Scientific Institution, reading rooms 139
Market Place council office 168–9
Museum in former sexton's cottage 106
Police Station, Ash Walk 201
Police Station, Station Road 201–2
Police Station, The Avenue 201
Police Station, 32 Bread Street 202
Portway House council offices 169
Post Office, Angel Inn 225
Post Office, 70 Market Place 225
Post Office, Station Road/East Street 225–6
Three Horseshoes Yard library 141
Town Hall 40–2
Woodcock Road swimming baths 240
Workhouse 169

Westbury

Laverton Institute, council offices 170–2
Library in Oddfellows hall, Bratton Road 141–2
Police Station, Edward Street 202
Police Station, Station Road 203
Post Office, 14/16 Edward Street 226
Post Office, 26 Edward Street 226–7
Swimming baths, Church Street 240–2
Town Hall 42–4
Westbury House, Edward Street, library 142

Westfield House, council offices 172
Workhouse 172

Wilton

Kingsbury Square council offices 173
Library in former Quaker meeting house, South Street 143
Police Station, Salisbury Road 203
Police Station, 43 Russell Street 203
Post Office, 11 Kingsbury Square 227
Post Office, South Street/West Street 227
Post Office, 4 West Street 227
Town Hall 44–5

Royal Wootton Bassett

Borough Fields library 144
Cemetery lodge council offices 175
Council offices in former National school 175–6
High Street council offices 174–5
Manor House council offices 175
Police Station, Station Road 203–5
Police Station, Manor House 204–5
Post Office, 21 High Street 227
Post Office, 33 High Street 227
Purton Workhouse 173–4
Purton Institute 174
Sessions hall, Station Road 88–9
Town Hall 45–6

Index of Architects

Biographical information on the architects listed here, unless otherwise indicated, comes from the two volumes of 'Architects and Building Craftsmen with work in Wiltshire' (Pamela M Slocombe, Wiltshire Buildings Record, 1996 and 2006) or the 'Index of Wiltshire Architects' by Julian Orbach (prepared as part of his work on the new Wiltshire 'Buildings of England' and available online at julianorbach. weebly.com.)

In the early 19th century the county surveyor, reporting to the quarter sessions, had responsibility for county bridges and for the few buildings then under county control, mainly the prisons at Fisherton (Salisbury), Marlborough and Devizes.* But the range of buildings managed by the surveyor expanded as the century progressed and was accelerated further with the formation of the county council in 1889, such that in the end many public buildings were designed in the county surveyor's office. A separate role of county architect was created in the 1920s and lasted until the 1990s after which that function within the county council more or less ceased. Salisbury had a city surveyor while it retained its autonomy and Thamesdown Borough had an architect's department from its formation until a similar date.

Sometimes the individual who designed a particular building for one of these departments cannot be readily identified and in such cases must remain anonymous within the more general designation of 'office of…' Where architects are individually identified the building's entry comes under their name, but sometimes a building attributed to a particular county surveyor or architect may in practice have been designed by an unidentified member of their staff.

The number at the end of each entry indicates the page(s) on which the building description is to be found. The list includes the architects, where known, of both standing and demolished buildings.

* WRS50 – *The Letters of John Peniston, 1823-30*

Adye, Charles Septimus, 1841–1906, of Bradford on Avon, Wiltshire County Council's first county surveyor from 1889. Widespread practice across the southwest in church restoration and new buildings. In practice from c1880 with Henry Weaver (qv) and from 1889 working with Adye's son Herbert.
Police Station, George Lane, Marlborough 1899 (192)

Gorsehill House, Swindon, conversion to Police Station 1905 (198)

Allom, Thomas, 1804–72, of London where he designed houses and a church on the Ladbroke estate.
Workhouse, Calne 1847–8 (150)

Baker, Orlando, 1834–1912, born Gloucestershire, moved to Swindon 1870,

emigrated to Tasmania 1890. Designed houses and nonconformist chapels in Swindon and in 1911 the Custom House in Hobart, Tasmania.
Purton Institute (Wootton Bassett) 1879–80 (174)

Baldwin, Thomas, 1750–1820, city architect of Bath, 1775–1793, where built prolifically.
Rebuilding of Town Hall, Devizes 1806–08 (23)

Bertram, Bertram & Rice of Oxford. Little seems to be known of the work of this partnership, which is a shame because the Swindon council offices are of considerable quality.
Council offices, Euclid Street, Swindon 1936–8 (162)

Beswick, Alfred Edward, 1885–1959, son of Robert (qv), in practice in Vancouver but returned to Swindon c1925 to continue father's practice as RJ Beswick and Son, with increased emphasis on church building and restoration over a wider area.
Partial rebuilding of Mechanics' Institute, Swindon 1930 (with father Robert) (133)

Beswick, Robert James Rick, 1856–1931, born Manchester but in practice in Swindon c1874–1925, mainly designing commercial buildings.
Reading Room, Rodbourne Road, Swindon 1904 (135)
Partial rebuilding of Mechanics' Institute, Swindon 1930 (with son Alfred) (133)

Binyon, Brightwen, 1846–1905, of Ipswich but born Manchester. Became architect to Swindon School Board 1879 and thereafter built mainly schools in the town.
New Town Hall, Swindon 1891 (36)
Extension to Mechanics' Institute, Swindon 1892 (133)

Blore, Edward, 1787–1879, of London. Initially a topographical artist, he started his practice in the 1820s and thereafter designed numerous country houses and churches as well as extensively for Marlborough College.
Town Hall, Warminster 1832 (41)
Literary and Scientific Institution, Warminster 1838 (139)

Blount, George Leo William, 1870–1932, of Salisbury. Pupil of Henry Weaver (qv), his practice was mainly churches, schools and commercial buildings.
Young Art Gallery, Salisbury 1913[1] (104)

Bothams, Alfred Champney 1861–1931, of Salisbury. In practice from 1883, assistant city surveyor 1889, succeeded his father John Champney Bothams as city surveyor 1902–8. Designed many buildings in Salisbury in both roles, and the practice he established continued into 1960s.
Alterations to form Police Station, Endless Street, Salisbury 1883 (195)
Alterations to Guildhall, Salisbury 1896–7 (attributed) (33 note 88)
Library, Chipper Lane, Salisbury 1905 (130)

Bowden, Frank I, 1901–78, county architect from c1940 until 1966, also an artist and later consultant to Wiltshire Historic Buildings Trust.[2]
Police Station, Corsham 1951 (188)
Police Headquarters, Wilton Road, Salisbury 1955 (196)
County Police Headquarters, Devizes 1962 (190)

Brandt Potter Partnership, formed 1967 when John Brandt joined the Potter & Hare partnership of Robert Potter and Richard Williams Hare. Focus on church work.
Redevelopment of King's House, Salisbury, for Salisbury Museum 1981 (102)

Broadhead, Bob, last Wiltshire county architect, to c1999.
Library, Bradford on Avon 1990 (114)

Bromley, William Harris, builder and architect working in Corsham area from c1870 to c1910.
Town Hall, Corsham 1883 (16)

Bruges Tozer, of Bristol, established 1973 by James Bruges and Howard Tozer; still active in 2023 though original partners retired.
Police Headquarters, Hampton Park, Melksham 2002 (193)

BTA of Warminster. Founded by Barrie Taylor as Barrie Taylor Associates in 1970; later taken over by David Sharp. Practice continues.[3]
Remodelling of Civic Centre, Warminster 2011 (170)

Burrough & Hannah
Council offices, Monkton Hill, Chippenham 1967 (151)

Capita Symonds, founded 2004, large architects and general services group with an office in Swindon borough council offices for duration of their work there.
Pinetrees Library, Swindon 2011 (136)

Cockerell, Samuel Pepys, 1754–1827, of London, best remembered for Sezincote, an Indian–influenced country house in Gloucestershire.
North Wing to St Edmund's College, Salisbury 1790 (158)

Cole, Eric, joined practice of John Middleton and opened office in Cirencester 1930; later expanded in various partnerships with offices in several towns, including Swindon from 1950s; died 1980.[4]
New Town Hall, Cricklade 1933 (19)

Coleman Hicks Partnership, of Kidlington Oxfordshire. Established 1979 with a varied workload from individual houses up to large supermarkets, of which a number have been completed for the Co–operative Society including that at Highworth.[5]
Brewery Street Library, above new supermarket, Highworth c2000 (122)

Cooper, William, architect and auctioneer of Henley, Oxfordshire. Designed several workhouses in the late 1830s.
Workhouse, Marlborough 1837 (156)

Creeke, Christopher Crabbe, 1820–86, born Cambridge but moved to Bournemouth c1850 and responsible for much development there.
Workhouse, Chippenham 1858–9 (151)

Cropper, Edward, Post Office architect, designed at least 20 across the country in 1910s and 1920s.[6]
Extension to Post Office, Regent Circus, Swindon 1911 (222)

Currivan, Tony – see Newland, Nic

Davis, Charles Edward, 1827–1902. Practised in Bath from c1849 and became surveyor of works there in 1862, a position he held until 1900. Varied buildings in Wiltshire including several parsonages.
Market House, Trowbridge 1862 (64)

Davison, Thomas R of London but with practice in Swindon.
Victoria Institute, Trowbridge 1902 (won in competition) (137)

DKA, originally David Kent Architects of Bath; undertook numerous public building and schools projects from 1993 onwards.
Monkton Park council offices, Chippenham 2002; refurbishment 2013 (152)

Drew, William Henry, c1837–1905. Swindon architect with large practice, later with his son Edward, in commercial and domestic building in and around the town.
Bath Road post office, Swindon, alterations 1901 (221)

Dyke, David Nicholas, 1881–1969, architect in Office of Works, assistant chief architect by 1939, had designed 'over 100' post offices and telephone exchanges by 1930.[7]
Chipper Lane, Salisbury, telephone exchange 1936 (221)

Evans, Aaron, practice in Bath begun 1978 and now substantial and wide-ranging.
New Library, Calne 2001 (117)
New Police Station, Polebarn Road, Trowbridge

2004 (201)

Evans, T L, of London. Not a qualified architect but formerly clerk of works to Sampson Kempthorne, a main designer of workhouses, and himself designed several. His design for Wilton workhouse was refused because he was not qualified.
Workhouse rebuilding, Westbury 1836–7 (172)

Feilden & Mawson, large practice with London and provincial offices.
Salisbury Law Courts 2009 (82)

Fildes, Geoffrey, 1888–1963 of London, son of painter Sir Luke Fildes.
Antrobus House, Amesbury 1925 (112)

Fitzroy Robinson Partnership, of London. Large practice founded 1956, taken over by Aukett Associates in 2005.
Council offices, Browfort, Devizes 1985 (154)

Fogg, Thomas Holt, 1880–1918, born in Derbyshire[8] but came to Chippenham in 1909, various commissions but killed in First World War.
Neeld Hall, Chippenham 1911 (15)

French, Alex & Partners, large Bristol commercial architecture practice founded 1930s by Alex French.
County Hall extension, Trowbridge 1972–5 (167)
Community Campus, Corsham 2014 (119)

Fuller, Thomas, 1823–1898, of Bath. Numerous works in Bath area, Bradford town hall his most prominent, before emigrating to Canada c1857 where he won competition to design Canadian parliament building. Later chief government architect there.
Town Hall, Bradford on Avon 1855 (8)

Gibberd, Frederick & Partners. Large London practice established 1935 by Sir Frederick Gibberd, 1908–1984.[9]
Library, Park, Swindon 1964 (136)

Gillinson, Barnett & Partners, of Leeds, specialists in public swimming pools.
Oasis leisure centre Swimming Pool, Swindon 1976 (240)

Goodridge, Alfred, 1828–1915, of Bath. Worked initially with father Henry; later works in Bath and Trowbridge.
Town Hall, Trowbridge 1889 (38)

Gould, John, believed to have designed many of the buildings for the Tottenham Park estate, Savernake.
St Peter's School Marlborough, now library 1853 (125)

Greatrex, Roland Ivor, born 1915. Designed post offices for ministry of public building and works.
Roundstone Street Post Office, Trowbridge 1966 (224)

Halliday & Anderson, of Cardiff. George Eley Halliday 1858–1922, and Anderson.
Swimming Baths, Westbury 1888 (240)

Hammond, John, of Marlborough.
Bridewell, Marlborough 1787, attributed (191)
Rebuilding of Town Hall, Marlborough 1792–3 (26)

Hamp, Henry Joseph, 1857–1939, born Wolverhampton but became borough engineer and surveyor for New Swindon.
Market Hall, Commercial Road/Market Street, Swindon 1891 (63)

Harding, John, of Salisbury, in directories 1867–99, extensive practice in South Wiltshire.
Alterations to 40 St Ann's Street Salisbury for Salisbury & South Wiltshire Museum 1864 (99–100)
Hamilton Hall, Salisbury, reading room 1871 (129)

Harding, Michael, of Salisbury, son of John Harding. With his father from c1890 and continued until 1937; diocesan surveyor by

INDEX OF ARCHITECTS

1907.
Hamilton Hall extension, Salisbury 1889–90 (129)

Hardy, C R, of the Property Services Agency.
Conversion of Alexandra House, Salisbury for law courts 1984–5 (81)

Harrison Patience Architects, of Putney, London. Practice specialising in light–weight tensile membrane structures, as used in Swindon. May have had a short life in the first half of the 1990s.[10]
New Market Hall, Swindon 1995 (64)

Hawks, Henry Nicholas, died 1911, architect to Post Office division of the Ministry of Works, designed at least nine post offices.[11]
Chipper Lane Post Office, Salisbury 1907 (220)

Hepworth, Philip Dalton, 1888–1963, of London. Had previously designed Walthamstow town hall, equally monumental.
County Hall, Trowbridge 1938–40 (166)

Hill, William, 1827–89, of Leeds. In practice from 1851 and said to have built over 100 nonconformist chapels.[12]
Corn Exchange, Devizes 1857 (56)

Hopper, Thomas, 1776–1856, of London. Leading architect of country houses and public buildings.
Alterations to Guildhall, Salisbury 1829–30 (33)

Howard, Sydney. Surveyor to Bradford on Avon Urban District Council in the late 19th century.
Swimming Baths, Bradford on Avon 1898 (232)

Hunt, Edward, of Alresford, Hants.
Workhouse, Harnham (Alderbury/Salisbury) 1836–7 (160)
Workhouse, Wilton 1836–7 (173)

Ingleman, Richard, 1777–1838, of Southwell. Specialist in asylums but also designed other buildings.
Town Hall, Westbury 1815 (43)

Jones, Daniel c1796–1866, & **Charles**, 1798–1852, of Bradford on Avon. Sons of John Jones and primarily builders. Daniel said to have done much work for T H Wyatt (qv) and Charles to have built numerous toll-houses.
Town Hall, Melksham 1847 (28, 192)

Judd, E W, architect with Ministry of Public Buildings and Works.
Sheep Street Post Office, Devizes 1969 (215)

Kempthorne, Sampson, 1809–73, architect to Poor Law Commissioners from 1835, produced model workhouse plans and subsequently designed 30+ before emigrating to New Zealand in 1841.[13]
Workhouse, Warminster 1837 (169)

Kendall, Henry Edward, 1776–1875, of London. Pupil of Thomas Leverton and probably also of John Nash; varied practice with early work in Lincolnshire.
Workhouse, Semington, Melksham 1836–9 (157)

Kendall Kingscott Partnership, established Stoke Gifford, Bristol 1962 by John Kendall. Practice focussed on larger–scale commercial projects.[14]
Alterations to Magistrates' Courts, Swindon 1989–90 (83)
Wiltshire & Swindon History Centre, Chippenham 2007 (94)

Kirby, Major Arthur D, of Wyvern Design, Chippenham.
Bewley House offices, Chippenham 1968 (151)

Larkham Design of Salisbury. Much work of domestic scale.
Amesbury History Centre 2023 (92)

Loring–Morgan, J, Swindon borough architect c1947–65.

Magistrates' Courts, Swindon 1964 (83)
Art Gallery extension to Swindon Museum 1964 (105)

Luck, Gordon, Wiltshire County Architects.
New Library, Corsham 1969 (119)

Mantell, Edward Walter, of Swindon. Active in Swindon area in 1850s and 60s; he may have moved elsewhere later.
National School, later council offices, Wootton Bassett 1861 (175)

Moffatt, William Bonython, 1812–87, of London. In partnership with George Gilbert Scott from 1836 and built about 50 workhouses between them, mostly in the south west; produced improvements to Kempthorne's standard plans. Partnership broken 1845–6; Moffatt had some further work but imprisoned for debt in 1860 and practice then ceased.
Workhouse, Amesbury 1837 (by Moffatt alone) (148)
Workhouse, Mere 1838–9 (with George Gilbert Scott) (157)

Newland, Nic & Currivan, Tony, of Swindon Borough Architects. Newland was head of design and construction.
New Library, Swindon 2008 (135)

Niblett, Francis, 1814–83, Gloucestershire. Built numerous churches in that county.
Market Hall/Town Hall, Malmesbury 1848 (24)

Nicholls, George B, of Birmingham.
Workhouse, Harnham (Alderbury/Salisbury) rebuilding 1877–9 (160)

Oliver, Charles Bryan, 1850–1918, of Bath.[15]
Town Hall, Calne 1886 (11)

Overton, Samuel, Architect and builder of Marlborough. Agent to the Savernake estate and built in that area, particularly schools.
Alterations to Town Hall, Marlborough 1867 (26)

Peniston, Henry, 1833–1911,[16] of Salisbury. County surveyor in succession to his father and grandfather; appointed 1858 in competition with others including Henry Weaver (qv)[17] but resigned c1864 over criticism of his work.
Police Station, New Canal, Salisbury 1858 (195)
County Police Station, Devizes Road, Salisbury 1859 (195)
Police Station, Edward Street, Westbury (attributed) 1860s (202)

Peniston, John Michael, 1807–58, of Salisbury. County surveyor, succeeding his father in 1848; also city architect. Substantial body of work mostly in and around Salisbury; died suddenly after manoeuvres with Wiltshire Militia.
Police Station, Stallard Street, Trowbridge 1854 (199)
Police Station, Burnham Road, Malmesbury 1855 (190)
Police Station, New Road, Chippenham (probably by him although his son may have worked on it) c1857 (186)
Police Station, Ash Walk, Warminster (probably by him although his son may have worked on it) 1857 (201)

Pilkington, William, 1748–1848, of London but born near Doncaster.
Guildhall (Council House), Salisbury 1795 (to plans of Sir Robert Taylor (qv) but some alterations) (33)

Pinfold, Cyril George, 1907–83, Ministry of Works architect, designed post offices in the 1950s as well as telephone exchanges and other buildings.[18]
Post Office, Chippenham 1959 (212)

Pollard. Quoted as of Frome but no evidence of this from directories; possibly George Pollard (1767–1838) of Taunton.
Alterations to Market House, Devizes 1838 (55)

Ponting, Charles Edwin, 1849–1932, of Marlborough. Substantial practice, mostly in

Wiltshire, including much church restoration as diocesan architect for over 40 years; also surveyor to Marlborough College for 30+ years and Salisbury Cathedral architect for 16.
Rebuilding of Town Hall, Marlborough 1901–2 (27–8)

Powell, J George, Wiltshire county surveyor by 1911 until early 1920s.
Police Station, Station Road, Wootton Bassett 1912 (204)
Hill Street offices, Trowbridge 1913–14 (166)

Reeves, Charles, 1815–66, of London. Built 64 court houses as architect to the County Courts; also 44 London police stations as architect to the Metropolitan Police.
Court Hall, Trowbridge 1854 (86)

Roberts, Edward, 1819–75, of London. May have assisted Sampson Sage (qv) on the old town hall in Swindon.
Mechanics' Institute, Swindon 1854 (133)

Sage, Sampson, born 1799 in Somerset but moved multiple times and was in Swindon from early 1840s to c1861; little of his work identified there.
Old Town Hall, Swindon 1853 (34)

Scott, Sir George Gilbert, 1811–78, amongst the most prominent, and prolific, of all Victorian architects. Early partnership with Moffatt (qv) produced numerous workhouses (see that entry).
Workhouse, Mere 1838–9 (with William Bonython Moffatt) (157)

Seccombe, Henry Edward, 1879–1955. Architect in the Post Office division of the Office of Works. Worked on c30 post offices in the south west and Wales as well as numerous sorting offices and telephone exchanges.[19]
Victoria Road Post Office, Swindon 1935 (attributed) (222)
Post Office extension, Bradford on Avon 1936 (attributed) (211)

Sharpe, John & Associates, of Chippenham
District Council offices, Trowbridge 1974 (168)

Sidell Gibson Architects. Large London practice.
Marlborough Workhouse conversion 1999 (156)

Simmons, John & Associates, of Bath.
Civic Centre, Trowbridge 1974 (168)
Redevelopment of Market House, Trowbridge 1974 (65)

Smith, Cyril Herbert, born 1879, of Calne. Partner in Smith & Marshall. Appears to have done limited work in Calne area.
Carnegie Library, Calne 1905 (115)

Smith, John James, 1848–1915, of Swindon from c1870 to c1900. Various works in Swindon of which the baths may be the most important. Retired to Devon c1900.
Faringdon Road Baths, Swindon (237)

Smith, P G, of the Office of Works. Little seems to be known about his other work.
Church Street Post Office, Melksham 1969 (219)

Smith & Light (perhaps members of the town corporation).
Jubilee Building, Chippenham 1889 (118)

Smith, William, of Trowbridge. Architect and builder, active by 1842 and through to 1890s, particularly building chapels and schools.
Stallard Street warehouse, later council offices, Trowbridge 1878 (165)

Stanley, William Henry, c1857–1933, of Trowbridge. Started in Trowbridge as part-time surveyor to the urban district council and developed a local practice of generally modest-scale work. Left Trowbridge on retirement in 1924.[20]
Post Office, Bradford on Avon 1901 (211)

Stanton Williams of London, founded 1985 by Alan Stanton and Paul Williams. Large

international practice.
New building at Council House, Salisbury 2010 (160)

Stent, William Jervis, 1815–87, of Warminster. Prolific architect of nonconformist chapels but other buildings also, particularly in Warminster and Westbury.
Alterations to Westbury House, Westbury 1850s (attributed) (142)
Athenaeum, Warminster 1858 (140)
Temperance Hall, Chippenham 1863 (117)
Laverton Institute, Westbury 1873 (171)

Strapp, John, engineer to the London & South Western Railway 1853–70 when he resigned over a financial irregularity.[21]
Market House, Salisbury 1859 (61)

Stride Treglown, large practice with numerous offices.
County Hall alterations, Trowbridge 2012–13 (167)

Tanner, Sir Henry, 1849–1935. With the Office of Works from 1873, became principal surveyor in 1898 and knighted in 1904. Large number of post offices associated with him but some, including Swindon, he may have just approved the drawings for.[22]
Conversion for Regent Circus Post Office, Swindon 1900 (attributed) (222)

Taylor, Sir Robert, 1714–88, of London. Apprenticed as sculptor but changed to architecture c1754 and developed successful practice; knighted 1782.
Guildhall, Salisbury 1795 (posthumous – see also Pilkington, William (qv)) (33)

Thamesdown Borough Architects; various architects.
West Swindon Link Centre library 1985 (136)
Wat Tyler House council offices, Swindon 1985–6 (163)
Even Swindon Library 1990 (136)

Thompson, John Bell Langhorn, c1891–1961. Swindon Borough Surveyor from 1924–48.
Coate Water swimming pool and diving stage, Swindon 1935 (239)

Thomson, James, 1800–83, of London. Built in London and elsewhere but most noted in Wiltshire for association with Joseph Neeld of Grittleton for whom he built extensively in Chippenham, Grittleton and surrounding area.
Town Hall, Chippenham 1833 (14)

Underwood, Charles, c1791–1883, of Bristol. Successful practice in Bristol after early bankruptcy in Cheltenham.
Home Mills, Trowbridge, later museum, 1862 (106)

Walker, Thomas, 1882–1953. A Scot, trained in Hawick before moving south. Wiltshire County Architect 1921–47.[23]
Polebarn Road Police Station, Trowbridge 1926 (200)
Salisbury Road Police Station, Wilton c1926 (203)
Gorse Hill Police Station, Swindon 1928 (198)
Station Road Police Station, Warminster 1932 (201)
County Library offices, Trowbridge 1934 (138)

Walters, G, of Salisbury City Council.
Conversion of Salisbury Market House to Library 1975 (62)

Weaver, Henry, of Devizes. Born probably c1815, practising from c1840, thereafter large Wiltshire practice until late 1880s. County surveyor by 1865, in partnership with Charles Adye (qv) from c1881.
Alterations for Wiltshire Museum, Devizes 1872 (95–6)
Police Station, Eastcott Hill, Swindon 1873 (197)
Alterations to Police Station, Stallard Street, Trowbridge 1874 (200)

Weedon, Harry, Partnership. Harry Weedon in partnership in Birmingham from 1912 but later became prominent cinema architect. Post–war practice focussed on

factories but in 2023 Weedon Partnership handled a range of large-scale projects.
Council offices, Beckhampton Street, Swindon c1975 (163)

Wilde, John, of Ivybridge, Devon. Work at Trowbridge for Hydrock Developers.
Alterations to Civic Centre, Trowbridge 2011 (168)

Wilkinson, George, 1814–90, of Witney, then Dublin from c1840. Designed over 30 workhouses in England and Wales, then invited to Ireland to design all of Ireland's proposed 130 workhouses.[24] Later worked on other buildings there before retiring back to England.
Workhouse, Devizes 1836–7 (153)
Workhouse, Malmesbury 1837–8 (155)
Workhouse, Purton (Wootton Bassett) 1837 (174)

Wilson & Willcox of Bath. James Wilson (1816–1900) and William John Willcox (1838–1928), in partnership from 1865, Willcox having probably been a pupil of Wilson. Willcox also county surveyor for Somerset, c1886 to 1908; Wilson opened London office from 1850. Successor partnerships lasted until the 1970s.
Corn Exchange, Swindon 1866 (designed by Willcox) (34)

Wiltshire County Architects. County architects during the period covered by the buildings listed below (though designs may have been by their staff) were Frank I Bowden (qv) to 1966, Stanley H Townrow 1966–79, Robert Haynes 1979–86. In 1989 the architect's department was absorbed into Property Services.
Melksham Library, Lowbourne 1964 (126)
Devizes Library, Sheep Street 1968 (121)
Amesbury Library (113)
Chippenham Timber Street Library 1973 (119)
Warminster Library, Three Horseshoes Yard 1982 (141)
Chippenham Magistrates Courts 1996 (72)

Wiltshire County Council Property Services Department. Individual architect not identified.
Extension to Swindon Magistrates' Courts 1994 (83)

Woodbridge, C J. Architect in Post Office division of Office of Works.
Post Office, Calne 1953 (211)

Wyatt, Thomas Henry, 1807–80, of London. A leading Victorian architect who designed over 400 buildings, many in Wiltshire including much church building and restoration.
Assize Courts, Devizes 1835 (74)
Salisbury Museum, King's House, south-east wing 1851–2 (102)
Market House, Warminster 1855 (65)
County Militia Stores, later Police Station, Devizes 1856 (190)
Bleeck Memorial Hall, Athenaeum, Warminster 1879 (140)

Notes

1	BoE mistakenly attributes this to Gilbert Blount, who died in 1876
2	Dates from FreeBMD and Ancestry websites; information on art from Sulis fine art website, all accessed 28/11/2023
3	BTA website accessed 28/11/2023
4	Website of Eric Cole Architecture accessed 28/11/2023
5	Company website accessed 2/12/2023
6	British Post Office Architects website
7	British Post Office Architects website; Purpose-built Post Offices, Jonathan Clarke, English Heritage 2008; FreeBMD
8	FreeBMD

9   Company website accessed 29/11/2023; FreeBMD
10   Entry for Sandy Patience on 'Linkedin'
11   British Post Office Architects
12   Leeds Libraries Heritage website accessed 29/11/23
13   Workhouses.org.uk
14   Company website accessed 29/11/2023
15   Kelly, Somerset, 1914 & 1919; FreeBMD
16   FreeBMD and 1881 census
17   Devizes & Wiltshire Gazette 1/7/1858
18   British Post Office Architects; FreeBMD
19   British Post Office Architects
20   Wiltshire Times 21/1/1933; FreeBMD
21   Managing the Royal Road: The London & South Western Railway 1870-1911, David Anthony Turner, unpublished PhD thesis, University of York 2013.
22   British Post Office Architects
23   Dictionary of Scottish Architects
24   Workhouses.org.uk

www.ingramcontent.com/pod-product-compliance
Lightning Source LLC
Chambersburg PA
CBHW060929180426
43192CB00044B/2815